On Other Grounds

SUNY series, The Margins of Literature
Mihai I. Spariosu, Editor

On Other Grounds

Landscape Gardening and Nationalism In Eighteenth-Century England and France

Brigitte Weltman-Aron

State University of New York Press

Cover photo: A detail from Hubert Robert (1733–1808). *Vue du Bosquet des Bains d'Apollon lors de l'abattage des arbres* [View of the Grove of the Baths of Apollo during the Felling of the Trees], oil on canvas (124 x 191 cm), 1774/75. Versailles, Musée National du Château. © Réunion des Musées Nationaux. Courtesy Art Resource, NY.

Published by
State University of New York Press, Albany

Printed in the United States of America

For information, address State University of New York Press,
State University Plaza, Albany, NY, 12246

Production by Marilyn P. Semerad
Marketing by Michael Campochiaro

Library of Congress Cataloging-in-Publication Data

Weltman-Aron, Brigitte, 1961–
On other grounds : landscape gardening and nationalism in eighteenth-century England and France / Brigitte Weltman-Aron.
p. cm. — (SUNY series, the margins of literature)
Includes bibliographical references (p.).
ISBN 0–7914–4805–3 (alk. paper) — ISBN 0–7914–4806–1 (pbk. : alk. paper)
1. Landscape gardening—England—History—18th century. 2. Landscape gardening—France—History—18th century. 3. Gardens—England—Philosophy—History—18th century. 4. Gardens—France—Philosophy—History—18th century. 5. Nationalism in gardens.
I. Title. II. Series.

SB470.55.G7 W46 2001
712′.0942′09033—dc21 00–026554

10 9 8 7 6 5 4 3 2 1

for
Dragan

Contents

Acknowledgments

The project of this book started in a graduate seminar taught by Peggy Kamuf, in which we read Rousseau's *Julie ou la Nouvelle Héloïse*. I was intrigued by Rousseau's description of Julie's garden, and thought that my incipient idea was fresh and new. Little did I know! Years later, I am deeply indebted to all the friends and guides who helped me find my way out of a maze of my own doing. I want first to acknowledge the example that Peggy Kamuf's critical work and performance as a teacher has always represented for me. She made the role of researcher an attractive position to aspire to, and one I wanted to emulate. She has given me confidence by her constant support and by her friendship.

All the readers of my manuscript generously contributed to its final shape by their questions, comments, and stylistic nuances. I particularly want to thank my colleagues and friends Tina Chanter, Catherine Jones, Jonathan Krell, Leonard Lawlor, and Lisa Rosenthal, for their helpful suggestions. Clay Tanner's help in editing and printing this manuscript was invaluable. I also wish to thank the editor of the series, Mihai Spariosu, and James Peltz, acquisition editor at SUNY Press, for their unfailing support of my project.

Several grants allowed me to devote time to research and writing: I benefited from the Undergraduate Research Opportunities Program at the University of Minnesota, Morris; I received two faculty development grants at the University of Georgia; and one faculty research grant at the University of Memphis. I am indebted to the students who helped me gather indispensable documents, particularly Tamara Marwitz and Barry Flippo. It is with gratitude that I acknowledge the help of the Réunion des Musées Nationaux in France in facilitating the reproduction of Hubert Robert's *Vue du Bosquet des Bains d'Apollon*.

At earlier stages of its development, my book has also benefited from the encouragement and constructive criticism of Edith Farrell and Michel Baridon. Doris Kadish in particular has always been available with friendly advice. I also wish to mention those who have given me the emotional support I needed during the writing of this book, especially Anna Klobucka and Isabelle Gros.

My parents, Ghislaine and Marcel Weltman-Aron, have continuously supported my intellectual endeavors. But I have mostly benefited from my exhilarating exchanges with Dragan Kujundzic. This book is dedicated to him.

Introduction

The Seeds of Discord

One would think that nature is made in France otherwise than in the rest of the world.
—Rousseau, *Julie ou la Nouvelle Héloïse*

A study on landscape gardening in France during the second half of the eighteenth century immediately raises the question whether gardening was then a French or an imported art. In the last decades of the century, the predominance of the theory and practice of the English landscape movement on both sides of the Channel seems to invalidate in advance any serious claim of specifically "French" techniques or doctrines of gardening. It has been repeatedly argued that the French zenith in gardening was reached under Louis XIV, under the guidance of Le Nôtre, but that this preeminence gave way in the next century to the widespread influence of the English style, including in France. Therefore, is it legitimate to postulate a specific French landscape style of gardening near the end of the eighteenth century? If we superimpose on this question the common assessment of each style—the French style is (more) artificial, whereas the English style is (more) natural— we have furthermore a summary of the evolutionary history of landscape gardening toward a greater natural awareness. In other words, the difference between styles is not a sheer aesthetic difference. On the contrary, embracing the English style is often described as a progressive sign in itself, because the appreciation of nature "for its own sake" in gardening is constructed as the very position of modernity. This view is important, because during the eighteenth century, English authors were precisely expounding a history of gardening leading toward a necessary termination, the English style, in order to demonstrate that their nation was evidently progressive and free, not under an absolutist and tyrannical rule, as in France. Indeed, critical studies on landscape as a mode of political discourse abound, although today they do problematize the ideological underpinnings of such assertions. French authors or gardeners of the eighteenth century may seem inevitably condemned to repetition, either that of a misguided former style of their own, or that of the new, foreign style. This book partly remarks this inevitability, or rather reiterates that unavoidable repetition, but it also analyzes the resistance which it met in France. I examine the anxiety of influence that the repetition of English principles represented for French authors, and the ways in which French treatises circumvented it.

The position of French authors was made all the more difficult since they actually agreed with English analyses that promoting a limited artistic involvement in a garden was an apter way of understanding nature. This agreement, however, is expressed very cunningly by French authors, in a way that denies English precedence and authority as much as it accepts it. Two acclaimed interpretations of the need to modify formal French gardens may be considered as paradigmatic of the forms taken by the French resistance to the English model. The first was highly influential among French authors: in *Julie ou la Nouvelle Héloïse* (1761), Jean-Jacques Rousseau presents Julie's garden, the Elysée, as a compelling alternative to traditional French gardens. Hubert Robert provides a second interpretation in four paintings (1774/75) that depict one of the first initiatives of King Louis XVI, that of the felling of the trees of Versailles, undertaken between 1774 and 1776. The best-known representative of the French style, Versailles, is here revealed in a process of utmost upheaval and transformation.

Rousseau's novel was largely praised and imitated immediately after its publication, and his contemporaries' numerous allusions to Julie's Elysée attest that Rousseau's interpretation of gardening struck a sympathetic chord in them. The Elysée is a secluded, quiet, overgrown and lush place, with sounds of trickling water and singing birds competing for the attention of the delighted visitor. It induces revery, meditation and simple pleasures through a profound, though not labored, solicitation of the senses:

> I was struck by an agreeable sensation of coolness which dark shady trees, an animated and vivid greenness, scattered flowers everywhere, the murmuring of water and the singing of a thousand birds brought to my imagination at least as much as to my senses; but at the same time I thought I saw the wildest, the most solitary place in all nature, and it seemed to me that I was the first mortal who had ever entered this desert. (Rousseau 1964, 471)[1]

Rousseau is generally credited for having given the French the poetic legitimacy of a less artistically filtered appreciation of nature. This indicates his transcription as well as his amplification of an existing feeling among his contemporaries. The description of the Elysée testifies to a dissatisfaction with the geometrical style favored in parks designed under Louis XIV. Rousseau deplores the monotonous taste for symmetry and straight lines, and for alleys with a long perspective, which were characteristic of the French style. He denounces the excessive costs involved in the French style as an unnecessary display of the vanity of the garden's owner. Rousseau endorses instead a more "natural" conception of gardening, that is to say, an unobtrusive participation of the gardener in his art: "The error of so-called men of taste is to want art everywhere, and not to be pleased if art does not appear; whereas the veritable taste consists in hiding it; especially as far as the works of nature are concerned" (482). This seems a typical "English" argument; yet, Rousseau, in his mixed response to the adoption of English features, is a good representative of French essays on landscape gardening. Although he writes that symmetry is "an enemy of nature and of variety" (483) and suggests that "nature is made in France otherwise than in the rest of the world" (481), he is not entirely laudatory when he tackles the English style. When he talks of Stowe, one of the most celebrated achievements of English gardening for English and French authors alike, Rousseau is not struck by the greater naturalness of the park, but rather by a different sort of unnaturalness. In Saint-Preux's words, "It is a composition of very beautiful and very picturesque places, the aspects of which have been chosen in different countries, and of which everything appears to be natural, except its being assembled" (484). Likewise, Rousseau declares in a note that Le Nôtre, Louis XIV's renowned landscape designer, knew "what gave life to nature, and interest in its spectacle" (483). In fact, Julie has diverted from the more stately French park a smaller space for her own garden, and consequently different principles are shown to coexist, not to cancel each other out. This is therefore a way to suggest an ongoing legitimacy to the French style ("for strangers," Julie says [474]).

These positions are generally shared by Rousseau's French contemporaries. They indicate that the growing taste for a limitation of art in gardening found a widespread support in France. Yet, the evidence of a changing taste does not imply that French authors were willing to endorse fully English criteria, even though it is clear that the literature on gardening in France found its inspiration both in treatises written in England and in the layouts executed in England and in France after these new principles. For French authors, then, the lesson of Rousseau's representation of a garden such as the Elysée is the possibility of distancing oneself from French designs, while giving oneself leave to criticize the English style, apparently in order to propose a third way of gardening.[2] This example will be heeded by French authors writing on landscape after Rousseau.

The viewer of Hubert Robert's pictures is not struck by peacefulness, but by an intense human activity involving the felling, uprooting, and cutting of old trees (Figure 1). The measure was necessitated by the gradual decay of the trees planted under the reign of Louis XIV (Francastel 53). In his rendering of the scene, Robert insists on the human labor necessary in order to construct a park, and as a result, gardening is visualized not as an artistically pleasing *result* (a beautiful, green garden), but as a somewhat painful *process*. Treatises on landscape gardening of the end of the eighteenth century emphasize the fact that new, "natural" gardens must provide a sense of nature's constant self-modification, rather than achieve a totalized artistic object for the enjoyment of the viewer. Robert powerfully conveys an impression of transitoriness, even though in his painting he clearly ascribes to man the task of managing it.

Furthermore, his paintings represent some of the numerous sculptures for which the park of Versailles was particularly famous. Some statues are fallen from their pedestals as if they were antique

Figure 1. Hubert Robert (1733–1808). *Vue du Bosquet des Bains d'Apollon lors de l'abattage des arbres* [*View of the Grove of the Baths of Apollo during the Felling of the Trees*], oil on canvas (124 x 191 cm), 1774/75. Photo: RMN. Versailles, Musée National du Château. © Réunion des Musées Nationaux.

sculptures. Thus, they contribute to the motif of decay and ruin suggested by the pictures.[3] At the same time, the paintings either depict the palace in the background, imposing and more permanent than the wounded vegetal remnants in the front, or they show the perspective of the Grand Canal, that testimony to human labor and willful arrangement of the landscape. In the foreground of the two paintings held in the Museum of Versailles, the royal family is represented, the king speaking to other figures, pointing to the operation in process, in a way which reassures the viewer that the ongoing destruction is planned and controlled. Robert had been commissioned by Louis XVI to do the paintings of the felling of the trees (de Cayeux 15), and he was later to be given the position which had been held by Le Nôtre, that of "Designer of the Gardens of the King," a position that had been suppressed since Le Nôtre's death (de Cayeux 18). Both distinctions are a sign of confidence and indicate an authorized transmission of power, a continuity rather than a rupture. About Robert's paintings, de Cayeux argues that "There is nothing dramatic in this 'felling,' in this temporary destruction of an aged scenery" (72). Indeed, although the representation of this scene could be felt to foreshadow a deep stylistic transformation in the landscape, the inclusion of the palace and of the statues in the antique style fosters instead an impression of permanence, or repetition of the same under superficial, "temporary" changes.

The sweeping vogue of English landscape gardening would seem to demonstrate conclusively that a change of some kind occurred. Yet, it is important to realize the persistence of continuities within the project of transformation of French parks. In the case of the replantation of the park of Versailles between 1774 and 1776, for instance, it has been shown that "On the whole, one finds that the new park was replanted following the same principles as those which had prevailed under the reign of Louis XIV. In 1776, there was a sheer replantation" (Francastel 54).[4] Even though some parts of the park were subsequently transformed under Louis XVI in deference to the new style, as was done in the case of the *bosquet* of the Bath of Apollo in 1778 (under the direction of Robert), it appears that the additions and transformations often used former features, which were therefore reframed, rather than discarded. Throughout this book, I recognize the evidence of a repetition ("a sheer replantation"), and at the same time, I analyze the common claim, then and sometimes even now, that the theory and practice of gardening have been thoroughly transformed during the eighteenth century. I have consistently paid attention to the ways in which authors of treatises on landscape gardening, perhaps without their knowledge, expound claims of novelty while remaining within the compass of tradition.

I address the assertion that stylistic changes in landscape gardening took place, as a point of entry into the larger question of the belief in progress, that is to say, a change for better conditions, which is a view generally shared by authors of the Enlightenment. The faith in the overall good effects of progress has been problematized in our time, for instance by focusing on those who are, deliberately or de facto, excluded from the benefits that progress is believed to bring about. In that sense, the case of landscape gardening in the eighteenth century is exemplary. First, because, in W. J. T. Mitchell's words, "Landscape as a cultural medium . . . naturalizes a cultural and social construction, representing an artificial world as if it were simply given and inevitable" (Mitchell 2). The proclaimed "return to nature," which is found in numerous treatises of the time, also gives an additional legitimacy to the project of the Enlightenment. Naming nature as the ultimate field of investigation, the purpose of knowledge and the possibility of progress, and all those aims as coextensive with modernity, serves to naturalize and validate the ends of the Enlightenment itself. It also serves to obfuscate various appropriations and dispossessions, including that of man's "natural" environment. My position capitalizes on the critical work which brings to the fore the effects of the equation between "nature" and "modernity."[5] I also expose the nationalist underpinnings of eighteenth-century treatises on landscape gardening. These treatises display in an exemplary fashion a link between nature and nationalism, which is a potential risk of the pursuits of Enlightenment or modernity. If landscape becomes such a debated question in the eighteenth century, it is also because it is conceived or represented as the crux of—unless it is the pretext for—the reflection on man's relation to the world. This is why treatises on landscape gardening of the period are not only a mode of political discourse, but aim to bring together philosophy, science, arts, politics, and ethics.[6] I address these issues by concentrating on the ways in which French and English writers concur or differ in their treatment of the topic.

One way to resist the description of irresistible change and development toward the appreciation of nature, which is claimed by eighteenth-century histories of landscape gardening, is to point out disregarded repetitions that contradict the posited teleology. In the first chapter, I argue that instead of endorsing a unidirectional progress toward a greater natural awareness, a progress that supposedly happened at a specific historical time, it could be said that the Western garden has always presented within itself concurrent rustic and architectonic features, which can be traced to the Renaissance interpretation of the Classical garden. This repetition was largely ignored during the eighteenth century (and sometimes still today), partly because of the appeal of periodical stylistic novelties as a metaphor for political changes, and partly because the proposition that "moderns" understand nature in unheralded ways is in itself pleasant and convincing.

This overwhelming appeal or conviction means that French authors of the eighteenth century are unwilling to accept their assigned position as one of mere repetition of English principles. Like their English counterparts, they assert that they are promoting "new" views and techniques. What interests me in the assessment of the claim of change, therefore, is how French authors of the eighteenth century react to the English discourse of an inevitable progress toward the English style, which is described as at one with nature. There is a resistance to the English style in French treatises on landscape gardening, which makes them both part of, and in excess of, the English landscape movement. In the second chapter, I analyze various forms of resistance to the English model, particularly in terms of a negotiation between change and repetition. While layouts of eighteenth-century gardens in France might suggest a simple repetition of English theories, the analysis of French treatises demonstrates instead another form of repetition, namely the appropriation of the English evolutionary discourse. French treatises use, for their own purposes, the arguments proposed by the English in order to keep open the history of landscape gardening, which they argue will end in France, not in England. The repetition in question is further complicated by the adaptation and transcription of English strategies of resistance to the overwhelming seventeenth-century French style, which French authors could find in English treatises. I argue that this gesture of resistance is motivated by patriotic or nationalist concerns regarding the safety of the "French" soil. The challenge for the authors of landscape treatises is to promote new English principles of gardening, while containing a phenomenon that they feel is a threat to the integrity of the French land. In particular, I analyze how they define nature in a way that can be made familiar and indigenous, purely "French." What is natural is consistently thought in terms of the national, and French treatises on landscape gardening participate in the reflection on the national territory, which is also addressed in other essays of the time.

I have narrowed down my inquiry to the study of French treatises written for the most part in the 1770s (by Watelet, Morel, Girardin, and Carmontelle, among others), because this period marks the end of one regime of French colonial policies, until the British disastrous defeat of France during the Seven Years War (which included the French loss of Canada), and the beginning of new orientations regarding the acquisition of other colonies, for example in the South Seas. The victory of Britain created a profound insecurity regarding French territories, in particular as far as their economic usefulness and their contribution to the formation of French identity were concerned. This context explains why landscape gardening treatises written in France contest the fashion of the English style as a form of invasion of the French land. In the third chapter, I establish a parallel between this concern and analyses found in Raynal's widely read essay on European colonialism (first published in 1770). Raynal favors measures that would counterbalance British imperialism at the end of the eighteenth century, in order to rectify what he interprets as a wish to occupy French territories. This chapter also examines the French "discovery" of Tahiti, as recounted by contemporaries (Bougainville, Diderot, Raynal), in order to assess a characteristic double discourse concerning the annexation of other lands. While the French strongly reject the perceived ambitions of the British on their own territories, they are ambivalent when it comes to the status of lands like Tahiti. However, they do represent figures of resistance to annexation in general, and I argue that the fascination with the primitive, or origins, or savage man, reveals an unease about the effects of colonialism, as much as a nostalgia for a "Georgic" past. I contrast the seeming adequation posited at the time between deaf-mute and savage men, with the elaboration of a teleology in which authors like Diderot and Condillac waver in their determination of stable poles for plenitude and lack, origin and end, nature and civilization. Not only do these essays evince doubts concerning the uses of territory as such, but the legitimacy of territorial gains to "civilized" Europe is also interrogated. This questioning takes place at the same time as treatises on landscape gardening assert that a liberation from the French style is a metaphor for liberation itself.

The emancipation of the garden implies the appropriation of the surrounding landscape, which becomes, as it were, incorporated in the garden, through various devices, such as the *ha-ha* (or a ditch which is not visible when viewed from a certain angle, as opposed to a fence). The project of tearing down fences, like that of abstaining from altering too forcibly the shape of trees and shrubbery, is relished as a figure of liberty. However, inasmuch as it becomes a method for transforming the surrounding landscape into a vast panorama, a spectacle to be discovered and enjoyed by the viewer, or a "formulation of liberty as panoptic control" (Bermingham 1994, 84), the project of the early English movement is not entirely opposed to some of the effects of the French formal style. The analysis of effects is the object of the fourth chapter. I first analyze claims according to which, during the eighteenth century, the new garden provided altered modes of visualizing space, in order to foster a different awareness of the position of the spectator within, and not simply outside, the picture contemplated. It is generally assumed that the French style organizes the landscape as an image to be viewed from a distance. I examine a common opposition made between the French and the English styles in terms of intelligibility as opposed to sensibility (forms which address the senses, not the mind). This opposition has often been related to philosophies or epistemologies that were respectively contemporaneous to the French and English styles, namely Descartes's and Locke's. I question this attribution precisely at the point which concerns a supposed difference in the experience of visualization. I argue that the attribution of the French style to Descartes neglects a division within the structure of the garden which precludes an entire "Cartesian" effect. This division demonstrates the persistence of the

Baroque within the design of the formal garden. It is questionable, in any event, whether the geometry of the French style can simply be assigned to a Cartesian epistemology. Likewise, visualization for Descartes does not entirely escape the sensible contingency and proximity that geometrical features in the French style are supposed to proscribe.

What does not correspond to formal elements in the French style is generally ignored in the descriptions of eighteenth-century authors. However, in terms of the effects sought for in the new style, the difference is mostly one of degree. What eighteenth-century authors strive for is not so much to avoid effects, but to systematize their efficacy. In particular, they focus on ways to capture the viewer's attention, which they say is not solicited enough in the former style. The desire to substitute a narrowly focused view to the large prospects of the former style corresponds to that attempt. Analyses on attention, memory, and reminiscence were available to eighteenth-century authors. Locke is the first indispensable reference, but I have mainly examined Condillac's work, in order to explore further what Jacques Derrida has called a double gesture of inauguration and rupture in Condillac (Derrida 1980, 42). Condillac's complex relation to repetition and novelty (especially in connection with the different philosophies of Descartes and Locke) aptly fits the ambivalent relation that French authors of the eighteenth century entertained toward the French formal style as well as the English landscape movement.

French treatises define a landscape that should not only be pleasing to the eye, but involve all the senses, and represent cultural landmarks that reinforce man's participation in the spectacle, and ensure the legibility of the landscape. Hubert Robert summed up the notion that landscape has the power to act upon the senses and, through the senses, on the mind, when he reportedly gave the king the following interpretation of his paintings (representing, it will be recalled, the felling of the trees in Versailles):

> What is your objective, Majesty? It is not to have a geometrical shortcut of this vast scene, but to cause your soul to recall the extraordinary sensation that it feels when it looks at this dead nature, at these monuments of arts, which, isolated, do not have a pleasant aspect any longer and seem to participate in the ruin of the first. (de Cayeux 72)

Not only does the effect of the garden shift its emphasis from "geometry" to "sensation" and "the soul." In Robert's analysis, the appropriation of the space for the beholder rests on a sentimentalized narrative, in which the response of the viewer is solicited by intricately weaving an appreciation of nature with cultural reminiscences. This figurative appropriation, or domestic colonization of space is clearly legitimized in eighteenth-century treatises.

Such an appropriation may seem unavoidable, since it is unquestionable that there is no apprehension of lanscape that is not culturally or technically mediated by man. But in the last chapter, I make a historical leap and analyze the recently completed projects of the French landscape designer Gilles Clément, particularly in the André Citroën Park in Paris. He has summed up his gardening principles under the general denomination of "garden in movement," and the difficult task of the gardener as that of "managing mobility" (Clément 1990, 99). Clément does not believe in the possibility of simply breaking away from the gardening tradition. His cogent explanations of various processes of natural acclimatizations and growths constitute perhaps the most obvious tie of his project to tradition. Still within the compass of eighteenth-century treatises, the gardener effaces himself behind his recorded observations of natural forms of development. However, Clément's project becomes particularly compelling in its profound lack of investment in a potential or ideal spectator's desires and reactions. In Clément's analysis, a gardener should organize, after the fact, nature's spontaneous and therefore unplanned outbursts. In a garden, the gardener does intervene, but he comes as an afterthought, which does not predetermine the direction of natural growth. Therefore, this attempt, if it does not entirely preclude a visual appropriation of the space of the garden, powerfully seeks to fight man's urge to sentimentalize nature. At the same time, it erases the codes providing the garden's legibility. For the ultimate assumption of Clément's garden is that of man's fundamental absence. Nature lives on, always where it is unexpected ("getting out of the space assigned to it" [Clément 1990, 69]), without the necessity of man's watchful gaze, and even without the need of man's existence. Whereas the French and English styles alike, whatever the differences in their concepts, organized the garden around man's needs or pleasure, Clément's project thinks gardening beyond the human scope. This recent assessment of landscape gardening provides us with the possibility of considering landscape as a space that cannot be possessed, though it can be temporarily used, an environment that can be lived in, not ravished. In his layouts, Clément makes irrelevant the vantage point of nationalist conflicts, and the discussion of precedence and authority, two positions that were so urgently debated in eighteenth-century treatises. Instead, he invites us to think about a land that would not be a territorial possession, and lets us reflect, therefore, on other grounds.

Chapter 1

Natural Nature

> Nature did everything, but under my direction.
> —Rousseau, *Julie ou la La Nouvelle Héloïse*

> The second half of the eighteenth century reacts to the industrial revolution by a return to Antiquity and by a return to nature.
> —Jean-Claude Lebensztejn, *Zigzag*

TRANSITIONS OR SIMULTANEITY: A POLITICAL AND PHILOSOPHICAL QUESTION

Voltaire begins the fourteenth of his *Philosophical Letters* (1734), entitled "On Descartes and Newton," with an allusion to his own position, that of a Frenchman in exile in England: "A Frenchman arriving in London finds quite a change, in philosophy as in all else" (Voltaire 1961, 60). Although the "Frenchman" is of course not simply Voltaire, "On Descartes and Newton" provides legitimate grounds for biographical parallels, dealing as it does with various responses on the part of governments or authorities toward writers and philosophers, two terms of an equation which are, as it turns out, central to the argument developed in this letter. One of the questions the letter particularly asks us to consider is, Is there such a thing as "philosophy"? Or only "philosophies," in the plural? The second question, perhaps more difficult to answer, and which is woven into the discussion of the first, could be paraphrased thus: Can there be a philosophy, not to say philosophy in general, without reference to the national? Exile is probably conducive to such an inquiry, because it gives the French philosopher Voltaire the fiction of not belonging; exile suspends, though it does not entirely cancel, his national appurtenance, or "deterritorializes" him. Voltaire narratively transposes his position of exile, neither here nor there but in between, into that of the impartial observer of local usages. But the fact that his geographical displacement from France to England is thematized at the beginning of the fourteenth letter is not indifferent, in that it announces his discussion of a linear progression toward knowledge and philosophy. In that respect, moving to England is also getting closer to truth. In the fourteenth letter, Voltaire consistently emphasizes the oddity of simultaneous yet incompatible scientific systems, proposing instead to consider systems as consecutive, in successive transition toward truth.

The philosophical differences between France and England that Voltaire mentions at the beginning of the letter are particularly exemplified by the figures of Descartes and Newton, whose principles seem at first to have nothing in common ("some tremendous contrarieties" [60]). In this letter, "Descartes" and "Newton" designate the respective scientists, or "philosophers" as Voltaire says (a biography of each is provided [61–63]), but they also are the best representatives and the leading names of French and English philosophies.[1] Underscoring the incompatibilities of principles between the two could suggest that, according to Voltaire, *philosophy* always really is *philosophies* in the plural, and furthermore that it is nationally marked (French philosophy, English philosophy). This would mean also that Cartesianism can be embraced at the same time that another philosophy, Newton's for example, is followed elsewhere: certainly, the first pages of the fourteenth letter make it clear that France, at least its scientific elite, is Cartesian, whereas England has rallied to Newton's teachings.

Up to a point, this analysis follows Fontenelle's argument in his celebrated essay "The Elogium of Sir Isaac Newton" (1728), an essay which also plays an important part in Voltaire's assessment of nationally marked philosophy. As the permanent secretary of the French

Royal Academy of Sciences, it was incumbent on Fontenelle to write an essay commemorating the life and works of a member after his death. This was the case of Newton, whose election as a foreign associate of the Academy occurred in 1699 (Fontenelle 1978, 468). The Academy's very decision to choose Newton as an associate would seem at first to complicate Voltaire's division between a Cartesian France and a Newtonian England. In fact, however, Fontenelle concurs with Voltaire's view: he points out that Newton's Philosophy "hath been adopted throughout England, it prevails in the Royal Society, and in all the excellent performances which have come from thence" (465–66); meanwhile, he also expresses "Cartesian" misgivings, in particular, as is well known, about Newtonian attraction, of which the essay says that it is "a notion exploded by the Cartesians, and whose condemnation had been ratified by all the rest of the Philosophers; and we must now be upon our guard, lest we imagine that there is any reality in it, and so expose our selves to the danger of believing that we comprehend it" (454).[2] Thus not only can Fontenelle talk about Newton and Descartes, as Voltaire will, as "These two great men, whose Systems are so opposite," he also finds an enduring, equal merit in both in the rest of the sentence: "These two great men . . . resembled each other in several respects, they were both Genius's of the first rank, both born with superior understandings, and fitted for the founding of Empires in Knowledge" (457). In the following page, he shows in effect that both philosophers have the defects of their qualities, which he sums up thus: "The self-evident principles of the one [Descartes] do not always lead him to the causes of the phenomena as they are; and the phenomena do not always lead the other [Newton] to principles sufficiently evident" (458). One of the consequences of this assessment is to suggest the valid coexistence of the two systems. Fontenelle's postulate of a simultaneity of principles has the consequence of avoiding the devalorization, or lack of currency of French science, whose primary position is not affected by Newton's successes in the essay.

Voltaire points out the evidence of scientific coexistence, and therefore does not entirely disagree with Fontenelle; yet it would be closer to his position to remark that in his letter, philosophy in France is posited as held back, because it is *still* Cartesian. This philosophical delay or backwardness in France is made clear when Newton is said to have overturned Descartes: "This famous Newton, this destroyer of the Cartesian system . . . " (Voltaire 1961, 61). The destruction of Cartesianism has not so far—and it is noticed in Voltaire's account—been suitably registered by French philosophers, such as Fontenelle. Yet, Voltaire does not say that Newton merely "destroyed" Descartes, for he also calls him Descartes's successor: "Descartes made as great progress, from the point at which he found geometry to the point to which he carried it, as Newton did after him" (63). In other words, Newton has not entirely followed a route other than Descartes's, and he has also benefitted from some of the discoveries of the French philosopher, especially in mathematics and geometry. Voltaire's initial bafflement as to the possibility of the incompatible simultaneity of both systems gives way to a teleological reasoning. As Voltaire puts it, Descartes "taught the men of his time how to reason, and how to fight him with his own weapons" (64).[3] In that view, Descartes's philosophy leads to Newton's, and becomes also an indispensable link to an assessment of Newton's philosophy.[4]

Voltaire's attention to links that lead to the present moment of knowledge, and beyond it, to an ongoing, open-ended progress, is one of the philosophical assumptions shared by other contemporaries. As the article "Encyclopédie" (*Encyclopédie* V, 635) puts it in its opening paragraph, the term *Encyclopedia* comes from the Greek and means "chain of knowledge [enchaînement de connaissances]." Therefore, paying heed to the *chain*, to its links, is also a way of describing the cognitive process itself. If, for Voltaire, French philosophy is in a manner of speaking the past of English philosophy, then such a position complicates his initial evaluation of incompatibility ("tremendous contrarieties" [60]) between French and English philosophies. Voltaire avoids in this second estimate both the rejection of Descartes and the endorsement of the viability of simultaneous opposed principles. Thus his investment in expounding the "change" he mentioned at the beginning of the letter, is not a way for him to endorse concurrent different usages, but signals a clear transition in knowledge. His proposed sequence from Descartes to Newton has implications for his understanding of philosophy, not as plural and coexistent, but as a continuous dispelling of errors, toward a final universal enlightenment, he himself, perhaps, being such a contributing link—indeed, his *Eléments de la Philosophie de Newton* (1738) are widely acknowledged as having been instrumental to the acceptance of Newton's principles in France (Gillispie 430).

However, it should be emphasized that Fontenelle himself is far from being opposed to the project of dispelling errors, since for him, Descartes has eminently done so in the case of scholasticism. It is in fact because of Descartes's successful eradication of scholastic "errors" that some of Newton's positions, such as attraction, should be rejected in Fontenelle's view, because they are considered as scientifically regressive. Therefore paying attention to the chain or to the transition to the next, more enlightened link might not be sufficient. Voltaire goes further by suggesting that the discussion of philosophy is overdetermined, by pointing out that its assessment is seldom free of—in fact is likely to be intertwined with—national claims and preferences. Fontenelle's essay certainly suggests that the postulated currency of French science is at the same time an investment in the status of "France." This consideration goes beyond the case of Descartes and Newton. Fontenelle recalls for instance a "great contest between M. Leibnits and him [Newton], or rather between Germany and England" (Fontenelle 1978, 448).[5] For Voltaire, the appeal of a universal science and knowledge has to be calculated while taking into consideration such statements as Fontenelle's. Voltaire wonders whether it is possible to avoid the returns and dividends of a successful system to a specific nation.

Voltaire addresses the issue when he assesses the reception of Fontenelle's *Elogium* in England. Immediately translated in no less than at least four different versions, the essay enjoyed a success testifying to the admiration evinced in England for Newton (Gillispie 442). Voltaire obliquely proposes, though, that part of the appeal of Fontenelle's essay to an English audience was due to an awareness of the Cartesian convictions of the French Academy of Sciences, which constituted an additional flattering circumstance: "The eulogy on Mr. Newton that was delivered by M. de Fontenelle before the Académie des Sciences has been read with eagerness, and has been translated into English" (Voltaire 1961, 61). As we have seen, however, even if Fontenelle's eulogy can be partly said to testify to scientific equanimity, it does not exactly offer a teleological scientific development from Descartes to Newton, or from error to truth.

Voltaire continues to record the effect of Fontenelle's speech in these terms:

> In England they looked forward to the judgment of M. de Fontenelle, expecting a solemn declaration of the superiority of English philosophy, but when they found him comparing Descartes to Newton, the whole Royal Society of London was aroused to indignation. Far from acquiescing in such a judgment, they criticized the discourse. (61)

Voltaire interprets the disappointment of the Royal Society at Fontenelle's unexpectedly balanced eulogy as what would now be called a nationalistic reflex: "Several even (and those by no means the most philosophical) were shocked at the comparison for the sole reason that Descartes was a Frenchman" (61). Voltaire's bracketed remark is indicative of the terms in which he wants to locate the assessment of philosophy, that is neither in "England" nor in "France." In effect, the remark illustrates and denounces the kind of link often made, for example in Fontenelle, between philosophy and nationality: "for the sole reason that Descartes was a Frenchman." Such a link is precisely what Voltaire wants to put into question, for example when he avoids the simple opposition between Descartes and Newton. In an article, "Cartesianism," published decades later in his *Questions sur l'Encyclopédie* (1770), Voltaire reaffirms this position and writes a programmatic counter proposition to nationalism in/as philosophy: "One must be true; one must be fair; the philosopher is neither a Frenchman, nor an Englishman, nor even a Florentine: he is of every country" ["de tout pays"] (Voltaire 1962, 230). The philosopher should not be thought of as nationally anchored, which has implications for philosophy, acquiring in this gesture a universal relevance. This explains why Voltaire defends as it were a philosophy in exile ("de tout pays"), and argues for conditions to promote thinking as universally relevant.

At the same time, Voltaire exemplifies in the fourteenth letter the need to traverse the question of the national before such thinking can be effectively put into some form of operation. For his parenthetical remark on some English scientists' reactions against Descartes seems to acknowledge that philosophy all too easily slips into, or remains caught in national, not to say nationalist pulls, which is what is really holding it back, and what it does not always know how to avoid. Indeed, this remark might first of all be applicable to himself. For example, in the case of Fontenelle's eulogy, he did not fail to point out some English philosophers' narrow-mindedness and nationalist reactions. Voltaire could also have underscored in the telling of that episode the fact that Fontenelle felt it necessary to justify his praise of a foreign genius by comparing him to a French prominent figure, and partly used Newton's legacy as a means to reaffirm the validity of the Cartesian heritage. But Voltaire does not make that comment. In fact, he himself followed the structure of Fontenelle's example when he compared Descartes and Newton in the fourteenth letter. Later on, he is even more severe when he writes: "In a criticism made in London of M. Fontenelle's discourse, somebody dared say that Descartes was not a great geometrician. Those who talk in this way may reproach themselves for beating their nurse" (Voltaire 1961, 63). Voltaire's indignant comment introduces the notion that Descartes is the beginning and Newton the continuation of the path to truth. Even though he will subsequently underscore a number of Descartes's shortcomings (for example: "I will not deny that all the other works of M. Descartes swarm with errors" [64]), Voltaire seems to resent the disparaging comments made in England, symmetrically mirroring here the reaction of the Royal Society to Fontenelle's *Elogium* ("were shocked" [61]). *Shock* at the other's *daring* always risks preventing the possibility of the impartial, "true" and "fair" position that Voltaire recommends, and it is so for Voltaire himself. However, Voltaire importantly recognizes the nationalist parameters involved in the attempt to assess fairly a great scientific figure like Descartes or Newton, perhaps even as he at times repeats them. The letter precisely shows that the philosophical recognition elicited by true scientific principles or accomplishments is intricately linked to a political gain, which returns the scientist's success as a national advantage. This conjunction is problematized by Voltaire. His distrust of simultaneity, or the coexistence of opposed principles and his endorsement of transitions toward universal truth is therefore also for him a way out of nationalism. At the same time, the temporality of knowledge he endorses also has political effects.

Neither Descartes nor Newton, nor even Voltaire, can be blamed for not anticipating what our own contemporary science tells us about universal truth or compatible opposed systems, as Koyré often mentions in his *Newtonian Studies*, evoking for example Einstein's theory of relativity or the wave theory, which is not Newton's theory of light, while not invalidating it (97). The legacy of the Enlightenment has not lost its appeal, above all because of its discourse on human rights and social justice. But studies such as Horkheimer and Adorno's on Enlightenment have made it impossible not to be attentive to some ominous ideological consequences lying behind the appeal to progress and the universal, in particular the instrumentalization of knowledge toward domination.[6] Critics today generally problematize the recourse to categories such as "transitions," for example, because they betray an inherited, "enlightened" teleological desire to establish the stages of a neat process, which in turn tends to presuppose a progress toward perfection, truth, even when it is acknowledged that this moment of perfection is still just a promise. Yet, just as Voltaire had shown in the fourteenth letter, the current critical distrust of "transitions" does not always preclude a repetition of the very categories it denounces.

PROBLEMATIZING "TRANSITIONS": LANDSCAPE GARDENING

Eighteenth-century authors who, in France and in England, wrote on landscape gardening, are like Voltaire in the sense that they pay a close attention to the question of "changes." The fact that the emphasis on transitions is linked to a faith in the advent of perfection or truth is clear in the respective statements made by two important authors on gardening. The first is Jaucourt, who wrote the article "Jardin" for the *Encyclopédie* in 1765, and who affirms the absolute primacy of Louis XIV's landscape designer, Le Nôtre: "He never had an equal in this area and still has not found his master" (*Encyclopédie* VIII, 459). The second, Horace Walpole, asserts in the *History of the Modern Taste in Gardening* (1771) that in England, "We have discovered the point of perfection. We have given the true model of gardening to the world; let other countries mimic or corrupt our taste" (35). These two contradictory pronouncements already illustrate a point which will be examined later at greater length, that is the extent to which their authors are caught in the kind of nationalistic reflex Voltaire represents in the fourteenth letter.

Walpole's title explicity relies on the possibility of presenting an evolution, a series of transitions, or "history" of the process toward the "point of perfection" he celebrates. Jaucourt also unfolds his version of the history of landscape gardening. He first retraces the long antiquity of landscape gardening, with a Pagan heritage (for example the Gardens of Babylon, one of the Wonders of the World) as well as a Judeo-Christian ancestry (the garden of Eden). Still he holds the view that "It is under this prince [Louis XIV] that this art was on the one hand *created*, perfected by la Quintinie for utility, and by le Nôtre for pleasure" (459, my emphasis). This tendentious statement is written before a case for impartiality is made, in a mode that recalls Voltaire's vantage point from which to philosophize a-nationally. Likewise, Jaucourt attempts to secure an "impartial" position from which to evaluate landscape gardening: "Let's take an impartial look at our century" (460). This injunction is followed by an opposition between France and England "today." In France, landscape gardening is found to be in decadence: "How do we decorate today the most beautiful sites of our choice, out of which le Nôtre would have known how to derive marvels? We use a ridiculous and petty taste" (460). On the contrary, on the other side of the Channel, landscape gardening is flourishing: "The same is not true of a neighboring nation, where gardens of good taste are as common as magnificent palaces are rare" (460).

England is therefore achieving now what used to be France's advantage. It is noticeable that while Jaucourt believes that France has "degenerated" ("However, since the death of this famous artist [Le Nôtre], the art of his invention has strangely degenerated among us" [459]), he does not mention the possibility, let alone the actuality of an imitation, or contagion of landscape gardening practices between France and England.[7] On the contrary, he consistently maintains the irreducibility of French and English practices, and even principles in landscape gardening. France, in this estimate, is not part of, nor does it benefit from the success of the English garden in England. As was the case with Voltaire, "England" is clearly more than the name of a country; it is also a temporal marker on a teleological line toward progress and a better, universal understanding (landscape gardening in France is in decadence, and now flourishes in

England). As such, "England" comes after, or is the successor of "France."

Jaucourt and Walpole, therefore, respectively refer to a stylistic change which tends at the same time, especially in Walpole's *History*, to be represented as progressive. It is undeniable that their description of a change in taste taking place in the eighteenth century is accurate. The change is conventionally explained as a transition from an appreciation of artistic to natural effects in a garden. To some extent, when historians document that change, they tend to repeat Walpole's gesture—that is, they present an evolution or "history" of forms in landscape gardening.[8] But what they criticize today is the irresistible unidirectional temporality endorsed by Walpole in his recording of transitions. They agree that changes took place, but qualify the temporality of their occurrence. In other words, they importantly "rewrite history." This is the case in John Dixon Hunt's indispensable analyses of the landscape gardening movement in England, and some of his prominent figures, such as William Kent. Hunt often stresses the limits of the concept of transition in landscape gardening by showing the influence of precedents, the time taken for implementing changes, and the complexity of the modalities of stylistic transformations. For example, when he studies the part played by Italian gardens in the formation of the English landscape movement, he recognizes that a transition took place during the eighteenth century from an appreciation of art to a privilege given to "the effects of nature," but he immediately qualifies this statement: "Yet these changes in taste did not proceed with that unfaltering momentum which historians seem to impute to them; indeed, it is relatively easy to find evidence that contradicts the apparently pleasing story of the advance of nature at the expense of art" (Hunt 1986, 90). In effect, Hunt's final remark helps explain why it is difficult, even today, to escape the contagious enthusiasm of Walpole's celebration of the transition from the French to the English style, since the version of what could hastily be termed a "return to nature" is, in Hunt's words, a "pleasing story" in itself. In other words, it is difficult to resist corroborating the view of an inevitable progress or teleology in the recorded movement from art to nature in eighteenth-century landscape gardening, because the celebration of the primacy of nature in gardens corresponds to our sense of being "moderns," as W. J. T. Mitchell remarks in his essay on "Imperial Landscape": "As a pseudo-historical myth, . . . the discourse of landscape is a crucial means for enlisting 'Nature' in the legitimation of modernity" (13).[9]

Clearly the view of change as progress is now most notably put into question by critics. Hunt and others are wary of defining stylistic changes according to a semantics of evolution (for the better). If the recourse to the notion of "transitions" is not altogether eliminated, it is importantly modalized. We mentioned Hunt's qualification, in which the examination of transitions is typically inflected toward the investigation of past or concurrent practices to a given form or movement. Such studies show that a form or movement may hark back to previous modes or compete with others, and not necessarily usher in a new occurrence or conceptualization. The revision of the chronology of landscape gardening movements disturbs the apparent logic of a necessary progression from "art" to "nature," or from the French to the English style during the eighteenth century. In her study of the picturesque garden in France, Dora Wiebenson argues for instance that gardens on both sides of the Channel presented some supposed "English" features concurrently, rather than successively. On other occasions she upsets and inverts the postulated progression from France to England.[10] Hunt also notes that in England by 1728, "the invocation of variety as a specific English need—in contradistinction to the French love of uniformity—was routine." However, he immediately adds that this polemical view was not doing credit to the actual practice of the French style, a style that is called "former" in terms of conventional chronological periodization: "Actually, the French garden did not by any means lack variety: among the bosquets and compartments of Versailles and Marly the experience of diversity and surprise would have been just as striking" (Hunt 1987, 28). Such a recognition undermines the unfolding narrative of historical change, from a former French model to a newer English style. It also puts into question the stability of the boundaries separating different styles of gardening, by undermining the very coherence within, and opposition between styles.

CLASSICISM IN QUOTATION MARKS: AN ITERATION

Remarkably, though, the numerous demonstrations as to the untenable notion of transition in landscape gardening do not prevent critics from using that very category. While the concept of transition as progressive change or novelty is criticized, the term is still widely used. In "Jardins et paysage: Existe-t-il un style anglais?" Michel Baridon starts his analysis by indicating that the modalities of stylistic transitions have lately been extremely complicated and refined by critics, with the expected implication, therefore, that the very word *transition* is not fully satisfactory. But he still points out that he considers what he continues to refer to as "the problem of transition" from the French to the English style to be an important issue (Baridon 1986, 432). What might be interpreted as a relapse happens because Baridon's study of a convergence of politics, science, and aesthetics in landscape gardening (an approach to which I am indebted) examines the different forms that each style uses to represent or translate onto "nature" a specific political and philosophical imaginary. Studying the details of these different forms (he links for example the "gothic myth" to the very shape of the English garden: "the immemorial English countryside with its forests, its waters and its Nordic horizons" 436) implies emphasizing difference as such between styles. Baridon asserts for example that "[the political myth] functions in an altogether different way in English gardens" (435). While not in disagreement with Baridon in his description of stylistic differences, I would like to pay heed to his initial complication of the strict separation of each style, and argue that different politics may not preclude analogous politics of representation.

In stressing separation or "the problem of transition," no matter how much the term is refined, critics risk repeating the very historical positioning of the eighteenth-century texts on landscape gardening that they are interpreting today. In these texts, as we saw for example in the case of Jaucourt and Walpole, one object of the emphasis on transitions was to locate one's position on a line of progress toward perfection. This is another way of saying that history progresses, that changes are themselves progressive, and by the same token universally applicable, as Walpole implied when he said: "Let other countries mimic or corrupt our taste" (35). Baridon's argument seems to follow a similar line when he proposes that the English model "was necessarily to become universal" (Baridon 1986, 432). Emphasizing the inevitability of a transition to a new occurrence has the effect of ignoring what repeats an already (historically) given form or concept, or of disregarding the synchronism of different forms. It could be argued on the contrary that stylistic variations coexist with unchanging gardening structures, and that these recurring structures are precisely used to convey to the spectator such notions as "nature" or "power." This suggests that there is an iteration in the uses to which the garden or landscape is put, whatever the power structure.[11] In fact, Baridon's study shows this even as he speaks of differences. Even though, as we saw, he posits that "[the political myth] functions in an altogether different way in English gardens" (Baridon 1986, 435), he first says of Versailles that it is "a transposition through images of the influence [*rayonnement*] of monarchy" (434), and then of the English parks that they "were becoming the relays of a decentralized power" (435). If we disregard the issue of various forms, it appears then that far from "functioning" differently, the two styles evince a similar attempt to effect a political translation onto "nature."

Furthermore, even the difference in forms may be contested in some respects. The forms chosen or the functions attributed to a garden in the West can be said to have been repetitive ever since Roman classicism, itself adapting or quoting characteristics of the Greek or even the Egyptian garden (through Homer). This model was given in turn an authoritative interpretation during the Italian Renaissance, based on the reading of ancient writings. The Renaissance interpretation became then the indispensable reference for further garden designs.[12] Through the interpretive reading of the classics in the Renaissance, a model was to be consistently upheld: "garden scenes with temples, smaller buildings graced with busts or statues, and the happy, almost preternatural congruence of grove, water and villa" (Hunt 1986, 14).[13] It is because the two seemingly incompatible views of nature, as either rustic or architectonic, are already contained in the classical garden in its Renaissance interpretation, that the English as well as the French styles could find an inspiration in it.[14] It is important to emphasize that the interpreted classical garden offers no stylistic unity, but distributes two heterogeneous demands within a single space. This inner division is a fundamental structuring factor of the garden in general in the West. In fact, both the French and the English styles may be said to take their cue from that model by presenting *at the same time* rustic and architectonic elements. Certainly, the best-known example of the French garden, Versailles, may seem more architectonic than rustic. Yet, Le Nôtre has been shown to have integrated, especially in such parts of the park as the *bosquets* or the labyrinth, elements which parallel English aesthetic claims of liberty, surprise, sinuosity, and process in their gardens.[15] Thierry Mariage also points out that in the first half of the seventeenth century, gardeners paid close attention to the constraints of the site and the surroundings of the garden, in a mode that anticipates eighteenth-century claims in England.[16] Conversely, the celebrated English garden, Stowe, shares some elements with French designs, particularly because of its emphasis on sculpture, inscriptions, and monuments. This does not mean that the two styles are the same, and that the total desired effect of an English or French garden is identical. The iteration in question is a repetition with a difference. But the common reference to some elements of the classical garden in both styles revises the apparent solidity of the delimitation between, or the coherence within separate styles. In fact, what seems invariable in landscape gardening is that whatever the style considered, elements have consistently been borrowed from the model of the classical garden, in order to bring about an age's sense of its own modernity. Hunt has aptly defined two possible assessments of the transformations in landscape gardening: on the one hand, we can "be seduced by the lures of a Whiggish garden history which sees English connoisseurs moving surely from the lures of art to the liberties of nature" (Hunt 1986, 91). Yielding to that seduction also means, as we have seen, repeating history by repeating the "Whiggish" description of history as progress. On the other hand, Hunt, who retraces the history of Italian gardens from 1600 to 1750, goes on to say that

> It is far more useful to chart the different kinds of relationships that were held to be possible between art and nature. . . . While these may readily be located along a graph of an accelerating tolerance of natural over artificial effects, their significance lies less in that teleology than in the sheer range of aesthetic attitudes that were available to garden visitors during the seventeenth and eighteenth centuries.

The constant interplay of responses to art and to nature is inscribed within the classical garden, and is also found to function as the very future of Western landscape gardening.

I should add that I am aware of the importance that Chinese gardens assumed for landscape gardening during the eighteenth century, in order not to repeat the "Eurocentric bias" Mitchell mentions in his essay, "Imperial Landscape": "The intrusion of Chinese traditions into [English landscape aesthetics] is worth pondering further, for it raises fundamental questions about the Eurocentric bias of that discourse and its myths of origin" (9). Mitchell rightly points out that Chinese art constituted a challenge to Europe, which explains why the Chinese example was either appropriated or simply disregarded by historians of "progress" like Walpole. In fact, the interpretation of Classicism by the Renaissance was so overwhelming as to make it a threat to creativity, or invention. Basil Guy has shown that at the end of the seventeenth, and during the eighteenth century, the example of "China" was consistently invoked in France in order to bring about "the dissolution of tradition" (Guy 1963, 102). He explains the dissenting aspect that Chinese art could represent to Europeans in these terms:

> The arts of China influenced European designers . . . by constantly presenting to their eyes the example of an art which was the antithesis of Renaissance classicism. Here were innumerable art objects, painted with a triumphant disregard for symmetry and perspective. . . . The whimsical and fantastic element in such paintings . . . made a strong appeal to those who wished to relax from classical discipline. (164)

In that sense, Chinese gardens could be perceived as a desirable alternative model to European gardens. Yet, the very recourse to "Chinese gardens" evidences a displaced desire, for they prove appealing through an intermediary interpretation by European authors. In fact, the desirability of Chinese art is always filtered through European standards. This is the case in William Chambers's *Designs of Chinese Buildings* . . . (1757), which posits for instance that

> The perfection of their gardens consists in the number, beauty, and diversity of these scenes. The Chinese gardeners, like the European painters, collect from nature the most pleasing objects, which they endeavour to combine in such a manner, as not only to appear to the best advantage separately, but likewise to unite in forming an elegant and striking whole. (Hunt and Willis 284)

Likewise, Chambers's *Dissertation on Oriental Gardening* (1772) is, in Hunt's words, as much an essay on "Oriental designs" as it is "a vigorous contribution to an English gardenist debate that reached its peak in the 1790s" (Hunt and Willis 318). And the very appeal for the inclusion of "art" in gardening (for example: "Art must therefore supply the scantiness of nature. . . . The Chinese are therefore no enemies to strait lines . . . " [Hunt and Willis 319]) shows that Chambers is still within the parameters of the Renaissance interpretation of gardens, even as he invokes a supposedly other example. Furthermore, Mitchell indicates that in a history of landscape gardening which narrates a progress toward "nature," the "other" of landscape gardening traditions, such as the Chinese, is excluded from the narrative sequence, or from history: "Chinese landscape is prehistoric. . . . The 'other hand' of landscape . . . is preemancipatory, prior to the perception of nature as such" (12).

Recognizing (elements of) Roman classicism through Renaissance as an invariant in Western landscape gardening helps explain a few apparent contradictions. It first allows one to understand why "nature" has, seemingly so incompatibly, been defined at times as geometrical and at others as ungeometrical, two opposite appreciations that were to become standard references to the French and the English styles respectively. In 1638, Jacques Boyceau writes in his *Traité du jardinage selon les raisons de la nature et de l'art*: "All of which things, as beautiful as we may choose them, will be flawed and less agreeable if they are not ordered and placed with symmetry and good correspondence, for Nature also observes it in her so perfect works" (Baridon 1995, 192). On the contrary, Girardin posits in his own treatise, *De la composition des paysages* (1777), that geometry and symmetry are "against nature" (68). Instead of ascribing this difference to a historical "evolution" in the appraisal of nature, it is possible to interpret these contradictory definitions of "nature" as already contained or inscribed within the model of the classical garden, or as different available quotations of the classical garden.[17]

In a study on the use of the rock and the pillar in the eighteenth century, Monique Mosser has perceptively shown in her examination of the doric pillar that in some cases the architectonic was chosen precisely as a symbol of the most natural. This helps understand why the architectonic has not always been seen as a contradiction to nature. She notes that "above all, the 'archeologism' of that form has been emphasized" (Mosser 1983, 59). This is because the doric order was "considered as the most ancient of the classical orders." But she immediately adds an important argument: "and, as such, it was the one which contained most obviously in its forms the trace of its natural origins" (59). Indeed, in the eighteenth century, classicism functions as the model for the most civilized as much as a pointer to the most natural, if not the most natural itself, in that it is closer to "nature," compared to our own historically degraded state. Furthermore, Mosser's comment shows that the very opposition between architecture and rustic nature, which is urgently posited by most authors of landscape gardening in the eighteenth century, collapses in the case of the doric pillar. For it is used precisely, in spite of being obviously architectonic, because it is "a primitive order," "a pure order," in other words because "in sum, it is the order which can best be allied to the forms of nature" (59).[18]

Finally, a common reliance on the example of antiquity also explains why the supposedly stylistically opposed French and English gardens presented some common features (in particular imitations of classical monuments or sculptures). Here is most visible the kind of "double bind" involved in the political theory of *translatio imperii*: power is geographically displaced, history moves forward, while thematically and concretely, power takes up figures from the past in order to construct itself and project itself in the future. Iteration is both promoted and denied.

Instead of repeating that sometime during the eighteenth century, there was a transition in France from the French model to the English style, I would rather speak at this stage of a recycling of forms or concepts in landscape gardening. Versailles is again a good example, because additions to the park were so steadily made from the moment it was constructed. Yet, as Jean de Cayeux's study on Hubert Robert shows, work in Versailles was as much a matter of displacing and reframing existing elements as providing additions. This is the case of three groups of marble statues representing Apollo served by nymphs, known as "The Bath of Apollo." Robert used the statues sculpted in 1675 by Coustou, Girardon, and Marsy for Louis XIV (de Cayeux 73), but he displaced them in a new frame created for them between 1778 and 1781 (de Cayeux 165). In fact, the frame changed—in 1675, it was a grotto made with shells—, but the statues remained the same. Simone Hoog mentions that the artificial frame (which included sculpted rock) was built in order to promote the new English style (93). When she considers the "Bath of Apollo," Miller comments on what is in effect the coexistence of two opposed styles, not the replacement of a "former" style: "The present grove constitutes a surprising tableau amidst Le Nôtre's garden. . . . Here the mysteries of nature, embedded in the obscurity of the enveloping grotto, are juxtaposed with the apogee of classicism represented by Girardon's white marble statues" (76). Robert's recycled "Bath of Apollo" undermines in its very conception the teleological claim of histories of landscape gardening, such as Walpole's. It is not that the "tableau" remains always the same, but that its very image only needs to be displaced and reframed in order to convey appropriately a sense of novelty. The statue of Apollo differs from itself. We have here a temporal perspective in which, in the words of a profound philosopher of history, Walter Benjamin, "what is newest does not change" (Buck-Morss 97).[19] It is possible to expand Miller's above-mentioned remark on "the apogee of classicism." While it refers in Miller's sentence to seventeenth-century French classicism, it can also be taken to represent the iterable figure of Classicism in the Western garden. The different location of and decoration around that figure are allowed to define "a new style," while the figure itself remains, like an obsessive memory.

TRANSITIONS: A RETURN

We have seen that the authors who promote a history of landscape gardening unfolding in a series of transitions to a next, better stage, disregard the ways in which a new style repeats the classical reference, the model of a garden. In fact, they ignore repetition as such, repetition in the sense of recycling, not identity, as we saw in the case of the "Bath of Apollo." Since I have been stressing so far the extent to which such a repetition is omitted or silenced, it might come as a surprise that I shall now turn to a close reading of precisely the opposite claim, that a transition has taken place, a claim I have been in some measure working against up to this point.

The argument is made in French treatises on landscape gardening written in the 1770s.[20] These treatises celebrate the disappearance of the French style and the advent of a new style. Their descriptions of gardens rely on actual layouts. Among other contributions, Morel designed the parks in Guiscard and Ermenonville, Girardin laid part of the grounds in Ermenonville, Watelet worked in Moulin-Joli, and Carmontelle in Monceau.[21] An important question for these authors and for their readers today is how to name the new style they are describing. Walpole is of the opinion that they evince a clear propensity to "mimic" the English style, when he says that "The French have of late years adopted our style in gardens" (22). The French authors in question disagree with that view. Both responses relate the aesthetic, taxonomic discussion to the "politicization" of nature that Baridon discusses in "Jardins et paysage."

But in taking at face value and reading closely both adversarial positions as far as a stylistic change is concerned, I am still within the parameters of my discussion of "transition." My object was first to point out a silenced repetition behind a claim of change in gardening practices. I now come back to this claim in order to investigate it as a form of denial, the effects of which need to be interpreted. I will next address the ways in which Walpole's assessment of an imitation—that is, a repetition of the English style in France—is not merely denied in French treatises, but rhetorically addressed. By this, I mean that French authors imitate the figure of repetition itself in their treatises. To Walpole's suspicion, they respond by foregrounding the process of imitation and repetition, in a first step. Then they reject the position of indebtedness, by presenting their conceptions as the path to the future, in a way which adopts while diverting for its own purposes the "Whiggish" history French authors are writing against. They also bring to the fore, *en abyme*, the debt of the English to the French. Thus they return the very accusation of imitation to the sender, in a return which is also a circuitous repetition of an earlier English gesture.

Let us examine first how the imitation of English principles is addressed. Eighteenth-century French authors expound principles that are hardly original and, on the contrary, rehearse current, common arguments. They cannot be original because they write after these arguments have already been long in circulation. They often choose to admit it, when, like Girardin or Carmontelle, they recognize that the topic has long been debated before them, particularly by the English. Carmontelle starts his short description of the *Garden of Monceau* (1779) by stating:

> We do not have the pretention of giving here a theory, or precepts; it would be ridiculous, coming after the work published in England by Sir Thomas Wathely [*sic*], under the modest title *Observations on Modern Gardening*. That book contains the true principles of these kinds of gardens. (2)

This indicates that French treatises enunciate a *doxa* about landscape gardening, a summary of current ideas. Moreover, English treatises on landscape gardening were often translated and made available in France almost at the same time as their publication in England, and reciprocally.[22] Thus not only can these treatises hardly be said to express original ideas, they moreover integrate stock notions about landscape gardening that might have been written by English authors against a "French" perspective to begin with. This repetition is apparent in the consideration of Le Nôtre's accomplishments in French treatises of the 1770s, because like their English counterparts, they critically assess the issue of the emphasis of artificial effects in a garden.

THE FRENCH AGAINST THE FRENCH STYLE

At the beginning of his article, Jaucourt defines a garden as a "site artistically planted and cultivated, either for our needs or for our pleasure" (459). The acknowledgment that the work of the landscape gardener is artistic is a commonplace in treatises on gardening. In his *Théorie des jardins* (1776), Jean-Marie Morel repeatedly refers to the landscape gardener as an "Artist" (for example 24). Or Girardin calls him a "Composer" (for example 10). Yet, the expressed necessity of writing treatises on landscape gardening arises largely from the wish to rectify false assumptions regarding the amount of involvement of the artist in his work.

Jaucourt praises Le Nôtre for his good taste and art (459); about the Versailles gardens he says: "It will always be true that much art, genius, and intelligence were necessary in order to embellish, to a singular point of perfection, one of the most uncultivated sites in the kingdom" (460). But Girardin is more severe in his estimate of Le Nôtre's accomplishments: "This is called symmetry. Le Notre introduced it in gardens, and Mansard in buildings; and the extraordinary part of it is, that if you were to inquire what was the use of it, no *spe-*

cial jury could determine" (123–24). This is a good example of an integrated English argument on the French style: Hunt has shown that the English landscape garden movement was directed against "its supposed formality" (Hunt and Willis 8). Girardin lists some negative characteristics, which ranks him among the detractors of the French formal garden:

> [T]hen followed the plantation according to the rules of cold symmetry; the ground was laid smooth at a great expence, the trees were mutilated and tortured in all ways, the water shut up within four walls, the view confined by masy hedges, and the prospect from the house limited to a flat parterre, cut out into squares like a chess-board. (3–4)

In his first chapter, "Of Symmetrical Gardens," Morel is in agreement with Girardin that symmetry and geometry are to be avoided because they "mutilate" and otherwise disfigure nature (they are "against nature," Girardin says [68]). Morel makes the point that a false analogy has been drawn between architecture and landscape gardening (6), and that an effort has been wrongly made to "link by a mutual correspondence the building, which he [the architect] made the principal object, to the Garden which seemed to him only to be the accessory" (6). The perception of a geometrical link between the mansion and the garden, and therefore the consideration that the garden follows an architectural pattern in the French formal style is already conventional in these treatises. This view has important counterimplications for their understanding of nature.

Jaucourt remarks quite the opposite approach in English landscape gardening: "One does not pretend to provide in those sites the smallest, and even the most beautiful works of art" (460). He underscores here an important perceived difference between French and English gardening—in France, Le Nôtre has overemphasized art, whereas in England, landscape gardeners tend to deny themselves the self-evidence of art. For Jaucourt, the landscape gardener's self-denial prevents beauty in some measure ("even the most beautiful works of art"), yet authorizes another, certainly better understanding of nature, for it awakens a sense of its beauty that is as unmediated as possible: "Let us take advantage of her liberalities [nature's], and let us be content with using industry to vary her spectacles. May waters bring groves forth and embellish them!" (460). The reproach, therefore, mostly addressed to Le Nôtre, is not that he used artifice in his layouts but that he never exerted enough self-restraint in his conceptions.

In the treatises considered here, the assertion that there have been false assumptions about landscape gardening generally precedes a plea for an unobtrusive artistic involvement. The artist's work, it is said, should aim at seconding nature, his function must be supplementary, not contrary to nature. Jaucourt underscores this function when he praises the English garden for showing "only nature modestly adorned and never made up" (460). The artist sometimes adds to, sometimes removes from nature, while using mostly nature's "materials" (such as trees, water, rocks), making nature a "supplement" to itself. The supplementary logic also divides nature from itself, as is made obvious in a letter written from England in 1750 by Mme du Boccage. There, she sums up the relation of nature to itself in a landscape, when she mentions that "They [the English] even make canals run in a serpentine form, *that they may appear the more natural*, and cast unequal shades upon the banks, which are covered with green turf and trees, *in the form in which they are produced by nature*" (Wiebenson 26, my emphasis). Mme du Boccage points out here that form is both natural and an appearance, that is to say, a contrivance, of nature: form may be one of nature's productions, and an artefact, which however purports to be taken for nature.

Not only nature, however, but the artist also is a supplement. The supplementary logic explains why the "Artist" is at times modestly assumed to be only nature's assistant ("be secondary to it [la seconder]" [Morel 90]), and on other occasions said to have superseded it. Morel writes for example that the landscape gardener succeeds "in appearing to have done nothing, . . . in persuading that everything depends on felicitous chances and the disposition of the location" (348). The best art is here the art that conceals itself, again giving an appearance of nature without presuming to be too evident: "they [the beauties of nature] must, on the contrary, carefully hide the art which produced them" (381). But on the other hand, this is a proud modesty, in the sense that the landscape gardener, through his self-denial, also rivals nature, and even "makes" it: "One [the Gardener] creates, so to speak, Nature, since he uses the same materials, disposes them in the same order, and uses the same means as she" (374). For Morel, unlike a painter who represents nature, a landscape gardener "creates" it: "One makes reality, and the other, representation" (374). Therefore, nature can, in that respect, become quite subservient to the artist: "Nature, which he has, so to speak, subjected to his orders, yields to his will, shares the labor with him, completes and perfects the work" (378–79). Such definitions invalidate a strict opposition between nature and culture. Rather, "landscape mediates the cultural and the natural. . . . It is not only a natural scene, and not just a representation of a natural scene, but a *natural* representation of a natural scene, a trace or icon of nature *in* nature itself" (Mitchell 15).

WHAT MAKES NATURE NATURAL

The attention to supplementarity evinces one important component of the appeal to nature in landscape gardening treatises: nature may function as a precedent, a model, yet at the same time, at stake is not merely the reproduction or *mimesis* of preexisting elements. In his *De la Composition des paysages* (1777), René-Louis de Girardin talks of "chosen nature" (72) as the task and purpose of the landscape gardener, but he soon adds that "a landscape . . . is a site which is chosen or *created* by taste or feeling" (72–73). Earlier in England, William Gilpin had used a striking formulation, when he talked of a "probable nature" (6). In effect, it could be said that the treatises investigate what makes nature natural, and determine that what the landscape gardener should aim at achieving is the *creation* of *natural* effects, an antithesis that is fundamental for the authors considered.[23]

Morel gives a good example of such an investigation when he inquires into the natural formation of a terrain. It will be remembered that for Jaucourt, a garden is a "*site artistically* planted and cultivated." In that respect, Morel emphasizes the necessity to consider primarily the site, a position that Girardin agrees with: "Before you begin the work, make yourself well acquainted with the surrounding country, and make sure that the terrain necessary to complete your design is appropriate" (21). Watelet is also of the opinion that "The nature of the terrain must essentially contribute to determine the character of the scene" (62). In fact, we have seen that such questions had long since been taken into consideration. Boyceau, for example, devoted sections of his treatise to the respective merits of level and unlevel sites (Hazlehurst 32–33).[24] But Morel seems to go further: he inquires into "the principal causes that determine the form of the terrain" (91), because, according to him, it is by understanding the causes of natural forms, which in turn produce certain effects, that nature can be "created" for some predetermined purposes by the landscape gardener. Morel concludes at the end of his investigation that "Such is the general course [marche] of Nature in the formation of the terrain, and such is the rule that the Artist must follow when he proposes to have it undergo some changes" (95).

This statement shows that the artist must follow nature at the very moment when he is in the process of altering it; the artist is not expected by Morel to copy strictly speaking, but to be verisimilar to nature's "marches," a recurring word in his treatise that also indicates the essential self-transformation, the constant formation of nature. For Morel, *physis* undoubtedly is, before man's intervention in landscape, but it is in a state of perpetual motion, it is not arrested, there for man to imitate it: "Varied in her forms, rich and proportionate in her unequal dimensions, she infinitely modifies herself" (23). This formulation will recall "materialist" views of nature, such as they are summed up in d'Holbach's *Système de la nature* (1770). D'Holbach asserts for example that "all the phenomena of nature are due to the diverse movements of the various materials it contains. As a result, like the Phoenix, it is continually born again out of its ashes" (I, 63). Moreover, d'Holbach's third chapter is entitled "Of matter, of its different combinations and of its diverse movements; or of nature's course [marche]" (65), the last phrase being repeatedly used by Morel. Morel does not exactly recommend copying or selecting from nature's plenitude and plenty in landscape gardening. Rather, man should emulate and even rival nature in his art, and in particular he should imitate its perpetual motion and modification. Watelet also proposes for the gardener to emulate a motion that he sees as characteristic of nature: "Movement, that spirit of Nature, that inexhaustible principle of the interest it triggers, will cause him to wish ceaselessly to animate the landscape he will arrange" (109).

The task of the landscape gardener is to reproduce modification, as the very principle of nature. The effect of the gardener's intervention consists therefore in representing in the garden the temporality or historical difference with itself of a terrain, not only its (spatial) "motion" or transformation.

THE EXEMPLARITY OF WATER

Water is generally found to convey best the notion of what Watelet calls "the liberty of movement" (68). For Morel, water's "liberty" is warranted by its free and uninterrupted "circulation," a word he often has recourse to in his treatise: "The perpetual circulation of the waters, ceaselessly reduced to vapor and pumped by the action of the sun, that universal principle of activity and movement, is a physical effect that is well-known and noticed by the least attentive men" (91).

Authors of landscape gardening treatises are in agreement when they define water as a key "material" of nature. Again, this argument is hardly new, either as a requisite element in gardens, or in its suggested associations. But Morel's interest in water stems from his observations on the formation of the terrain. He shows in that respect that water is not only an element of decoration or convenience in a landscape. It importantly contributes to its very form. It does so first with the action of rains: "It is they which shape the mountains, which smooth out their angles, which procure for them that harmony in forms and that softness in contours. It is they which link, by an imperceptible union, all the different slopes among themselves and with the level parts" (92). Gathered at the bottom of slopes, water serves to "perfect the forms" of the terrain (93). In nature, landscape is forever perfecting its forms, reacting to itself with itself, and it is this effect of fluidity, this harmonious circulation that the landscape gardener should achieve in his art. The difficulty for the landscape gardener consists in striving to achieve what is transitory, what is in the process of transforming itself: "All the forms, to which the gardener proposes to subject it [the terrain] must bear the imprint of their action [the waters], or at least must not present effects which contradict it, if he wants to give them a character of truth" (96). What the landscape gardener must attempt to provide is not only a phenomenon that seems natural (which would be merely artistically rendering a certain end result of "nature"), but the link between cause and effect that a natural phenomenon makes visible: "Whatever their diversity and variety, the forms which do not seem to be the effect of a physical cause must be rejected" (100). The process of formation must be perceptible in landscape gardening. In Morel's analysis, if water is one of the factors that naturally shapes a terrain in the form that it has and that it will have, then it follows not only that it will look natural to incorporate water to a landscape, but that the dynamic action and reaction between water and terrain must be perceptible, which will ensure the credibility, and therefore, naturalize, the artificial terrain ("bear the imprint of their action . . . if he wants to give them a character of truth"). Again, by suggesting that what must be rendered is this link between cause and effect, Morel insists that he is referring to an "action," or an ongoing tension which has to be made manifest in the garden.

Morel's position about nature finds a complement in Girardin's negative assessment of symmetry and geometry, one of the effects of which he indicates thus: "By taking the straight line for the basis of his art, the builder finds, it is true, in the square [équerre], the perpendicularity [l'aplomb], and the perpendicular, level straight line, the principle of construction, because *the straight line is that of immobility*" (20, my emphasis: translation omitted). If the straight line, that is if geometry is immobility, it is by the same token at odds with nature, which is movement itself:

> But the architect composer [i.e., the landscape gardener] must work for the movement of the eyes, and even of the soul; so, when he wants (if I may say so) to *immobilize* everything on a straight line, and enclose everything by angles, he obviously acts against the nature of movement, of sight, of strolling, and against all the picturesque varieties that the different sites may offer. (21, translation omitted)

Girardin's understanding of the site as movement and unbounded variety parallels Morel's considerations on the terrain. Both authors read the site as in perpetual motion, and nature as self-transformation, circulation, and fluidity, and Le Nôtre is to blame in their view because his art contradicts this characteristic, it freezes what should be let flowing, it immobilizes what should be kept in motion.

REPEATING THE ENGLISH: A RHETORICAL GRAFT

The arguments French treatises rehearse in order to condemn the French style are clearly familiar. Likewise, the injunctions to the

French landscape gardener of "today" appear to be merely a transcription, or the repetition of similar techniques or principles recommended in England earlier or at the same time. If we only look at Whately's *Observations on Modern Gardening*, which was a well-known reference for French authors, and compare its table of contents with Morel's, the similarity is striking, in particular in the discussion of nature's "materials." After his description of the terrain and what presides to its formation, Morel talks "Of Waters" (chapter 8), "Of the effects of vegetation" (chapter 9), "Of Rocks" (chapter 10), "Of Buildings" (chapter 11). Whately also discusses the "materials of the art of gardening" with the same subdivisions: "Of Ground," "Of Wood," "Of Water," "Of Rocks," "Of Buildings." The similarity of construction between English and French treatises leads Hunt, for example, to call Girardin's treatise "the most authoritative French treatise on the English landscape style" (Hunt and Willis 42). In terms of genre and style, he is certainly right, yet his assertion cannot account for the following statement in Girardin: "Therefore I will not discuss here ancient gardens, or modern gardens, or English, or Chinese gardens . . . I shall only treat of the methods to embellish or enrich nature, the combinations of which, varied to infinity, cannot be classed, and equally belong to all ages and all nations" (8–9). Such a statement, which is also found in diverse forms in other authors of the same period in France, denies that the treatise rehearses English landscape gardening principles, in fact shows a relationship to the "English" which is rather adversarial than imitative. Jaucourt and Carmontelle, for instance, share the view that some principles regarding the involvement of art in landscape gardening have already been successfully theorized and executed in England. This conviction is then what urges them first to contain English gardens in England and then to redistribute in some measure to "France" what is apparently so indisputably an English achievement. Carmontelle says for example that he proposes

> some reflections on the new Gardens, and observ[es] that our wealth, our customs, our tastes, and our climate being different to those of the English, our Gardens must not be a servile imitation of theirs, but must be composed with these differences in mind. (2)

Again, there is no question that Hunt is right in his assessment that the English landscape garden "dominated Europe in much the same way that the French garden of Le Nôtre had done earlier" (Hunt and

Willis 39). Nor can it be contested that French theoretical treatises on the new style often "took their cue from English writers: Watelet's *Essai sur les jardins* (1774), for instance, is dependent upon Addison and Whately" (Hunt and Willis 39). The next chapter will investigate, still in keeping with Voltaire's observation, the nationalist character of the French authors' denial, a nationalist reflex which is further complicated by the appeal to a universal criterion (in Girardin's words, "all ages and all nations"). Yet, I would contend that Girardin's position is paradigmatic of a specific graft that has been effected from English authors. What will interest me above all is a rhetorical graft that, if analyzed, can begin to account for Girardin's claim that he is not talking of English gardens when he actually seems, for all intents and purposes, to be talking of English gardens. There is visible the process *en abyme* I mentioned earlier. What the French treatises repeat in their very recognition and denial, at the same time, of a repetition of English principles and practices, follows closely a similar double gesture they found elaborated in English treatises on landscape gardening.

Chapter 2

National Nature

> The recurrent metaphor of landscape as the inscape of national identity emphasizes the quality of light, the question of social visibility, the power of the eye to naturalize the rhetoric of national affiliation and its forms of collective expression.
>
> —Homi Bhabha, *Nation and Narration*

ENGLISH RESISTANCES TO THE FRENCH

The occupation of one's national territory by foreigners during a war is one of the clearest cases of the loss of one's liberty. Symbolically, the vogue of a foreign style of landscape gardening could be associated with such a disenfranchisement, perhaps more readily than any other aesthetic instance, because at stake was the concrete transformation of the domestic soil by a foreign form. The reliance on the French style in the seventeenth century perceptibly constituted a serious cultural threat to early eighteenth-century English authors writing about principles of landscape gardening. Therefore, at the beginning of the century, they were in a situation comparable to that of the French authors writing in the 1770s: the English had then to deal with an influential French style, and the French were later to have to come to terms with the widespread English style. Focusing on theories rather than practices allows one to become aware of a strong resistance to an overwhelming or "invading" model. This resistance was first uttered by English authors. If we consult English treatises on landscape gardening, it becomes apparent that their French counterparts used them not only in order to imitate and borrow the same principles in gardening, but to repeat the very formulation of an argument against the danger of contamination by the other. Such an argument, together with the rhetorical means proposed in order to counteract the contamination, are proposed by English authors such as Walpole or Whately, or even earlier authors, such as Pope.

To begin with, English authors gave the French the example of a dual assessment of gardens on their soil. If we only follow as a characteristic example the argument made against geometry by English authors, we can observe that geometry often divides itself in two, into the foreign and the domestic. This is a way for them to distinguish between what can be regarded as their own, national achievements, as opposed to designs influenced by foreign accomplishments. Horace Walpole's *History of the Modern Taste in Gardening* (1771/1780) testifies to this dual assessment. First, it should be noted that as long as he considers the French style in France, Walpole does not have a serious objection to geometry, as is made apparent in his playful remark that "when a Frenchman reads of the garden of Eden, I do not doubt but he concludes it was something approaching to that of Versailles, with clipt hedges, berceaus, and trellis-work" (Walpole 4). As a consequence, Walpole concludes that "it is thus that the word *garden* has at all times passed for whatever was understood by that term in different Countries." But what bothers him is the thought that the French style should have been overwhelming in England, and adopted by "our ancestors" (21). To circumvent the force as much as the appeal (the fashion) of this intrusion and of the foreign contamination of the English soil, Walpole has recourse to a gesture adopted by earlier eighteenth-century writers on landscape gardening in England. He first diminishes England's reliance on the French style by giving numerous examples of a home-grown symmetry.

Walpole invokes as a precedent a celebrated literary figure, Alexander Pope, who had enthusiastically embraced the new English style. Walpole declares, in his assessment of the geometrical French style: "Trees were headed, and their sides pared away; many French groves seem green chests set upon poles. Seats of marble, arbours and summer-houses, terminated every vista; and symmetry . . . was so essential, that, as Pope observed, each alley has a brother, / And half the garden just reflects the other" (11). This slightly misquoted reference might induce Walpole's reader to think that Pope is talking here of a garden located in France—Walpole has just mentioned "French groves" and ends his sentence with Pope's disparaging assessment of symmetry. If we read Pope's quotation from *An Epistle to Lord Burlington* (1731) in context, however, it is clear that Pope is alluding instead to a geometrical style located in England—his comment that "Grove nods at Grove, each Alley has a brother, / And half the platform just reflects the other. / The suff'ring eye inverted Nature sees, / Trees cut to Statues, Statues thick as trees" (Pope 144), is supposed to be the description of an Englishman's grounds, "Timon's Villa." F. W. Bateson, the editor of Pope's *Epistle*, says that "the identification of Timon is one of the most difficult and complicated of the problems connected with Pope. . . . Timon is almost certainly nobody in particular—a personification of aristocratic pride" (Pope 142). The editor also remarks that Pope's image of Timon's Villa "is intended to comprize the principles of a false Taste of Magnificence" (Pope 142). With their descriptions, both Pope and Walpole strive to contain the anxiety they feel at the domination of a foreign style by referring to it as the poor taste of their own domestic achievements.

For Pope does not merely rehearse the French impact on English gardening practices. Earlier in the *Epistle*, he contrasts the masterpiece of the French style, Versailles, to the very recent English accomplishment, Stowe, and favors Stowe in the comparison: "Nature shall join you; Time shall make it grow / A Work to wonder at—perhaps a STOW. / Without it [Sense], proud Versailles! thy glory falls" (Pope 139). This opposition allows Pope to celebrate present-day English accomplishments (Stowe), which become more adequate to the demands of his time than Versailles in terms of reason ("Sense") and in aesthetic terms ("a Work to wonder at"). This gesture is a way for Pope to minimize the powerful influence of the French style in England, by splitting geometry in two, a foreign geometry as opposed to a domestic geometry: on the one hand, there would be the geometry of "proud Versailles," and on the other, a home-grown symmetry, certainly outdated and to be ridiculed, as in Timon's Villa, but still

English. Indeed, Hunt retraces as one factor for the emergence of the English landscape movement in England a reaction against the early domestic Tudor geometrical garden (Hunt and Willis 2).

Dividing geometry into the foreign and the domestic is also a way for earlier authors to allow for England's potential or actual greatness in landscape gardening, while diminishing England's reliance on the French style by giving examples of an English geometrical style. Batty Langley's *New Principles of Gardening* (1728) states for example that "If the Gentlemen of *England* had formerly been better advised in the laying out their Gardens, we might by this Time have been at least equal (if not far superior) to any Abroad" (Hunt and Willis 178). This implies that not only can geometry be said to be split in two (foreign against domestic), but that the English style is correlatively made to divide itself, the achievement of Stowe being, in Pope and others, the preferred way to oppose the English garden to itself (the new style against geometry). Twenty years after Langley's treatise, William Gilpin used words that parallel his, but he was more hopeful, because such grounds as Stowe's enabled him to distinguish between a detestable former English style and a felicitous modern English design: "Our Gardens for the most Part were laid out in so formal, aukward, and wretched a Manner, that they were really a Scandal to the very Genius of the Nation. . . . But *Stow*, it is to be hoped, may work some Reformation" (Gilpin 48). In this passage, even more decidedly than in Pope, the French precedent is all but silenced, and the "formal, aukward" taste is made into an unfortunate, but still indigenous part of the English heritage—"the very Genius of the Nation."

The fact that Walpole has recourse to this double gesture makes us aware of the rhetorical figure of repetition at work in his treatise just as he endorses the quite opposite notion of (gardening) history as an unfolding series of unheralded, singular moments. Like Pope and others, he emphasizes the poor domestic taste of the English in the past: "In Kip's views of the seats of our nobility and gentry, we see the same tiresome and returning uniformity" (Walpole 12). One of the effects of his long refutation of Sir William Temple's principles of gardening (expounded in *Upon the Gardens of Epicurus: or, Of Gardening, in the Year 1685*), is to show that the geometrical characteristics of the former English garden are due to misguided English theoreticians (Temple), rather than to the influence of the French style. Likewise, the English style is correlatively made to divide itself in two in Walpole, following the example of Pope and others. If Temple advocates wrong principles, Walpole argues, such is not the case of Milton, whose poem, *Paradise Lost* (1667), epitomizes the very principles of "modern gardening," "so minutely do his ideas correspond with the present standard" (Walpole 17). The prestigious ancestry of Milton's "ideas" is another way of circumventing the importance of Le Nôtre in earlier English gardens. Not only is the French style often described as a local, homegrown style. It also has been surpassed, if only in anticipation, by Milton, at a time that is contemporary to Le Nôtre's work in Versailles. In other words, the English style followed a wrong track in Walpole's estimate (Temple), but England can also be said to have discovered the right, modern principles at an early stage (Milton). Because English gardening is reinvested with historical priority and precedence in such an account, the French style becomes less threatening and overwhelming, and can in turn be discussed as a local, French aberration that never really affected the English soil: "It was not peculiar to Sir William Temple to think in that manner. How many Frenchmen are there who have seen *our* gardens, and still prefer *natural* flights of steps and shady cloisters covered with lead!" (Walpole 20). Indeed, historical priority is crucial to Walpole's argument, which traces an evolution of taste in England that traverses the French style and triumphantly peaks in the celebration of the discovery by the English of the "point of perfection" (Walpole 35).

FRENCH REACTIONS: DEFENDING LE NÔTRE

The poet Delille equitably declares in "Les Jardins" that "I do not choose between Kent and Le Nôtre" (Guy 1991, 96). After all, as Daniel Mornet has remarked, "Until the end of the eighteenth century, some people liked and even preferred the French garden" (219).[1] Walpole was of the opinion that because the English had found the "point of perfection," it implied that "other countries" would have to "mimic or corrupt our taste" (Walpole 35). One radical way chosen by some French authors to deny the need to imitate or acclimatize English principles in France is to consider that the absolute in landscape gardening has been reached by Le Nôtre. We have seen earlier that Jaucourt, who professes to be impartial in his assessment of landscape gardening, does mention that Le Nôtre is unsurpassed in some respects. But other authors are even more emphatic than Jaucourt. This is in particular the case of Antoine-Nicolas Dézallier d'Argenville, whose *Voyage pittoresque des environs de Paris* was first published in 1755, and had later editions with very few modifications in 1762, 1768, and 1779. Dézallier starts his treatise by announcing that "It is not a paradox to propose that the most beautiful gardens in Europe are those in France. Everyone knows that the beautiful art which teaches how to design them was born there under the reign of Louis XIV" (Dézallier 3). This statement is similar to Jaucourt's, and Dézallier's next comment testifies to a common silencing of the Italian heritage in landscape gardening: "That Prince, finding in Le Nostre a genius capable of carrying out his great ideas, sent him to Italy to perfect himself. The trip that Le Nostre took there in 1678 was, however, of little use to him" (3–4). Dézallier finds it necessary to support his praise of French gardens by a comparison with England, but his short analysis shows an obvious bias. To his own question, "Will England provide us with more beautiful objects in this genre?" (5), he answers in the negative, choosing not to mention Stowe, but listing on the contrary features which belong unmistakably to the French style and that are found to be unfortunately missing in England. For instance, "Kingsington, another Royal mansion, has neither the figures nor the fountains which are the soul of gardens. . . . The gardens of Hampton-Court are more regular, but very little adorned" (6). Dézallier's cursory examination of gardens in England ends with the opinion that "after this examination, it would be unfair not to grant France the superiority in gardens above all the other Provinces ["Nations," in later editions] of Europe" (9). As I have suggested earlier, this view, which consolidates once and for all France's preeminence in landscape gardening by grounding it in a prestigious past and by rejecting any foreign debt for its development, is extreme, and not entirely shared by authors such as Girardin and Morel, certainly not as far as the assessment of Le Nôtre is concerned. Characteristically, even Dézallier can relent and admit that English gardens may have some merits, provided they do not encroach on the French soil. This concession is found only as of the 1768 edition: "This decoration would not succeed in all climates; it requires a cool country, such as England, Flanders and Holland" (6). In other words, Dézallier is intent on affirming the uncompromised superiority of the French style, but slightly wavers and ends up accepting the English model when it does not affect the French soil. This double gesture of containment of the foreign abroad and celebration of accomplishments at home is similar to Pope's opposition between Versailles and Stowe. In a symmetrical gesture to Pope, too, and Walpole later (in their assessment of geometry), Dézallier attempts to divide the English garden in two categories: he wishes to contain the "Englishness" of the English garden and limit it to England, but on the other hand he confers praise on what looks French to him in England: "The gardens at Boughton, at a distance of twenty leagues from London, are distinctive only because they have nothing in common with the English taste" (7).

In his versified pamphlet against the English style, entitled "Epitre sur la manie des jardins anglois" ["Epistle on the mania of English gardens"] (1775), Chabanon claims that it is still legitimate to be, as he is, a strong partisan of Le Nôtre, by returning to the English the argument they use against "art" in French gardens: "But do speak with sincerity; / Have you, without care, without skill, / Polished the velvet carpet of your lawns? / What! This art seduces you and all other offends you?" (Chabanon 5). Chabanon points out other inconsistencies which do not correspond to the declared ambition to present a simple nature in English gardens, such as "hideous simulacra" or "the ridiculous image / Of these fake monuments that art has counterfeited" (10). He also gives the example of an English lord, who paradoxically cut down "the vigorous trees" (9) of his straight (geometrical, or "French") alley, in order to prepare the terrain for a so-called natural landscaping. For Chabanon, the accusation that the French garden is unnatural because it is too artificial is therefore not convincingly demonstrated by the very practices of the partisans of the new style. Both Dézallier and Chabanon defend Le Nôtre as indeed "ours," as the famous landscape designer's very name indicates.

FRENCH REACTIONS: AGAINST LE NÔTRE *AND* THE ENGLISH STYLE

Dézallier and Chabanon's resistance to the English garden is not adopted in these terms by Morel or Girardin. For one thing, like the

English authors we have mentioned, they do find fault with geometry in French landscape gardening, unlike Dézallier or Chabanon. But the two seemingly different approaches on the part of French authors could be said to represent two sides of the same coin.

In fact, Morel and Girardin insist at crucial points of their treatises that criticizing Le Nôtre and geometry does not entail endorsing the English style. Morel writes, for example: "From all those that I just reviewed, I exclude the symmetrical Garden" (Morel 203), because the symmetrical garden is not compatible with the principles he is expounding in his treatise. This seems to be a typical "English" argument. But Morel also repeats the rhetorical move of English authors, when he repeats the tactics of dividing a style, or a characteristic such as geometry, in two. He explains in that respect that there are really two types of French gardens: the first corresponds to the geometrical French style of the past, and the second, to the new style. In Morel's assessment of gardening in France, the repetition of Walpole and other English authors' rhetorical move (whose object, it will be recalled, was to promote a potential or actual nationally marked style, in response to an overwhelming foreign style) presents the similar purposes of counterbalancing the vogue of the English style. Therefore, unlike Walpole thematically (in what he says), but like him rhetorically (in what he does), Morel is dissatisfied with the new result and finds that the rejection of the symmetrical garden has brought about more harm than good: "Bizarre compositions have been substituted to the rejected symmetrical gardens; they have been filled with a multitude of buildings placed without order, distributed without taste, principles and intention" (393). This statement coincides with Jaucourt's estimate that in France, gardening has become decadent after Le Nôtre's death. According to Morel, this type of garden cannot be recommended in his treatise, because it is no less artificial than the symmetrical garden: "as if it were a means of rendering Nature" (394).

But unlike Jaucourt, who thought that England had taken over the talent of designing "gardens of good taste" (460), Morel does not oppose this misguided conception to landscape gardening in England. In effect, Jaucourt was describing three kinds of garden: two in France, one in England, the first French garden being the tasteful Le Nôtre garden, the second being a "frivolous" aberration (460).

According to Jaucourt, the tasteless French garden was increasingly found in France while the English pursued their own successful style in England. Jaucourt also presents a division used by English authors, in this case one between two French styles. Even though his discussion of French gardening "today" is not very positive, he valorizes at least one pole of the division, the former style promoted by Le Nôtre. But for Morel, who says he approves neither of past nor of recent gardening practices in France (be they in the new form or in the geometrical style), the conclusion of the examination of French gardening would be rather discouraging if it stopped at this point. But Morel does not stop here. On the contrary, Morel identifies the deplorable profusion, the accumulation of objects that was related by Jaucourt to the tasteless French garden of today, with what he calls either "modern gardens" or "English gardens":[2] "[T]emples, gothic churches, cemeteries, tombs, verses, inscriptions, allegoric and emblematic monuments, and all these buildings of imitation and caprice overcrowd *the modern Gardens, that take favor under the name of English Gardens*" (Morel 234–35, my emphasis). This denomination allows him to label as "English" a style he wishes to discard, not to endorse. Girardin follows the same line of argument, rejecting symmetry, on the one hand, while condemning the excessive "confusion" of the English style. For him, the "minute details of English landscape gardening . . . would only serve to foster confusion in your head and on your terrain" (Girardin 98). This diagnosis leads him to disagree with Jaucourt that there was once a symmetrical, elegant style in France, followed then by a tasteful English landscape gardening. According to him, both styles should be condemned:

> The dull magnificence of symmetry, made men run into the opposite extreme; for if symmetry has been abused by that ill-judged formality, which shut up and inclosed every thing, the irregular style was very soon abused likewise, and a vague and confused arrangement of objects only distracted the eye. (Girardin 11–12)

In fact, he thinks that if irregularity and disorder were sought as palliatives against geometry, they did not succeed in promoting a natural landscape: "[It was not perceived] that even if such an incongruous mixture were capable of any beauty in the details, the whole could never be natural nor verisimilar" (Girardin 12–13). Jaucourt could take no pride in the French gardening practices of his time. Morel and

Girardin do not disagree with his assessment, but the effect of their presentation is different, because, unlike Jaucourt, they ascribe the responsibility of the current decadent style in France to English principles. This allows them to downplay the success of the modern, English garden in France, while distancing themselves from past French achievements (Le Nôtre) that are too dated to be of use. At the same time, in the kind of dual gesture we have followed in English treatises (minimizing the foreign contamination, and valorizing the untainted national capacity), they insist that rejecting geometry need not imply discarding Frenchness. To demonstrate this, they promote a conception of the "natural" landscape, which they say has not been successfully grasped in the English theories of gardening, in connection with French contemporary accomplishments, mainly their own designs and layouts.[3]

DEFERRING THE "POINT OF PERFECTION": THE NEW FRENCH GARDEN (NATURAL GARDENS)

In a long footnote of his *History*, Walpole rightly assesses such positions as Girardin and Morel's as a defense mechanism, in other words as a denial. Girardin's claim that he is not dealing with "English, or Chinese gardens" (8) in his treatise can be juxtaposed to Walpole's contradictory remark that

> the French have of late years adopted our style in gardens, but chusing to be fundamentally obliged to more remote rivals, they deny us half the merit, or rather the originality of the invention, by ascribing the discovery to the Chinese, and by calling our taste in gardening Le Gout Anglo-Chinois. (Walpole 22–23)[4]

His point is well taken, as can be seen in Watelet's remark: "They say that this Nation [i.e., England] itself borrowed ideas for its gardens from the Chinese, a people too distant, too different from us, too little known not to give rise to extraordinary opinions and a lot of fables" (Watelet 50). Walpole exposes "the French" by showing the rivalry involved in the discussions of landscape gardening on both sides of the Channel. However, inasfar as he questions the validity of the French determination of an "origin," his remark is also telling, in that it strives to divest the Chinese as well as the French garden of all natural capability, which, in his view, only the English garden can be said to possess. Walpole goes on to say: "I think I have shewn that this is a blunder, and that the Chinese have passed to one extremity of absurdity, as the French and all antiquity had advanced to the other, both being equally remote from nature" (23). For Walpole, the French garden as much as the Chinese garden are erroneous assumptions that have been forever thwarted by the advent of the English style ("the point of perfection" [35]). With less lyricism, Whately concurs in that estimate when he starts his treatise by stating: "Gardening, in the perfection to which it has been lately brought to England . . . " (Whately 1). The fact that for both authors, *modern* and *English* are interchangeable terms testifies to a national pride that their French counterparts have apparently no grounds to feel "today." Therefore, does it follow that the French are inevitably reduced to mere "mimicry," in Walpole's terms (Walpole 35)?

The difficulty for the French authors considered here, as we have already mentioned, is that they are not ready to concede to any mimicry in their treatises. Girardin's example is characteristic in that respect. Throughout his treatise, he takes a harsh stance against Le Nôtre's accomplishments and against symmetry. Yet, he never refers to symmetry as the French style or the French garden. On the contrary, he does mention by name English gardens or English landscape gardening. He avoids the term *French* in connection with a style he does not approve of, because that would mean investing present-day French accomplishments with too negative a content. Correlatively, Girardin minimizes the value of the English style, in a move which parallels Pope's downplaying of the influential French style in his time. Pope counteracted "Versailles" by emphasizing the geometry of "our ancestors," as Walpole puts it, or in other words, of his countrymen. In a similar move, Girardin avoids associating "Frenchness" with geometry. This position is a way of depriving the English style of any authority and precedence, that is to say of "originality" (Walpole).

Furthermore, the denial that the English style is "mimicked" generally introduces claims by French authors that they advocate a "natural garden" in France. According to Girardin, the style he is promoting is not drawn after the English model but concerns itself with natural effects, which he finds are universal. Likewise, Morel insists: "The theory which I have just given is entirely founded upon Nature; it alone has furnished the precepts, the examples and the materials" (Morel 368). Morel and Girardin's descriptions of their own designs and layouts, especially in Guiscard and Ermenonville (Morel's chapters 12 and 13, and Girardin's chapter 6 as well as in the anonymous "Tour of Ermenonville"), are used as appropriately exemplary of the theory defended in their treatises. Incidentally, we may note that this gesture is symmetrically found in English treatises. Whately, for example, who quietly announces the preeminence of English gardening at the beginning of his treatise, examines several existing gardens and parks as he unfolds his principles. In particular, he is in the position to present some of the best representatives of English landscape gardening, when he writes the "Description of the Leasowes" (chapter 52), the "Description of Hagley" (chapter 57), and of course the "Description of Stowe" (chapter 59). Not only do Morel and Girardin valorize present-day French gardens, they also argue that they are the very embodiment of the natural landscape: "I meant only to give you a small sample of the variety and beauty which are to be found in nature" (Girardin 63) concludes Girardin's panorama of the grounds of Ermenonville. Such a position rectifies France's assumed inferiority to England in landscape gardening and refutes the argument that its own achievements are limited to the past.

It also testifies to an understanding of the merit of such gestures as an evolutionary discourse, as it is endorsed in Walpole's *History* or other English treatises. While French authors repeat this particular gesture, they choose to keep open the history of landscape gardening, in a contrary move to Whately and Walpole, who were describing the end of that history at the site of English gardens. Girardin mentions the change that he is confident his treatise will bring about—"The substitution of the most natural arrangement for that of the most forced" (149)—but he does not specify when and where this natural change will take place. However, he proposes in the span of several pages a temporal progression toward natural principles:

> Natural taste led people at *first* to suppose, that in order to imitate nature, it was sufficient to banish even lines. . . . When they wished *then* to introduce a greater degree of simplicity, it was thought sufficient to give back liberty to nature, and to place every thing at random. . . . It is therefore only by arranging with skill, or selecting with taste, that one can find what one was looking for—the true effect of pleasing landscape. This is the term; let us now explain the principles. (Girardin 12–14, my emphasis)

The temporal progression of this short narrative is unmistakable: "at first," "then," "now." The last part of this passage suggests in effect that the principles are available *now*. Ermenonville is one of the examples of the "pleasing landscape" he mentions. Girardin sets himself in the last sentence as the lawgiver in terms of landscape gardening, as if these principles were as yet unheard of, still to be provided. By this gesture which poses as foundational, Girardin refuses to acknowledge his debt to—let alone the possibility of derivation from—earlier or foreign principles. Girardin's principles are given now in French to the French and the "pleasing landscape" will be found (or already exists) in France.

Morel reconstructs a similar history:

> The Gardens of genre [i.e., English gardens] were, wherever the reformation in this art came about, wherever the revolution took place, *the first step* in the new opened prospect. Landscape gardening in these first moments resembles a new land which produces abundantly, but at first gives only wild plants and coarse grass; it is up to the true Artists to cultivate it, it is up to time to improve it. (Morel 394–95, my emphasis)

The metaphor of the last sentence is remarkable, and exemplifies the complex intricacies of nature and art at work in these treatises, since Morel's metaphor of the land that is cultivated in order not to produce wild plants is paradoxically proposed as a reference to the moment when nature will be given her due in landscape gardening. Morel's metaphor for nature, then, is culture. This growing up and coming of age in landscape gardening has not happened in that account with the English style. On the contrary, the English style is presented only as a first step, the first moment on the path to "nature's simplicity" (Morel 394) in landscape gardening. This reverses the position of English authors who celebrate such a simplicity in their own gardens, and applaud to the evolution away from the artificial French garden: "One returns to the simplicity of Nature only after having exhausted all combinations, just as one arrives at truth only after having gone through a long circle of errors: such is the course ["marche"] of the human mind" (Morel 394). As is the case in Girardin, the temporality of this accomplishment is somewhat uncertain in Morel's treatise: "But I foresee many obstacles to its advancement" (395).

It should be clear at this stage that Morel and Girardin's attempts to minimize any contagion of theory or practice between English and

French treatises or gardens, are not only made in order to advocate another, more natural type of landscape. In their arguments, the natural landscape becomes the equivalent of the new French garden. Such is the history they are presenting. Even more forcefully than Girardin, Morel anticipates that after the first step in the right direction constituted by the English garden, the advantage of adopting the right, natural principles will return to France. After alluding once more to profuse and confused English gardens, he adds that "I strongly doubt that, in a country fertile with great Artists [i.e., France], that in a century, where taste has made such progress, this novelty, which may have dazzled at first, can sustain itself for long" (Morel 358). In this passage, a genealogy is established in which the new, English style is described in the process of becoming already old, on the point of being taken over by a newer model, which as it turns out is the (new) French style. The English garden is not the answer, Morel says, it is only a temporary solution, an intermediary stage from geometrical excess toward "natural simplicity," but this second effect finds its fulfillment in France. Carmontelle displays the same moves when, like Girardin and Morel, he puts off the "point of perfection" of landscape gardening beyond the English style, and identifies it with French natural achievements:

> If we have had the desire of imitating the English gardens, it was only in order to escape the uniformity of ours, and our new Gardens will not always be poorly done, because they will not always servilely resemble those of the English. . . . When we move away from our old principles, we will have new ones, which will belong only to us. . . . We only need Gardens where nature presents itself in the most pleasant shapes. (Carmontelle 5)[5]

Clearly, Morel assumes that such an enlightened and principled version of the new garden will be achieved in France, in particular, because France is itself enlightened. There is an opposition, or progression, in Morel from English dazzling (358) to French enlightenment, "under the eyes of an enlightened Nation" (397). It is true that the context of this last quotation makes it clear that France tends to satisfy itself too easily with dazzling, which has the consequence of slowing down its own project of enlightenment:

> Isn't there reason to fear that these examples of a genre so frivolous [i.e., English gardening], so opposed to good taste, by multiplying with impunity under the eyes of a Nation enlightened, indeed, but enamored of novelty,

> might prolong the infancy of an art that is still only in the cradle? (Morel 397)

Yet in the last sentence, which is also the closing sentence of the treatise, there is at least the certainty that this new art, expounded at length in Morel's treatise, will sooner or later fully flourish in enlightened France. In fact, he says about his own work in Guiscard, that "there is not a single trace of straight alleys, though the woods were riddled with them; and the course [marche] of the terrain, altered everywhere, has recovered its natural bend" (270–71). Morel conceives of his design as a return to nature from the perspective of a misguided, geometrical style. This example allows him to substitute a natural French garden for an artificial French garden, in a way which forcefully outlaws all reference to the foreign. In these treatises, in other words, nature is really French. The project of enlightenment, by being coupled with a "natural bend," also gains additional legitimacy and becomes naturalized. The reference to enlightenment might seem at first to be incompatible with the wish for a mere national gain. In fact, of course, this incompatibility is only apparent, as we have seen earlier in Voltaire's analysis. At all events, the profound desire to obtain benefits for "France" is clearly perceptible in these treatises.

NATIONALISM IN GARDENS

The resistance to the English model is therefore articulated in nationalist terms which include and at the same time go beyond aesthetic considerations. Morel and Girardin agree that "Frenchness" must be upheld and protected from the risk, or even the danger, of English contamination, especially on French soil. Morel makes this sentiment quite explicit in the pages that precede his indictment of "bizarre compositions" (393), which are elsewhere identified by him as "English gardens" (235). This occurs when he discusses one effect of English gardens in France: "The Artist seeks to represent a foreign country, to transport on the terrain entrusted to him the customs, the forms, the productions and the constructions of another country or of another century" (Morel 391–92). Morel links here two crucial factors, the representation of the foreign, and the national terrain, which becomes in his estimate invaded by the foreign. He seems concerned that an alienation of the terrain from itself will take place because of foreign elements—"everything is borrowed from the foreign" (392)—and he formulates this striking conclusion: "This genre, by its overuse [l'abus], is perhaps the most dangerous of all, and cannot exist for long" (392–93). Morel equates the danger with the overuse, the surplus of such gardens ("l'abus"), but implicitly the danger is coextensive with the abuse suffered by the French soil, by those French terrains occupied by foreigners, if only metaphorically. His assessment of the landscape gardener in that context is noteworthy: his terms imply a breach of trust, a treachery on the part of the "artist" ("to transport on the terrain entrusted to him the customs . . . of another country"). A French terrain was "entrusted" to the landscape gardener, but he has betrayed it and submitted it to foreign modes, thus expropriating the terrain from itself. Morel's concluding remark that this situation will not, cannot last long is a defense mechanism that willfully affirms the possibility of the pure Frenchness of French landscape gardening.

Girardin can also be said to exorcize the imposition of foreign elements on the French soil when he discusses the introduction of foreign plants in France. He generally cautions against their use, not only for practical reasons, such as their cost, but because he finds that it harms the natural effect of the landscape: "As to foreign trees . . . they always accord badly with the trees of the country. Nature has planted every thing in the situation which is best adapted to it" (Girardin 101). Girardin addresses his cautionary advice against the foreign in the name of nature. Yet, it is clear that he recognizes the metaphorical, national implications of a foreign plantation. Like Morel, he especially wishes to prevent the mixture of the foreign and the national, which must be guarded against: "I should warn you against two errors which have crept into this subject of plantations. I mean foreign trees" (Girardin 100). Girardin, therefore, associates the natural with the national, and conversely links the foreign with the artificial. For if he cautions against the use of foreign trees in general, he emphasizes, on the contrary, the compatibility of foreign trees with buildings, that is to say with the unnatural: "It is especially in such a picture as this, that the color and the foreign shape of the trees would make it possible to introduce with most propriety some little temples, or buildings in a simple style; such as urns, obelisks . . . " (Girardin 78–79).

The restriction of legitimate grounds for the acclimatization of foreign plants in France is another way of expressing the fear of the English "invasion." The slip which occurs in Morel and Girardin from the description of natural effects to the delineation of national implications, may be ascribed to this anxiety. In a first step, they trace the origin of their principles to nature, which they often associate with universal, a-national values. For Girardin, nature's combinations "equally belong to all ages and all nations" (9). Morel agrees in principle that a natural landscape gardening should transcend the national, since "finding its model in Nature, [landscape gardening] should have been in all countries and all centuries invariable like her" (190). Yet, it turns out that "nature" becomes the equivalent of "Frenchness" in several passages of these authors' treatises.

The returns or benefits for a "nation" of positing an equivalence with nature were also elaborated by English authors on landscape gardening. As I have suggested earlier, French authors found examples of resistance to a strong foreign "occupation of lands" in the very treatises, the principles of which they were unwilling to credit. Whately, for instance, concludes his assessment of Stowe by a telling comparison. In his account,

> magnificence and splendor are the characteristics of Stowe; it is like one of those places celebrated in antiquity, which were devoted to the purposes of religion, and filled with sacred groves, hallowed fountains, and temples dedicated to several deities; the resort of distant nations; and the object of veneration to half the heathen world. (Whately 226)

With his prestigious analogy of Stowe to antiquity, Whately confirms the preeminence of English landscape gardening. And when he notes that like famous places of antiquity, Stowe attracts "distant nations," he also indicates that this superiority is not merely aesthetic, but involves national rivalry, and the wish for an internationally recognized supremacy. Such a position was already found in Gilpin's *Dialogue upon the Gardens at Stow* (1748), where one advantage of Stowe and such "productions" is, according to the protagonist Callophilus, "their Tendency to raise us in the Opinion of Foreigners. If our Nation had nothing of this kind to boast of, all our Neighbours would look upon us as a stupid, tasteless Set of People, and not worth visiting" (Gilpin 51).

What the respective examples of English and French treatises help bring to the fore is the extent to which the natural is consistently thought in terms of the national. We have seen earlier that Voltaire reflected on the possibility, which often turns out to be a challenge, of a-national philosophy. He showed that for such a philosophy to exist, it would have first to have traversed the national, but that this traversing would always risk not to be effected once and for all, since there could be, perhaps unavoidably, relapses in the national. Similarly, a wish for, or a declaration of national preeminence, which was precisely feared from the other and which prompted a response in the first place, consistently pervades the treatises we have discussed. I have described so far the rhetorical graft made by French authors for their own purposes, in particular their appropriation of an evolutionary discourse in order to represent the new French garden as the (chrono)logical continuation in the history of landscape gardening. This appropriation might seem to founder when it comes to translating to a French context the political metaphors that the English landscape garden movement intended its designs to convey. English authors expressed the view that the new style of gardening was a figure for, or the representation of the specificity of British politics, especially as far as they were defended by the Whig party. I will now repeat some of the arguments used to demonstrate the coincidence between landscape and local politics. This coincidence was argued from the standpoint that nature and British politics evinced a common trait—liberty.

NATURE AS LIBERTY IN ENGLISH TREATISES

Hunt has shown that the rejection of the formal French garden and the corollary English landscape garden movement were the continuation of earlier reactions against French authority: "Earlier pleas for less contrived scenery . . . were remembered and called upon to sustain the rejection of French authority in arts as in politics. It was an endorsement of liberty and tolerance against tyranny and oppression; democracy against autocracy" (Hunt and Willis 8). Hunt gives as an example a passage of Pope's *An Essay on Criticism* (1711), in which France and England are thus opposed: "The *Rules*, a Nation born to serve, obeys, / And *Boileau* still in Right of *Horace* sways. / But *we*, brave *Britons*, *Foreign Laws* despis'd, / And kept *unconquer'd*, and *uncivilized*, / Fierce for the *Liberties of Wit*" (Hunt and Willis 8). The fact that the English landscape garden movement saw itself in affinity with affirmations of liberty and preservation from absolutism, unlike in France, is apparent in Joseph Addison's articles. In *The Tatler* (No. 161, 18–20 April 1710), he opposes a "happy Region . . . inhabited by the Goddess of *Liberty*" to France, in which the river Rhone, "after having made its Progress through those Free Nations, stagnates in a huge Lake at the leaving of them; and no sooner enters into the Regions of Slavery [i.e., France], but runs thro' them with an incredible Rapidity, and takes its shortest Way to the Sea" (Hunt and Willis 140). In his poem *The Seasons* (1730), James Thomson shows the same congruence between the English landscape and freedom in politics. For example, he represents Lord Lyttelton walking through Hagley Park and "Planning, with warm benevolence of mind / And honest zeal unwarped by party-rage, / Britannia's weal" (Thomson 38). Conversely, in another poem, *Liberty*, he associates the excessive formality of French gardens with oppression: "Those parks and gardens, where, his haunts betrimmed, / And nature by presumptuous art oppress'd, / The woodland genius mourns" (Thomson 397). In that respect, Walpole reflects on the impossibility of ever achieving true English principles in landscape gardening in France, because of the regime of taxes in that country. As a result, he finds a direct link between the very form of gardens and a political agenda or executive power:

> As great an obstacle in France [as climate] is the embargo laid on the growth of their trees. As after a certain age, when they would rise to bulk, they are liable to be marked by the crown's surveyors as royal timber, it is a curiosity to see an old tree. A landscape and a crown-surveyor are incompatible. (Walpole 38)

Therefore, English authors provide a network of connections that establishes English landscape gardening as a metaphor for political freedom in England, while French gardens represent in their view absolutism or disenfranchisement in France. The most appropriate example generally given of a park that sets itself up as a testimony to English liberty is Stowe.

At Stowe, three buildings designed by Kent were particularly admired: the Temple of Ancient Virtue, with next to it, a Temple of Modern Virtue, built on purpose as a ruin, and the Temple of British Worthies, all found within a spot called the Elysian fields (Whately 220). Hunt has admirably demonstrated the intricacies of reminiscences involved in these constructions (Classical, Italian, gothic, that is to say, English).

> The Temple of Ancient Virtue, for example, was modeled on [Kent's] preferred classical Temple of Vesta at Tivoli, though with some glances both at other similar edifices and at the Mausoleum at Castle Howard, the first English imitation of this Roman temple style. The Stowe building therefore incorporates an allusion to the history of a particular building form. (Hunt 1987, 51)

As for the Temple of British Worthies, it was half classical and half-gothic (Hunt 1987, 51). Furthermore, Hunt points out that

> At least since the Glorious Revolution of 1688 the theory of a limited monarchy had been closely affiliated with the political thought of the ancients, mediated by a modern Italian thinker like Machiavelli. . . . In such a political vision, the revival of classical architecture in England becomes eloquent of a larger political geography, as London (in Toland's words) became "a new Rome in the West" and "could grasp at empire like Rome itself." (Hunt 1987, 57)

On the other hand, gothic ruins or monuments were a sign of "indigenousness," of harmony with "the native countryside" (Hunt and Willis 31): "[C]lassical temples . . . declared England's recreation of antique traditions, while gothic or *gothick* reminded visitors of native English values" (Hunt and Willis 34).[6]

In his dialogue, Gilpin had drawn a close parallel between the Temple of Ancient Virtue and the monument to the British Worthies. The first is represented as a monument to "great Heroes of Antiquity": "Illustrious Chiefs, who made Virtue their only Pursuit, and the Welfare of Mankind their only Study . . . bravely to defend a People's Liberty" (Gilpin 19–20). The description of the second monument shows that the same qualities (expressed, too, in similar terms) were shared by ancient local heroes: "This Place is called the Temple of *British* Worthies; and is gloriously filled, you see, with the greatest

Wits, Patriots, and Heroes, that are to be met with in our Chronicles" (Gilpin 28). The British worthies "pursued Virtue in the dazling Light in which she appears to Patriots and Heroes. . . . [They] battled for the State, ventured their Lives in the Defence of their Country, and gloriously bled in the Cause of Liberty" (Gilpin 30). This verbal adequation and interplay between the two monuments shows a movement of progress, at the same time as the heritage of classical values is thus conferred to England. Another passage makes the point more forcefully. The protagonist Polypthon notices a statue that reminds him of "a *Roman* Senator, sitting in his Curule Chair to receive the *Gauls*" (Gilpin 42). But Callophilus tells him that he is mistaken, and even that

> you have not yet honoured him according to his Dignity: he is nothing less, Sir, I assure you, than the Representative of a *Saxon* Deity. You see here Thor *and* Woden, *fabled* Gods with the whole System of your Ancestor's Theology. Walk round the Assembly, they will smile upon a true Briton. (Gilpin 42–43)

Gilpin suggests in this passage that the British "ancestors" of the present visitors of Stowe are invested with a stronger privilege or "dignity" than the prestigious Roman or classical "worthy." The poet Gilbert West establishes the same credentials in his poem on *Stowe, The Gardens of the Right Honourable Richard Viscount Cobham* (1732): "Or bold in Arms for Liberty they stood, / And greatly perish'd for their Country's Good: / Or nobly warm'd with more than mortal Fire, / Equal'd to *Rome* and *Greece* the *British* Lyre" (Hunt and Willis 218).

English authors show in their treatises a double attitude to the foreign—they may be appropriated (the Classics), or "Englished" (Hunt 1987, 79), or they are expressly rejected (the French), in a gesture that always endorses a nationalist confirmation of English preeminence "today." If English landscape gardening is construed as the representation or translation of political freedom in the space of a garden, it is also because the argument rests on the assumption that nature can be enslaved, therefore by contrast that it can be free, or adequately denote liberty. In fact, one of the most recurrent reproaches against the French garden is, in addition to its excessive geometry, the fact that it is walled in, enclosed, which is taken as another sign (another representation of imprisonment or absence of freedom) that absolutism is inscribed in the French style as much as it makes itself manifest for French subjects. About French parks, Walpole writes for instance that "Their parks are usually square or oblong inclosures, regularly planted with walks of chestnuts or limes" (14). The English landscape movement is conversely shown to free nature from its prison, in the same way that the Glorious Revolution freed the citizens:

> But the capital stroke, the leading step to all that has followed, was (I believe the first thought was Bridgman's) the destruction of walls for boundaries, and the invention of fossès—an attempt then deemed so astonishing, that the common people called them Ha! Ha's! to express their surprize at finding a sudden and unperceived check to their walk. (Walpole 25)

The ha-ha (or unperceived ditch) liberates the garden, and at the same time, the removal of obtrusive boundaries has the consequence of harmonizing the garden with what lies beyond it: "the garden in its turn was to be set free from its prim regularity, that it might assort with the wilder country without" (Walpole 25). In that account, a link is established between breaking free from built-in walls, becoming natural and becoming free, which implies that systematic associations are being made—the French garden is regular and walled in, therefore it is not natural, which implies that it connotes absolutism, whereas the English garden has abolished fences and rejected regularity, it has opened to the country outside itself, and consequently is natural and connotes political freedom. About Kent, Walpole pronounces the famous declaration that "He leaped the fence, and saw that all nature was a garden" (25). This statement deliberately eliminates any hierarchy, indeed any difference between nature and garden, for it is not only that the English garden becomes more natural than the French. What used to be beyond the garden, first becomes an extension of it through the ha-ha, before belonging to it ("all nature was a garden"), as part of the gardener's plan: "the contiguous outlying parts came to be be included in a kind of general design" (Walpole 25). The garden is not only liberated from its boundaries, it also becomes all-inclusive.[7] What used to be exterior to the garden becomes assimilated to it, drawn into it; in fact nature itself becomes totally encompassed within the space of a garden. This inclusiveness and this boundlessness are found to be adequate representations of

British political freedom. Liberty is made visible in the liberation from enclosures on the national soil.[8]

NATURE AS LIBERTY IN FRENCH TREATISES

Since English authors underscore the coincidence between trends in gardening and in politics, it seems that French treatises would ignore that connection, since repeating the English move might lead to an imprudent or unflattering assessment of French political liberty in the 1770s. Certainly, Morel's position is similar to Walpole's as far as the geometrical French style is concerned. For him, this style gives an effect of imprisonment: "One shut oneself in with iron gates instead of walls," he remarks about modern castles (Morel 223). And Walpole and Morel are in agreement with Kent's axiom that "*nature abhors a strait line*" (Walpole 30). But their common argument leads to different conclusions.

It was important for Walpole to underline that the "ha-ha" was an English invention (Bridgeman's), in order to show that the liberation of the garden from "French" boundaries had been performed by the English. Morel follows a different approach in his evaluation of the ha-ha, in which he aims to demonstrate that he is in effect more concerned with natural effects than those who say they promoted it. This allows him to show his reluctance to adopt openly English conclusions (the description of an evolution from enslaved to free nature, or from the French to the English style). He consistently displaces the discussion of liberty in each style by insisting that nature itself is liberty (Morel 21). Morel's proposition has the effect of putting into question the claim that free nature is due to the English model. He proposes instead generally valid statements such as: "Constraint is saddening and uniformity is boring: there is no grace without liberty, just as there is no pleasure without variety" (Morel 301). By stressing that nature gives a lesson in freedom that it suffices for the landscape gardener to follow, he refuses Walpole's politically self-serving interpretation.

Thus, while he endorses the notion that geometry is a representation of imprisonment, he also minimizes the effect of the ha-ha. Against the symmetrical garden, he says that "It is in vain that one imagines to have spared a part of this unpleasantness, by openings, or what is called *ha-has*; a coarse finesse that has never produced illusion" (Morel 17). Unlike Walpole, therefore, who considers that the ha-ha is "a capital stroke, the leading step" (Walpole 25), Morel scorns its use as a "coarse finesse," and not a real liberation, because according to him, it does still indicate an enclosure, and does not even give the illusion of an abolished boundary. The only advantage that is gained by the ha-ha, for Morel, is that it brings into the open the wish to do away with any "evident enclosure" (Morel 21). An enclosure is not acceptable, "because it always produces a secret uneasiness that creates the desire to cross it, whether this uneasiness be born of the very universal sentiment of liberty . . . " (Morel 17). Morel agrees that boundaries in a garden immediately convey an aspiration for liberty, but this aspiration is for him universal, and not a representation of English freedom. Moreover, the ha-ha is defined by Walpole as one of the origins of the English landscape movement, that is, the origin of a true understanding of the relation of the garden to nature. He constructs a stable, inevitable development from this originary moment to the final, unsurpassable achievement constituted by English layouts. But in a recurrent move in his treatise, Morel attempts to upset the certainty of such a history by showing that English practices are not the ultimate answer, but as always, an intermediate solution: the invention of the ha-ha "proves that all evident enclosure displeases" (Morel 21), but it is still a boundary, and as such must be replaced by Morel's model (a new French style), which is described as at one with nature.

When Morel discusses the ha-ha, he might in fact intend to denounce a French practice as much as an English principle. Thierry Mariage has shown that the ha-ha was used by Le Nôtre to extend the point of view: "The use he made of the ditches called *ha-has* or *sauts-de-loup* is well known. They exempted him from providing an enclosure and allowed for distant views" (Mariage 104). In fact, this practice was even theorized in terms that evoke Pope's "calling in of the country" in the widely read work by Dézallier d'Argenville, *La théorie et la pratique du jardinage* (first published in 1709). Mariage says that "At the chateau of Issy, [Le Nôtre] totally relinquished walls, or to quote the expression used by Désallier d'Argenville, the garden 'is united to the countryside'" (104–105). For Mariage, "Le Nostre did not isolate in the least the gardens from the general context in which they were inserted" (104), which therefore does not correspond to Morel's description of the French style as closing off the garden. It is not only that Morel adopts up to a point English generalities on the French garden, but that the style he opposes seems to be more removed in time than the classical garden of Le Nôtre. Baridon has shown the difference between two geometrical styles, corresponding to two successive practices in France: "Whereas the Renaissance garden accepts the enclosure as a line . . . the baroque garden will ceaselessly move back this enclosure in order to have the point of perspective enter into the garden itself" (Baridon 1995, 202). And Mariage says that because "the gardens of the 17th century as they came to us have lost their relationship to their surroundings" (6), we wrongly believe that they had no "opening onto space" (105). This suggests that Morel relied on non-current practices when he discussed the French style, in order to radicalize his own difference to it.

It also implies that Morel is aware, like his English counterparts, of the political implications of a discourse privileging an aesthetic awakening to the removal of visible barriers. But because Morel opens up the history of landscape gardening to include the achievement of the new French garden, he does not allow the English division between freedom and absolutism in nature to cast a disparaging light on his own project. On the first page of his foreword, on the contrary, he asserts that the French garden has freed itself, by itself, not with the help of English principles, when he underlines the liberating consequences of the principles he is promoting in the treatise: "But now that the *blindfold* of prejudice has been lifted . . . that landscape gardening wants at last to *break the fetters* of routine that have kept it in chains since its birth . . . " (Morel 1, my emphasis). The first part of the quotation also shows that French authors tend to trace to Enlightenment the pursuit of liberty in gardening and elsewhere, and not to a particular political system, as English authors did.

Morel certainly concurs with English authors in their assessment of the opening of the garden through the removal of artificial boundaries. In Ermenonville, he asserts that one of the effects of this removal is to promote continuity between the garden and its surroundings: "The destroyed walls of enclosure, as well as the gothic building which served as the court entrance, allow one to see the continuation of the valley in the direction of the South" (Morel 244). The reflection on what Morel calls the "frame" of the garden is a crucial focus of the "landscape movement," as it is represented in England or in France. Morel points out that establishing continuity in a "French" garden is more important than abolishing its geometry and promoting natural effects, since even the best landscaping could not counteract the ill consequences of a visible, closed frame:

> I suppose a delicious *bocage* which would be naturally linked with the parts that precede and follow it; transport it in an isolated place, which would not let one imagine anything beyond its enclosure; in a word, thicken, exactly close the frame, and immediately all its charm vanishes. (Morel 326)

Moreover, the lines which immediately follow indicate that the frame is in fact responsible for the whole effect of the garden, for a different frame seems to change the very form of a garden, even if its features remain the same:

> Displace this cool, rustic orchard, this voluptuous brook, choose another site, other surroundings: they will not produce the same impression any longer. It will still be the same extent, the same trees, the same waters, the same brook, and still the effect will be completely different; you will think you have caused them to take other forms. (Morel 326–27)

This effect of the frame would not be possible if nature itself did not display a principle of interweaving connections. Opening up the frame instead of closing a garden off spatially extends the characteristics of interrelation and interdependence of natural phenomena: "nothing being perfectly isolated in the scenes of Nature, each effect, each object depends on what surrounds it, and affects us differently, proportionately to what is next to it" (Morel 327). Morel gives several illustrations as an explanation of the function of the frame. He gives the example of his designs in Ermenonville and points out that he mostly linked different elements within the garden and opened the point of view beyond it, linking thereby the garden to its surroundings: "In short, everything was without unity and independent; the movement of the terrain was denatured everywhere; the view was obstructed on all sides . . . at the time when [Ermenonville] was entrusted to my care" (Morel 243).

It is important to recognize, though, that the represented opening up of the garden does not only respect nature's interpreted principles.

It also opens up quite another prospect in the treatises, namely a realization of the desirability of the French country, with its villages and its venerable old buildings. As the French say they liberate the landscape from the French style, the prospect of "France" presents itself ravishingly to their gaze. About one of the points of view in Ermenonville, Morel says: "The felled trees have uncovered a delicious site, terminated by a mountain distant of two leagues, and surmounted by a village, above which rises very high the antique, half-ruined tower of Mont-Epiloy" (244). The "delicious site" is by the same token appropriated by the gaze, perhaps differently but not in absolute discontinuity to the modes with which the French classical garden is supposed to operate.[9] In fact, by describing the surroundings of gardens, English and French authors on landscape gardening contribute to a reflection on the national territory. In the next chapter, we will examine other reflections on this question, regarding the uses and the appropriate size of a territory, its benefits or inconveniences. In that context, we will analyze some positions taken on the desirability (or not) of colonizing, that is, extending the national domain as opposed to another policy, which favors international relations, or power through money, not land. These questions were made all the more pressing by the international conflict of the Seven Years War and its outcome. Thus, the effort to reduce the appeal and the impact of English gardening theories in France was part of a wider concern regarding the prominent role of England in international politics after 1763.

Chapter 3

Trade Winds

> These semiotic features of landscape, and the historical narratives they generate, are tailor-made for the discourse of imperialism, which conceives itself precisely (and simultaneously) as an expansion of landscape understood as an inevitable, progressive development in history, an expansion of "culture" and "civilization" into a "natural" space in a progress that is itself narrated as "natural."
>
> —W. J. T .Mitchell, *Landscape and Power*

ANGLOPHOBIA

Why do authors writing on landscape gardening betray repugnance to what Diderot calls in another context the "English model"? My contention is that the insistence of numerous French authors that the French soil risks being "invaded" by the English, if only in the form of their gardens, can be traced to what most Frenchmen experienced as a trauma during and after the Seven Years War, when France lost almost all of its colonial territories to Britain. During that war and after the Peace of Paris (the 1763 treaty), Britain acquired Canada, India, East Florida, and Senegal, as well as the West Indian islands of St. Vincent, Dominica, and Tobago (Koehn 15). On the other hand, in 1763 the islands of Guadeloupe and Martinique were returned to France, after having been occupied by the British during the war. The colonial loss and the military defeat were severe psychological blows, and all historical accounts of the period concur in their admissions that France's foreign policies were oriented toward revenge against Britain, the support to the American insurgents starting in 1778 being largely viewed as the actualization of that wish for revenge (Tarrade I, 21).[1] Some authors have also pointed out that Anglophobic sentiments spread after the war across the political spectrum, including among the Liberals who had earlier propounded "Anglomania" in France.[2]

It is certainly necessary, as Georges Lefebvre indicated in his favorable review of Frances Acomb's *Anglophobia in France 1763–1789*, to keep in mind the difficulty of assessing the relation between Anglophobia and events such as the Seven Years War in terms of causality and consequence: was Anglophobia due to the war? or did it cause it? (Lefebvre 97). Such questions always have to be considered at the same time, never exclusively of one another. Likewise, some caution may be in order when contending that a link may be traced between the Seven Years War's aftermath and some nationalist positions found in French treatises on landscape gardening written in the 1770s. Certainly, gardeners' views are systemic, or contribute to a larger network of Anglophobic sentiments in that decade. It is another thing to affirm that they are solely the consequence of the war. Moreover, historians point out that the Seven Years War was only part "of a century and a quarter of intermittent warfare from 1689 to 1815, during half of which time the two nations [France and Britain] were actually at war. The contest was for world supremacy" (Stone 5). In that respect, it has been documented that in Britain, "by the early 1750s imperial anxieties and widespread francophobia had become mutually reinforcing" (Wilson 144). Kathleen Wilson demonstrates that cultural productions of the time reflected such anxieties:

> [The British plays of the 1740s and 1750s] marshalled the images and rhetoric of patriotism to make their case that English theatre was a crucial *bulwark* of national manners, language, morality, virtue and spirit—both an offensive weapon and a defensive *battlement* against "foreign" and especially French *contagion*, that could also contribute to British expansion abroad. (Wilson 137, my emphasis)

We have seen that treatises on landscape gardening had recourse to similar metaphors to protest against a perceived threat from the other.

The same rhetoric is also found in essays that discuss the struggle for maritime supremacy between the French and the English, as we will see in the case of Raynal's celebrated study of colonialism. In that respect, Wilson specifies that the felt need to expand Britain's empire was partly a response to a (real or imagined) threat to the national soil:

> In the context of these nationalistic anxieties and concerns, the anguish at the loss of Minorca in 1756 and the subsequent euphoria over the victories of 1758–60, which removed the French from the North American colonies, take on their full significance. The Seven Years War was the fulfilment and ultimate expression of mercantilist imperial aspirations. . . . Through the fears about French influence and cultural contagion, the war also allowed British global expansion to be seen as an ultimately benevolent and patriotic act. (Wilson 148)

Again, that sort of response to "France" on the part of the British seems to foreshadow the form taken by French criticisms of Britain's influence in the 1770s and 1780s. Even if it is agreed, then, that the Seven Years War is only one moment of an ongoing hostility between Britain and France, and one factor among others for nationalist reflexes, it is remarkable that the underlying resistance to the Englishness of the English garden is often conveyed in landscape gardening treatises of the 1770s in terms of a perceived threat to the integrity of the French *soil*. These terms are clearly analogous to those used to describe the endangered French colonies. While they strive to contain English landscaping practices, gardeners represent a desirable French territory (as occurs for example in Morel and Girardin's descriptions of Ermenonville), that unwittingly yet irresistibly draws attention to itself. The joined arguments of a desirability of and a menace against the French soil are attuned to a territorial crisis in and of "France," which was particularly acute after the Seven Years War.

This disquiet and crisis testify to a deep ambivalence about the uses or usefulness of territory as such. Jean Tarrade has shown that the economic wisdom of the time found it a danger for the mother country to send an excessive amount of emigrants to its colonies (Tarrade I, 14). Moreover, ideal colonies were considered those which provide what the mother country cannot produce, such as tropical plants (Tarrade I, 15).[3] This explains why the loss of Canada to the

British during the Seven Years War, even though it was the only "colonie de peuplement" (settlement) of France, was not deemed a serious loss by most of the enlightened public, and conversely, why the restitution of the "sugar islands" (the West Indies) at the Peace of Paris, was judged to be an important diplomatic success on the part of Choiseul. It is possible, as far as colonies are concerned, to gauge such an investment in uprooted mercantilism, against the populationist option, in Raynal's *Histoire philosophique et politique des Etablissements et du Commerce des Européens dans les deux Indes*.[4]

EUROPEAN COLONIALISM: RAYNAL'S *HISTOIRE DES DEUX INDES*

Raynal's assessment of the impact of colonialism and sea commerce on Europe has lately been receiving an increasing critical interest. Renewed attention to this encyclopedic, collaborative work was especially due to the documented extent of Diderot's contributions to it. Contemporary collaborators of Diderot's, such as Naigeon and Meister, had testified to Diderot's major participation in Raynal's work,[5] and these testimonies were investigated further at the beginning of the twentieth century by Anatole Feugère. But this research was facilitated and some of its results were confirmed after public access to the "Fonds Vandeul," that is to Diderot's manuscripts kept hitherto unpublished or partially published by his heirs, became possible.[6]

The complex ideological position of Raynal's work is partly due to the different contributors to the project. It is also the result of different modes of address. For one thing, Raynal sometimes adopts the stance of the enlightened philosopher, conveying eternal truth above and beyond the political turmoil of his age.[7] Indeed, the *Histoire* owes its fame to a radical political message which seems to anticipate the French revolution, and to views which appear to foreshadow decolonization. Yet, the work as a whole does not consistently uphold this revolutionary perspective. As far as decolonization is concerned, for example, it would be more accurate to say, as Bernard Papin notes, that the *Histoire* "condemns the excesses of colonization, but much more rarely colonization itself" (Papin 87). In fact, it has been convincingly argued that Raynal had ties with the Foreign Affairs and Bureau of Colonies in Versailles, and that the French colonial politics of the time is also for the most part the one reflected in, and defended by Raynal.[8] In that case, the *Histoire* is more pragmatic, less politically impartial than Raynal would have his reader believe in his philosophically minded mode of address. Therefore, Raynal's *Histoire* is aimed, in Jacques Chouillet's words, at "two categories of addressees: the oppressors and the oppressed. In the end, appeals to revolt are always subdued in the name of a reforming logic" (Chouillet 1991, 375). The number of contributors and this (at least) double ideological position explain why the work often presents irreconcilable statements, about colonialism and slavery in particular.

Current criticism of Raynal's work draws particular attention to its ideological complexities as well as to the specific questions of its authorship. It is certainly possible, as some have done, to insist on the common strategic goals of Raynal and his collaborators, toward what Hans Wolpe has called a "war machine against the regime of carelessness and amusement" (Wolpe 12). Consequently, Wolpe emphasizes "a fraternity of comrades in arms" (11–12) among contributors, and tends to refer indifferentiately to "Raynal" as the author of the *Histoire*. Others, on the contrary, have been more attached to tracing the coherence of a philosopher's thought in and out of the *Histoire*: this is Benot's position in *Diderot, de l'athéisme à l'anticolonialisme*, which tracks and comments Diderot's contributions in the light of his other works.[9] In fact, the most recent critical works on the *Histoire* address the necessity of taking into account the different effects of its authorship, without either privileging or dismissing the tactical appeal of "Raynal" for the eighteenth century. Conversely, the assessment of Raynal's work is found to be best conducted when it also takes account of what Chouillet calls "the problem of attributions" (Chouillet 1991, 374).[10] In the following pages, I will take these critics' conclusions for granted, but I will not contribute to the important reflection on the work's authorship. For reasons of practicality, I will instead indiscriminately refer to "Raynal" in my analysis. But I will sometimes make an exception for Diderot, who will be mentioned separately if I need to draw a more precise connection between Diderot's participation in the *Histoire* and his other writings.

CANADA AND GUIANA IN RAYNAL'S *HISTOIRE DES DEUX INDES*

Raynal, it has been argued, mostly defended Choiseul's colonial diplomacy, and helped promote it during and after the Peace of Paris. I will recount here Raynal's argument concerning the project of expanding the colony of Guiana, as a characteristic example of the complex way with which the *Histoire* approaches the question of territoriality. This project was conceived of as a compensation after the loss of Canada to Britain in 1759, during the Seven Years War: "The loss of that great continent determined the French ministry to seek for support from another, and hoped to find it in Guiana" (Raynal 1798, XIII, 293). Thus the two colonies are at times evaluated together in the *Histoire*. Raynal's discussion of the attempt betrays an ambivalence toward the appropriation of territories and their population. In reference to the advantage of territorial possessions, Raynal's position can be shown to fluctuate, as the example of his exposition of France's policies regarding Canada demonstrates.

Jean Tarrade makes the point that, at the time, "populationist theories . . . condemn colonies as a source of demographic decrease" (Tarrade I, 14). Raynal denounces the British rule over Canada in the name of this doctrine. He predicts more than once that Britain is not going to benefit from having gained Canada, calling it "the rage of extending their dominions" (Raynal 1798, XVI, 278). It is perhaps the case that his assessment of the possession of Canada by the British is not exempt of rationalization. Yet Raynal's conviction was widely shared by his contemporaries. It rests on the belief that a territory has natural limitations that it would be economically unsound to attempt to increase. The determination of these limits would also be, in that view, a function of the land's population. It was then commonly, but wrongly, assumed in France that the French population was decreasing—which caused alarm, as it seemed to prefigure a decline of the nation.[11] The belief that there is an ideal number of inhabitants for a given territory means that conversely, a nation could be overpopulated, which would be unhealthy, too.[12] Raynal's argument in Book X supports that general economic policy when he discusses the possession of Canada. According to him, Britain made a mistake by choosing to keep Canada over the "sugar colonies":

> It was reasonable to suppose that she [Britain] would give up the possessions she had gained in North America, as the advantages she might expect from them were distant, inconsiderable, and uncertain; and that she would be content with reserving to herself the rich colonies, the sugar colonies she had lately acquired, which the state of her finances seemed more particularly to require. (Raynal 1798, X, 483)

For Raynal, the fact that this obvious course of action was disregarded indicates a serious error of economic judgment. Britain has first of all lost the possibility of depriving France "of its richest trade" (Raynal 1798, X, 482). Strategically, too, he is of the opinion that the American War of Independence would have been impossible if the French had still been in Canada, because England "would have kept New England in a closer and more absolute dependence on the mother-country, a part of America that would always want to be supported against a restless, active, and warlike neighbour" (X, 482). This analysis shows that the War of Independence was partly prefigured in the terms of the Peace of Paris. Again from a military standpoint, he underlines the fact that Canada was a difficult position to defend for the French, and that the British might have derived benefit from that expenditure of energy: "Secondly, it would have contributed to weaken it, from its being under a necessity of defending Canada; a colony, which, from the nature of its situation, must be ruinous to a nation that had long neglected its navy" (X, 482). All these arguments, but especially the last, show that as a colony, Canada is onerous and without many advantages in itself. This implies that the French should encourage colonial policies which do not favor settlement, as had mistakenly been done earlier in Canada, but promote instead an essentially commercial colonization, as could be done in the West Indies.[13]

But at the same time, even though Raynal celebrates the economic as "deterritorialized," he betrays an anxiety about France that is expressed in terms of territorial possessions. In his account, the territory of "France" is irresistible, it calls invasion and appropriation upon itself. What is more, this fear is often articulated in terms of a "jealousy" evinced by Britain:

> The French islands [West Indies], on the contrary, which have already been once taken, attract the gaze, and incite the cupidity of a nation, highly dissatisfied with having restored them. Their regret makes us presume, that they will always be disposed to repair, by force of arms, the defects of their negotiations. (Raynal 1798, XIII, 301)

It is in the context of Britain's perceived hostile intentions toward the French West Indies that Raynal discusses the French government's attempted policy of expanding the small existing settlement of Guiana. It could be expected that such an undertaking would not fare well with Raynal's populationist and economic convictions. Raynal notes at first that the project "occasioned a general astonishment" (XIII, 290). But, as it turns out, Raynal rather finds fault with all that was poorly organized and carried out in the endeavor. He deplores, for instance, the avoidable loss of French settlers (XIII, 297; "sang français" [Raynal 1781, XIII, 41]), who died in the harsh climate of Guiana because of a too hasty preliminary assessment of the conditions on location. He also denounces the unequal conditions of access to property for white settlers in Guiana as "a political fault against humanity" (XIII, 294). After the disaster of the attempted settlement in Kourou, the question remained whether Guiana should still be cultivated and developed. Raynal, who recounts the failure of Kourou, offers an unqualified positive answer to the question, in a manner which is representative of the predominant position in the *Histoire* about Whites, natives or Indians, and Blacks.

Raynal tends to consider these future colonies as "desert regions," which will then be populated by "free men" (XIII, 293), that is to say by Whites.[14] But he often notes that Europeans are not able to work efficiently or to live long in these climates (XIII, 293–94, 302). This is why he suggests enlisting native or Indian populations ("collect these perpetually wandering people" [XIII, 303]). Raynal is aware, however, of the difficulties of such attempts, for the natives refuse to submit voluntarily to the conditions of a sedentary and agricultural life. But Raynal does not ever recommend the enslavement of the indigenous population. He endorses instead a more insidious violence, the effects of which will be apparent in the long run, when he suggests an assimilation to the European way of life through various "stratagems" (XIII, 304) in the name of the "benefits of civilization" (XIII, 304). This limited tolerance contrasts, however, with his second recommendation, ostensibly on grounds of a better productivity, to rely on Black slaves who would need to be acquired on purpose: "The feeble hands of the Indians will only bring forth commodities of moderate value. In order to obtain rich productions, it will be necessary to have recourse to the strong arms of the Negroes" (XIII, 304–305). This passage only would show that the *Histoire* is not consistently abolitionist and independentist. In fact, Raynal pleads for moderation in slavery rather than for its abolition in the case of Guiana, stressing for instance that the humanity of masters may be an adequate compensation for the loss of liberty: "[I]t would not, perhaps, be impossible to prevent the evasion of these unhappy victims of our cupidity, by rendering their condition supportable" (XIII, 305).[15]

Raynal seems to be contradicting himself when he condemns settling in Canada, only to favor it in Guiana. In his analysis, therefore, settlements seem both unsound and necessary. This happens because Raynal complicates the division that was then commonly made between the mother country and colonies, a division which established a strict complementarity between one and the others. Here is how Véron de Forbonnais defines the main advantages of a colony: "Thus the profit of the commerce and the cultivation of our *colonies* is precisely . . . all that they supply to our needs . . . all the surplus which they allow us to export" (650). Raynal shows that the division between "us" and "them" is first made possible by a "communication" between two colonies, which doubles that between the mother country and the colony. Forbonnais mentions the exchange of "needs" for "surplus" in the trade between the mother country and its colonies, but Raynal shows that such an operation is already at work between what he calls the Northern and Southern colonies. Raynal's full argument runs thus:

> It was essential to the southern colonies to have their roots for population and strength in the North, in order for them to trade the commodities of luxury for those of necessity, and keep open a communication that might afford them succours if they were attacked; a retreat in case they were defeated, and a supply of land-forces to balance ["un contrepoids" (Raynal 1781, XIII, 34)] the weakness of their naval resources. (Raynal 1798, XIII, 292–93)

During the last war, Raynal goes on to say, the "balance" or "bulwark to protect the French possessions" (XIII, 293) was Canada. Guiana, then, would replace Canada by making possible a protection for other colonies that Canada no longer affords. Guiana "might be able to resist foreign attacks, and, in course of time, to furnish a speedy assistance to the other colonies, when circumstances might require it" (XIII, 293). It becomes clear, therefore, that Raynal's argument does not completely run against settlement as such, since he justifies it in his discussion of "Northern colonies." Rather, Raynal is opposed to a settlement that would not be the double of another purely commercial colony. Canada in itself was not worthwhile, yet considered from a strategic point of view as a "bulwark" to the French sugar colonies, the perspective changes. Likewise, settlers may be a useless expenditure, but they are useful if they are articulated to an economic policy of access to, and availability of "luxury" products to the mother country. Raynal shows that the evaluation of the link between mother country and colony is blurring another tie, for the communication or exchange between them already doubles a similar communication between (at least) two colonies: communication proliferates.

It could equally be said, however, that communication divides (itself). The very semantics of the word *communication* suggests a link as well as a gap. In Raynal it also names a division, between colonies, or between a colony and the mother country. In the passage discussing Guiana in Book XIII, "communication" even becomes adversarial, the sign of a division between nations: "if they were attacked" (XIII, 292–93). Characteristically, the perception of a hostile English nation translates politically into the necessity for France to be sufficiently menacing in turn. French imperialism, which partly legitimated itself as a counterforce to the British empire, is often presented as purely defensive, unlike the British.[16] Or, French colonization is interpreted as a civilizing enterprise for the general benefit of humanity, not only France. For example, according to Raynal, the settlement of Guiana, which would entail "labours of tillage" (XIII, 301), is also a universally beneficial metaphor of a struggle against chaos: "It is in the clearing of the lands that consists the true conquest over chaos, for the advantage of all mankind" (XIII, 301). The economic appeal of a purely nomadic commerce is inextricably predicated in Raynal on its very reverse, on the fixity of territorial French possessions overseas.

COMMUNICATION: ALTERITY IN RAYNAL

Following the uses of the word *communication* as it relates to other terms in a dense network is helpful if we want to understand how what denotes an exchange is also what can suggest a division or even an aggression, as we saw in the context of Raynal's discussion of the "bulwark" to French colonies. It is as if "communication" were more easily conceptualized when considering its breakdown. One can begin to explain this once it is observed that "communication" is one of the meanings of "commerce."

Commerce is made synonymous with an exchange, an intercourse, a traffic. Commerce implies at first the evidence of at least two participants, of an other. As Raynal says in the introduction to the *Histoire*, exchange is first of all understood as "un échange *mutuel*" ("a *mutual* exchange," Raynal, 1781, I, 2, my emphasis). It was a commonplace at the time to say that commerce promotes peace.[17] The same notion is endorsed in Raynal: "A spirit of barter and exchange hath arisen in Europe . . . but [it] likes peace and tranquillity. A war, among commercial nations, is a conflagration that destroys them all" (Raynal 1798, VI, 350). In Yves Benot's words, such passages testify to an optimistic belief in "trading internationalism" (Benot 189), even though, as Benot also notices (190), an important part of the *Histoire* precisely demonstrates that colonial wars have taken place in spite of commercial ties, indeed often because of them.

In fact, commerce is often viewed not so much as a mutual exchange, but as a means to gain supremacy, or global ascendancy, as Choiseul's reported words in 1763 testify: "In the present state of Europe it is colonies, trade and in consequence sea power, which must determine the balance of power upon the continent" (Koehn 15). Raynal echoes this belief when he states that "these colonies have raised the nations that founded them, to a superiority of influence in the political world" (Raynal 1798, XI, 162). The aftermath of the Seven Years War partly explains why Raynal did not only defend the notion of an essentially commercial colonization (for example the French West Indies), though he found it economically more sound, but articulated it to the stability of French territorial possessions overseas. The justification of Guiana is not separable from that context. As Raynal indicates when he discusses the objectives of the French government in Guiana: "It never occurred to him [the French minister], that a part of the world, thus inhabited, could ever enrich the mother-country by the produce of such commodities as are peculiar to the southern colonies" (Raynal 1798, XIII, 293). This indicates that in spite of its geographical position, Guiana is expected to function as a "Northern" colony, not a profitable "Southern" colony.

Raynal's *Histoire* shows that if there is such a thing as an exchange, a communication, commerce between two parties, the returns affect the participants quite differently, elevating some, not all, to superiority, while it also may make the other redundant. This is how communication can be thought of in an economy of war or aggression, as Raynal did in his discussion of a "bulwark" to French possessions in Book XIII. Thus, he made explicit what remains latent in the functioning of commerce, optimistic declarations to the contrary notwithstanding. Coextensively with the proffered reciprocal exchange between two parties, commerce reveals a wish for domination, a disinterest in the other, even the ambition to eliminate the other.

This side of commerce names colonialist practices. It also designates imperialism, economic trusts, cartels, monopolies. Véron de Forbonnais's discussion of American colonies states a violence inflicted on the other, though he abstains from commenting on it. For him, the specificity of the American colonies consists in not having dissociated commerce from the cultivation of the lands. An ominous consequence for the indigenous populations follows that observation: "Therefore it was necessary to conquer lands and to expel the former inhabitants, in order to transport new populations there" (650). In Raynal, this projected disposal of the other and concurrent European usurpation are not completely ignored. If it is true that Raynal affirms the inevitability of decolonization, it is, however, very likely that he is mostly thinking of a decolonization such as the American War of Independence, namely of white colonists shaking the yoke of a European metropole.[18] In fact, Raynal's concern for non-Europeans is only episodic, generally in the form of humanitarian appeals for moderation where they are concerned. He focuses primarily on the effects of the "deux Indes" (the East and West Indies) on Europe, as the first sentence of the *Histoire* obliquely announces: "No event has been so interesting to mankind in general, and to the inhabitants of Europe in particular, as the discovery of the New World, and the passage to India by the Cape of Good Hope" (Raynal 1798, I, 1). The consequences of these discoveries, it is true, are shown to encompass the world, and not only Europe, because, Raynal says, they revolutionized commerce, including therefore relations between nations. But in spite of the recognition of mutual exchanges between East and

West, North and South, which created "new connections and new needs" (Raynal 1798, I, 1), Raynal's attention remains riveted to Europe: what the revolution in commerce has brought about is power, a power *over the world* that is still being negotiated and fought for among *European* nations. Moreover, global commerce is turning the world into Europe:

> I have said to myself: Who is it that hath digged these canals? Who is it that hath dried up these plains? Who is it that hath founded these cities? Who is it that hath collected, clothed, and civilized these people? Then have I heard the voice of all the enlightened men among them, who have answered: This is the effect of commerce. (Raynal 1798, I, 3–4)

Commerce is here defined as an enlightening, civilizing catalyst, which systemically ties it to a European ideal representation of itself. Commerce is, as it were, essentially European.[19] Europe is never really left behind on its voyage out to "les deux Indes," and this is why it is in keeping with the thrust of Raynal's work to summarize his project as he does: "[W]e must take a view of the state of Europe before these discoveries were made; we must trace circumstancially the events they have given rise to; and conclude with examining it, as it presents itself at this day" (Raynal 1798, I, 2).[20]

Throughout the *Histoire*, Raynal's diagnosis of the state of Europe is mixed. On the one hand, he acknowledges what he had at the beginning, that is that the farther Europe goes, the closer it actually believes it gets to an understanding of itself: "This great event [the discovery of the East and West Indies] hath improved the construction of ships, navigation, geography, astronomy, medicine, natural history, and some other branches of knowledge" (Raynal 1798, XIX, 486–87). Discovering the other becomes a pretext for increasing one's own knowledge.[21] However, it must be pointed out that what Europe has learned about itself is not always posited as a gain, and this explains the ambivalence felt by Raynal and other authors toward Europe's "epistemological profit of an increased knowledge about the world" (Van den Abbeele 1984, 43).

It is often pointed out that in the second half of the eighteenth century a disenchantment becomes perceptible in the generation of those authors who wrote the *Encyclopédie*.[22] What makes this disenchantment more acute is that it does not give rise to a counterwish, to a desirable alternative. As far as colonies are concerned, the question is not to renounce Enlightenment, the point is to think the inevitability of the globalization of Enlightenment, and to analyze the ways in which its revenues have so far been cashed in by Europe. As W. J. T. Mitchell points out in his study of "Imperial Landscape," "Empires move outward in space as a way of moving forward in time; the 'prospect' that opens up is not just a spatial scene but a projected future of 'development' and exploitation" (Mitchell 17). However, Raynal, for one, notes that the returns to Europe have not only been an accumulation. For example, the greater currency of gold and silver made available because of the New World has, as Raynal concisely puts it, a contradictory effect, that of "the evils attached even to the advantages [which we owe to the discovery]" (Raynal 1798, XIX, 488). This double effect is found at every level. For instance, if "national pride" has diminished, "lucrative speculation" has taken its place (Raynal 1798, XIX, 487). Such an exacerbated quest for profit, therefore, has developed at the same time national preferences have diminished, so that one evil has simply been exchanged for another. Conversely, the negatively marked struggle for profit had the positive consequence of fostering a greater civil and religious tolerance (Raynal 1798, XIX, 487). Positive and negative effects are therefore shown to be inseparable. Whatever they are, Europe, or as Van den Abbeele says differently, home, or yet again what he calls "the *oikos*," "does not remain selfsame" (Van den Abbeele 1992, XIX). This is the logic of the voyage, the detour of which alters the stability of what one calls home, even as this stability is posited and that alteration is denied (Van den Abbeele 1984, 43). Raynal's assessment of the contact between the New World and Europe is that of an ongoing alteration of both. For if the New World has helped confirm and strengthen Europe, Europe has also been disturbed, and found wanting.

COMMUNICATION: DIDEROT'S SAVAGES AND CIVILIZED

Diderot is one of the authors who think and pose anew the questions we have followed in Raynal: that of the returns implicit in the discussion of commerce and of colonies, and in particular the question of a revenue to Europe; that of Enlightenment, and of Europe and others;

that of communication, and of its breakdown. He does it in his contributions to Raynal's *Histoire*, as well as in other writings, in particular those he devoted to Tahiti, after Bougainville's account of his voyage there, as well as the publication of the narratives of Cook's voyages. Oceania was not part of Raynal's object of study ("les deux Indes"), yet he alludes to that recent space for colonization at the end of the *Histoire*.[23] Diderot constantly interrogates himself on the legitimacy of a return to Europe, as a passage he first wrote for the *Correspondance littéraire* (September 1, 1772), then published in a revised version in Raynal's *Histoire*, may exemplify. In the *Correspondance littéraire*, he ponders on the changes brought on the Old World by the New, a musing that is similar to Raynal's. But Europe remains a stable center from which comparison can be made, as well as the only object to be appraised: "Europe, *the only continent of the globe on which the eyes must rest*, seems to have taken too solid and too fixed a foundation to give rise [lieu] to rapid and surprising revolutions" (Diderot 1995, 593, my emphasis). In the reworked passage in the *Histoire*, the supremacy of Europe becomes slightly contested: "Europe, *that part of the globe which acts most over all others*, seems to have fixed itself on a solid and durable foundation" (Raynal 1798, VI, 350). In the second statement, although Europe is still paramount, others are mentioned, and need to be taken into account.

Like most of his contemporaries, Diderot acknowledges what he sees as the historical logic of a world in the process of becoming enlightened.[24] This view of "enlightenment" is predicated on an opposite notion, that of a liberation from "ignorance."[25] Transposed on a global scale, these antithetical terms often come to designate "civilization" as opposed to a "savage" (or "natural") state. A long Western "Georgic" tradition had been at the same time extolling the happiness and higher moral plane of those living in simplicity and ignorance.[26] This tradition could provide an easy grid of interpretation for "savages," also described as happy because of their ignorance and the limited range of their needs. In his *Voyage*, Bougainville had described the "enviable happiness" (Bougainville 269) of the inhabitants of "New Cythera" in a first reading of Tahiti. In that position, "civilization" is firmly determined to be "European," and marks "us" as morally corrupt, while we can long for what we perceive as our past in the present life of savages. Such a representation of savages generally conflates a childlike innocence and ignorance with a teleological discourse on the inevitability of becoming civilized (or European), a description that Diderot partly subscribes to.[27] On the one hand, he endorses a difference between savages and "us," or between ignorance and enlightenment. Yet he is certainly closer to Montaigne's tradition of opening up and contesting the opposition between savagery and civilization (for example in Montaigne's "Of Cannibals" and "Of Coaches"). Like Montaigne, he believes that Europeans have evinced savagery in the New World, as he writes for the *Histoire*:

> When a man hath crossed the line, he is neither an Englishman, a Dutchman, a Frenchman, a Spaniard or a Portuguese . . . he is a domestic tiger again let loose in the woods, and who is again seized with the thirst of blood. Such have all the Europeans indiscriminately shown themselves in the regions of the New World (Raynal 1798, IX, 264)

If savagery is shown to inhabit civilized man, does it by the same token compromise the very project of Enlightenment and its arguments in favor of proselytism?

This question is answered differently by authors who offer diverse analyses of the process or temporality of enlightenment. Voltaire, for example, in his chapter "Des sauvages" of his *Essai sur les moeurs*, has also recourse to a problematization of the opposition between savagery and civilization, which does not depend in his view on geographical location. This allows him to mention several kinds and degrees of savagery. In Europe, the poor, ignorant masses are called savages: "There are such savages throughout Europe" (Voltaire 1963, I, 23). In America, he points out, like Montaigne, that honor, courage, liberty make savages "*so-called* savages" (Voltaire 1963, I, 23, my emphasis). This repartition of, or division within savagery does not invalidate the pursuit of Enlightenment in Voltaire's analysis. For man is fundamentally "perfectible" (I, 24), and accessible to reason ("God gave us a principle of universal reason" [I, 27]). Unlike Rousseau in the *Second Discourse*, Voltaire does not propose to elucidate what prompted the historical and symbolic transformation of "savage and barbarous families" (I, 26) into "the most civilized [policées] nations" (I, 28).[28] It is sufficient for him to infer that a social drive has always and everywhere been at work in man in one form or another: "Man, in general, has always been what he is. . . . This is what never changes from one end of the universe to the other. Since the foundation of society always exists, there has therefore always been some society" (I, 25).

When reading Diderot, it becomes apparent that he often sustains two seemingly contradictory positions, which are to be negotiated, not reconciled. One is similar to Voltaire's assessment of a universal, inevitable drive in man toward civilization. Diderot's second position, however, attends to the consequences of affirming universality and inevitability. For such a position has a way, inevitably too, of comprehending and therefore annulling alterity in an all-encompassing and applicable description.[29]

On the one hand, then, Diderot does not disagree with Voltaire. It has often been shown that in his later writings, Diderot revised some of his primitivist conceptions, because of his recognition of undeniable benefits reaped by civilization, which forbid him to think in absolute terms, or to ascribe an unconditional superiority to savage life. In Raynal's *Histoire*, he notes: "It is not, however, that I prefer a savage to a civilized state. This is a protestation I have already made more than once" (Raynal 1798, VI, 467). Voltaire's assertion that perfectibility is universal is also paralleled in Book IX of the *Histoire*, in which Diderot argues that "[C]ivilization follows from the propensity which urges every man to improve his situation, provided there be no desire to compel him to it by force" (Raynal 1798, IX, 265). This claim is not without implications for the description and attention to others, non-Europeans, "savages."

Tzvetan Todorov has at times been criticized for accepting too readily the effects of enlightenment where others are concerned, in particular when he examined the "Conquest of America" in terms which seem similar to Diderot's account of civilization. On the one hand, Todorov and Diderot have in common an appeal to tolerance: civilization is acceptable everywhere provided that it is not imposed by force, Diderot says; and Todorov agrees: "A civilization may have features we can say are superior or inferior; but this does not justify their being imposed on others" (Todorov 179). In that statement, however, Todorov presents self-restraint as the (apparently only) warranty against the elimination of the other.[30] On the other hand, Todorov postulates that an ideal way of dealing with the other would consist in "an affirmation of the other's exteriority which goes hand in hand with the recognition of the other as subject" (Todorov 250). Todorov remarks in that respect that "to experience difference in equality is easier said than done" (Todorov 249). However, what makes it all the more difficult is that in his account, recognizing the other as subject is inextricably dependent on the proposition that the other is another "I": "But *others* are also "*I*"s: subjects just as I am" (Todorov 3). This last proposition may contemplate alterity as "exterior" but not as differentiated, differentiated from what *I* know about subjectivity for example ("subjects just as I am"), so that the phrase "difference in equality" becomes a promise that does not know how to fulfill itself.

This difficulty, or in Mitchell's terms, "the fantastic sameness of colonial representations of difference" (Mitchell 24), is also noticeable in Diderot's *Supplément au voyage de Bougainville*. He represents for example a Tahitian, Orou, in the pedagogical posture of native informant, and beyond that, of universal lawgiver, to an attentive French chaplain. In terms that Voltaire could have endorsed, the "Tahitian" Orou argues that man strives everywhere to promote his own interest:

> [A]nd, rest assured, however savage we are, we also know how to calculate. Go wherever you will, and you'll almost always find man to be as shrewd as yourself. He'll never give you anything but what's worthless to him, and will always ask you for what he finds useful. (Diderot 1992, 64)

Diderot tactically represents an *equal* finesse in the other, one that colonists often refuse to acknowledge, convinced as they are of their own superiority over the natives.[31] At the same time, however, difference in Tahiti is problematically addressed. For example, it has often been argued that in the *Supplément*, the represented Tahitian sexual politics translate above all a European male fantasy about "polygamous," or "free" sexuality. In such an account, therefore, alterity risks being appropriated and comprehended without a recognition of its specificity.[32] Edouard Glissant has pointed out the extent to which "understanding" the other has too often implied "comprehending," all-encompassing the other: "'[U]nderstanding' the other, that is to say . . . reducing him to the model of my own transparence" (Glissant 1996, 71).

Diderot is not, however, oblivious to that effect of comprehension. In the *Supplément*, on the contrary, he often underscores the mediacy with which the other is accessible to "me." He shows that the representation of the other "renders" him in terms which tend to dispose of his difference. In one passage of the *Supplément*, for instance, two French interlocutors assess the effect on a French audience of a Tahitian's anticolonialist speech: "The speech seems fierce to me, but in spite of what I find abrupt and primitive, I detect ideas and turns of phrase which appear European," one of two French interlocutors notes (Diderot 1992, 46). Tahiti is only accessible through a European translation. And it only translates Europe—in that case, Europe's ambivalence about the forceful annexation of other lands.[33] Even anticolonialism sounds European in the "ventriloquized" words of the other (Van den Abbeele 1984, 52). Against such moments of appropriation, or elimination of the other within an indifferentiated sameness, Diderot seems to propose another version of alterity. In that version, alterity would not be representable. The *Supplément* represents at times exchanges with another so different to the self that differences cannot be totally abstracted, but remain irreducible differences, apparently in a dissimilar mode, therefore, to the ways universalism understands "man."

Diderot pays attention to the translation of the other to the self by focusing on scenes of translation. He poses the question of understanding, not comprehending the other, by wondering how the French and the Tahitians understood, or communicated with one another. Here is Diderot's flourished emphasis of the difficulty that would-be colonists tend to make light of: if Bougainville understood that Tahitians could be anticolonialist, in the scene of the *Supplément* mentioned above, it was because

> it's a translation from Tahitian into Spanish, and from Spanish into French. The previous night the old man had made a visit to that same Orou to whom he called out the next day, in whose home knowledge of the Spanish language had been preserved for generations. Orou had written down the speech of the old man in Spanish, and Bougainville had a copy of it in his hand while the old man spoke. (Diderot 1992, 46)

This double translation, the result of which is, as we have mentioned, that it renders the other as European, shows that mutual understanding is always mediated, and is not warranted. Bougainville's *Voyage* shows a greater, though not as easily explained, fluency. Bougainville reports for example that as soon as his ships were within view of Tahiti, they were surrounded by the inhabitants' canoes: "All these people came crying out *tayo*, which means friend" (Bougainville 217).

It is a near indispensable component of a narrative of discovery to include a more or less thorough glossary, the other's words supposedly in the "original" (at least in an attempted phonetical rendition of it) and in translation.[34] Daniel Brewer has remarked that in such narratives the primitive is "unknowable until it is translated into language, set within a system of representation" (Brewer 1984, 53). Diderot, on the contrary, indicates the difficulty for translation of ever "meaning" the other. He does so most significantly in his rewriting of a passage from Bougainville. Bougainville had brought a Tahitian, Aotourou, along with him to France, and sent him back to Tahiti at his expense. His final comment about him was a wish: "O may Aotourou soon see his countrymen again!" (Bougainville 267).[35] In Diderot's treatment of the episode in the *Supplément*, this exclamation is expanded in a dialogue between A and B, two French interlocutors:

> A. Oh, Aotourou! How glad you'll be to see your father, mother, brothers, sisters, compatriots again! What will you tell them about us? B. Few things, which they won't believe anyway. A. Why few things? B. Because he conceived of few, and will find no term in his language that corresponds to those of which he has some ideas. (Diderot 1992, 40)

The return from the other risks being nil, because "no term" can adequately represent the other. And Diderot pursues the argument thus: "A. And why won't they believe him? B. Because in comparing their own ways with ours, they'll prefer to regard Aotourou a liar than to think us so mad" (Diderot 1992, 40). What makes understanding impossible in this case seems to be that a given cultural practice may not be translatable at all. The question of translation goes beyond the mere language barrier here, for the point is not that Aotourou's description would be absolutely out of the question, but that what he would describe would be unrepresentable, or seem mad, to his countrymen.

Another instance that translates and radicalizes the impossibility of understanding the other occurs in the dialogue between Orou and the chaplain. Communication may be threatened when two opposed cultural practices clash, as in the case of the Tahitian authorization, against the European prohibition of incest—at least, according to Diderot:

> The chaplain: May a father lie with his daughter, a mother with her son, a brother with his sister, a husband with the wife of another man? Orou:

> Why not? The chaplain: To say nothing of fornication, but incest, adultery! Orou: What do you mean by these words "fornication," "incest," "adultery"? (Diderot 1992, 60–61)

It might be objected that I am taking too seriously a clearly amusing passage in which the prudishness of the chaplain may be referred to Diderot's subtitle, "Dialogue between A and B on the inappropriateness of attaching moral ideas to certain physical actions that do not accord with them" (Diderot 1992, 35). However, Diderot earnestly tries to elucidate the ways in which sexuality serves public interest. He mostly fights the "inappropriateness" of the traditional discourse on "physical actions" by giving "an essentially economic explanation of Tahitian sexuality" (Papin 129). This is why legitimating a discourse on "physical actions" or sexuality does not prevent Diderot from rigidly codifying, in fact restricting anew sexuality itself, or conferring again "moral ideas to certain physical actions that do not accord with them." Therefore, it is also within these parameters that the chaplain's question has to be read, as an investigation of the functioning of sexual politics within Diderot's version of the Tahitian economy. In the dialogue just mentioned, where the word *incest* has clearly been paraphrased by the chaplain, Orou's last question about the signification of the term is not a lexical query, but a cultural puzzlement, as he testifies again later: "Tell me, then, what do you mean by 'incest'? The chaplain: But incest . . . " (Diderot 1992, 61). The tautology of the answer demonstrates the self-evidence of a concept or a practice which cannot account for itself and which prevents a successful exchange.

Diderot is first aware, therefore, of the possibility of misreading the other as transparent, identical, comprehensible. Conversely, he represents a way of avoiding that possibility when he exposes a breakdown in the exchange between self and other, an indication of the other's irreducible difference. However, Diderot's account of alterity does not stop here. In *The Location of Culture*, Homi Bhabha has shown that there is in fact no contradiction between that second position of Diderot's, that is to say the argument of radical otherness, or yet again cultural heterogeneity, and an investment in universalism, or in the commonality of humankind. For Bhabha, these two gestures can coexist in what he sums up as the agenda of "cultural diversity": such a view can combine "cultural exchange or the culture of humanity" with "a radical rhetoric of the separation of totalized cultures" (Bhabha 1994, 34). On the contrary, Diderot sustains an irreducibility or opposition between Europeans and non-Europeans, but only as a first step toward acknowledging a reinvestment in the other, on other grounds. Furthermore, his representation of a radical division and opposition is readdressed in ways that compromise the possibility of a polar separation between self and other.

The *Supplément* cautions against the literal understanding of the opposed poles "state of nature" and "civilization." These poles might have a conceptual validity, it is said, provided they are understood not to be necessarily descriptive of an "actual" reality, a position that is not unlike Rousseau's in the *Second Discourse*: "In the bleak and savage state of man, which may be conceived of and perhaps exists nowhere... A. Not even in Tahiti? B. No" (Diderot 1992, 69). The state of nature is therefore problematized, and so is the state of civilization. As far as man in civilization is concerned, the artificial in him has never entirely superseded the natural, nature has not been left behind: "Once upon a time there was a natural man; inside him was introduced an artificial man, and within his breast there then broke out a continual war, lasting the whole of his life" (Diderot 1992, 71). Such statements complicate, or even make redundant a simple opposition between Tahiti and France, or between the state of nature and civilization. Indeed, recognizing a tension, a "war," or in other words a difference within the self that can never be resolved, constitutes Diderot's analysis of what marks the human condition that is enlightened about itself.[36] Diderot promotes the thought of a spacing within, or "dialogicity," in Bakhtin's terms. One of the most obvious features of Diderot's writings is precisely his privileged use of a dialogic form (like the *Supplément*, which is entirely composed of dialogues). This prevents a monologic, totalizing thought from coalescing, and foregrounds alterity in his discourse. Diderot problematizes the opposition between self and other, and shows that alterity already inhabits the self. This is the case in the *Supplément*. It could be said that through exchanges between various interlocutors, Diderot's dialogues represent the general possibility for communication, commerce, intercourse to fail. In the dialogues between Orou and the chaplain, this happens when the "message" gets lost, misheard because it is culturally unheard of. But the whole essay/fiction generalizes the failure of communication, and the end is characteristic in that respect. The final dialogue between the two French interlocutors A and B, which is summing up all the previous insights afforded by the encounter between Tahiti and France (coming as it does after the Tahitian patriarch's address to Bougainville, and the dialogues between Orou and the chaplain), evinces several instances of misunderstanding or mishearing: "That's not quite right" (Diderot 1992, 67); "I wouldn't say that" (twice, Diderot 1992, 68: "Je ne dis pas cela"). The last sentences of the *Supplément* might be considered as the condensation of that interrogation by suspending the availability (and even the possibility of availing oneself) of a successful exchange. A and B wonder what the reaction of "civilized" French women would be when reading the dialogue between Orou and the chaplain, including therefore the advocacy and description of adultery, fornication, and incest: "B. What do you suppose they might say about it? A. I haven't a clue. B. And what would they think of it? A. Probably the opposite of what they would say" (Diderot 1992, 75).[37]

Two inferences can be drawn from Diderot's uncovering of alterity within the self. First, if difference or alterity is already experienced by civilized man within himself, then it is likely that any difference in itself between Tahiti and France will be sidestepped, or related to that fundamental inner division within the self. It will not be approached in its newness, but read within parameters of what alterity is known to be. Is it not what happens when Diderot discusses the "unheard" between France and Tahiti (in the case of Aotourou returning home, or in that of Orou and the chaplain's discussion of incest)? Radical irreducibility in such moments is never of another order than similar breakdowns between two Frenchmen, between French men and women, or within enlightened man: "a continual war, lasting the whole of his life." Todorov's ideal of "difference in equality" can be tested in Diderot's *Supplément*: there, "difference" seems to be apprehended only insofar as it is "equal" to my representation of it, when "I" can represent radical difference in its sameness to mine. Diderot's *Supplément* shows the difficulty of thinking difference in its difference.[38]

However, a second inference can be derived from Diderot's thinking on alterity. To begin with, the fact that civilized man is not identical to himself puts in question his privileged, centered position.

Moreover, there is a difference within Enlightenment, and this difference is also in Diderot's analysis, the other. The other has made enlightenment possible, and therefore, the other is not simply the other *of* enlightenment. About "the life and mores of savages," for example, Diderot writes in Raynal's *Histoire* that "It is perhaps to this knowledge that we owe all the progress that moral philosophy has made among us . . . we may say that it is the ignorance of savages which has enlightened, so to speak, civilized people" (Raynal 1798, XV, 682). The often proposed explanation for why ignorance taught anything and could be enlightening is well known—it offered a relativistic vantage point from which to judge European institutions. "Civilized" nations naturalized their own institutions, and the encounter with "savage" nations, or with men (almost) living in a state of nature, has taught Europe that its institutions were historically established, and therefore could be changed (Papin 127). But this is not all. Encountering alterity did not only rectify inadequate theories regarding European institutions by virtue of comparison with other customs and the recording of differences—which would have allowed for a fuller, richer, more complete Europe. Far from fulfilling an epistemological gap, "savages" have revealed a lack which in effect remains gaping within Europe, within its project of self-awareness and development. Diderot says that Indian nations furnished the historical opportunity for Europeans to realize that the European emphasis on itself in order to achieve enlightenment was really a blindness:

> So far moralists had looked for the origin and foundations of society in the societies they had under their eyes. . . . But since it has been perceived that social institutions did not derive either from the needs of nature, or from the dogmas of religion, since innumerable peoples lived independent and without a cult, the vices of morality and legislation have been found in the establishment of societies. (Raynal 1798, XV, 682).

According to Diderot, then, the "origin" of a self-same society is not to be looked for within itself, under its very eyes. On the contrary, positing the other as the origin is a way to make possible another history of the self. Diderot shows in effect that the origin of Europe is not or will not be European. His recourse to the other invalidates the self-same, self-identical assumptions that Europe tends to have about itself. But the statement that another history of the self is made possible by the other is inseparable from the discovery, through the other, of a difference within the self. In "Psyche: Inventions of the other," Jacques Derrida follows the conditions of possibility of "another invention, or rather an invention of the other that would come, through the economy of the same, indeed while miming or repeating it . . . to offer a place for the other [donner lieu à l'autre] . . . let the other come" (Derrida 1989, 60). The coming of the other also implies another "us":

> It can be invented only by the other who says "come" and to whom a response with another "come" seems to be the only invention that is desirable and worthy of interest. The other is indeed what is not inventable, and it is then the only invention in the world, our invention, the invention that invents us. For the other is always another origin of the world and we are (always) (still) to be invented. And the being of the we, and being itself. Beyond being. (Derrida 1989, 61)

The difference within the self is assessed by Diderot in terms of distance, of a spacing, what is considered not being anymore under one's eyes ("sous les yeux"). Discovering the other space of America forever opened up a space within Europe. Diderot shows that this spacing remains as a conflict, a war within the self, so that the self articulates differences, but does not resolve them. Glissant links "the question of the Relation and relativism as opposed to the absolute" (Glissant 1996, 38). In other words, in order for relativism to avoid being simply understood as various local applications of universal or absolute values (an understanding which corresponds to the project of Enlightenment), it is crucial to contemplate the question of the articulation or Relation. This articulation in general is a difference between, or a spacing within, it names and vouches for alterity.

And on that question, Diderot parts company with Voltaire. For he did not only anticipate, like Voltaire, the inevitability of the savage becoming civilized. He also detected in his French contemporaries traits that were for him evidence of a return to an earlier, primitive state:

> We feel the want of exercise, and go into the country in search of health. Our women begin to deserve the name of mothers, by suckling their own children; the children too are just rescued from the shackles of swaddling clothes. (Raynal 1798, IX, 275)

Diderot sometimes declares that civilization is the teleological outcome of savagery, and savagery the beginnings of civilization. Yet he describes here something different: civilization and savagery are shown to be intersecting, rather than simply polar oppositions. And man's historical trajectory will consist in encountering its other "state" (civilized, or savage): "In all the centuries to come, savage man will advance by slow degrees towards the civilized state; and civilized man will return towards his primitive state" (Raynal 1798, IX, 275). Man will have to meet, not assimilate, what to him is other. The Enlightenment has dwelt at length on the project of becoming civilized, on the advance toward civilization. What Diderot points out in this passage is that too little attention has been paid to the reverse, to what Diderot does conceive of as a "return" to the primitive. Yet, if both propositions (an advance, a return) are taken together, it becomes apparent that Diderot suggests here a simultaneous pattern of progression and regression that is incompatible with a teleological perspective. Bernard Papin has shown that for Diderot, the ideal point of happiness would be in between the savage and the civilized (Papin 17, 129).[39] Instead of an inexorable path to progress, Diderot advocates a convergence, a site where to meet the other halfway. This common space can be put in parallel with what Homi Bhabha promotes with the notion of "negotiation": "When I talk of *negotiation* rather than *negation*, it is to convey a temporality that makes it possible to conceive of the articulation of antagonistic or contradictory elements: a dialectic without the emergence of a teleological or transcendent History" (Bhabha 1994, 25). As Jacques Derrida's essay, *The Other Heading: Reflections on Today's Europe*, shows, what is being thought in "negotiation" has implications for the self as for the other, for the very concept of "subjectivity" (to return to Todorov's formulation): "*What is proper to a culture is to not be identical to itself.* Not to not have an identity, but not to be able to identify itself, to be able to say 'me' or 'we'; to be able to take the form of a subject only in the non-identity to itself or, if you prefer, only in the difference *with itself*" (Derrida 1992, 9).

This explains why one finds apparently contradictory statements by Diderot about the state of nature as opposed to that of civilization. On the one hand, Diderot needs to think "nature" as a separate pole to civilization, in order to postulate the possibility of the relation between the two. He does not need a separate nature any more when he thinks the inner division of the self. In that second position, Diderot does not emphasize the space to be negotiated, but the very contested, unstable locations, that in the first position are expediently represented as opposed "poles." In the second position, Diderot shows, as in the example of the civilized evincing savage traits (breast-feeding, exercising, etc.), that such a relation is already taking place, which affects the stability of, and even the possibility of thinking, a rigorous polarity between nature and civilization, or the hierarchical privilege of civilization.

COMMUNICATION: OF THE DEAF-MUTE

In his *Voyage*, Bougainville mentions that Pereire, who was known, in Rousseau's words, for teaching mutes "not only to speak but to know what they are saying" (Rousseau 1986, 243), examined the Tahitian Aotourou, who had been brought along to France. According to Bougainville, Aotourou had proved to be disappointing in one respect, because at the end of his stay of eleven months in Paris, he could not say more than a few French words (Bougainville 264). Pereire reportedly declared that Aotourou was physically incapable of speaking French ("he could not physically pronounce most of our consonants, nor any of our nasal vowels" [Bougainville 272]). It also appears that Pereire was present during some of Bougainville and Aotourou's "conversations." Characteristically, the account of Aotourou's restricted use of the French language slips into an analogy to the relation of the deaf-mute to language. Bougainville's analogy is neither random nor isolated. It was then a common occurrence to attribute similar characteristics to deaf-mutes and savages, first of all because both were determined to point closely to "nature."

They point to nature, yet are not in all rigor absolutely identical with it, since the "state of nature" is postulated by most philosophers primarily as a working "hypothesis": this is Diderot's position in the *Supplément* (1992, 69), and Rousseau's in the *Second Discourse* (1967, 169). It is true that Diderot, for one, departs from the understanding of the state of nature as hypothetical, by equating at times the present condition of savages with that of man in the state of nature. In the *Apologie de l'abbé de Prades*, he defines the state of nature as follows: "It refers, among philosophers, to the current condition of his descendants [Adam's], considered *in a herd* and not *in society*; a condition which is not only possible, but subsisting, and under which almost all savages live" (AT I, 454). In this text, the "possibility" or hypothesis is verified by the current condition of the savages, as well as it supposes the continuity ("subsisting") of an earlier existing condition. Rousseau appears to be more methodical, in that he maintains a conceptual distinction between a savage and natural state: "And it is for want of sufficiently distinguishing ideas, and observing at how great a distance these people [savage nations] were from the first state of nature . . . " (Rousseau 1967, 219). In fact, however, Rousseau has also recourse throughout the *Second Discourse* to verifications of his hypothesis of the state of nature in the reported present life of the savages, and often refers to man in that hypothetical state as "savage man."[40] As Jacques Chouillet points out, the purpose of positing a hypothesis in the first place is akin to a scientific experiment, the aim of which is to obtain "the model of a new humankind, rid of conventions and prejudices, reconciled with nature itself" (Chouillet 1973, 179). The position of savages, who are sometimes located at the origin, or in a more advanced stage of development toward civilization, illustrates well the conceptual complexity of the state of nature. Louis Althusser remarks that "Paradoxically, this state, ignorant of all society, *contains and illustrates in advance the ideal of a society to be created*" (Althusser 26). The state of nature may represent a nostalgia for a lost plenitude, but it also constitutes, in Althusser's words, "the end of history that is inscribed in its origin" (26). In other words, the concept of the state of nature depends on prior assumptions such as logic or teleology (when it evokes the origin, or the end), but profoundly unsettles their reliability. In another context, Derrida has called this "paradox" an "archeo-teleology" (Derrida 1992, 27). In the *Apologie*, Diderot justifies postulating a state of nature "when one proposes to discover philosophically, not the eclipsed greatness of human nature, but the origin and the chain of man's knowledge" (AT I, 454–55). Rousseau also affirms that the hypothesis has relevant effects for man today—"a state which, if ever it did, does not now, and in all probability never will exist, and of which, notwithstanding, it is absolutely necessary to have just notions to judge properly of our present state" (Rousseau 1967, 219). In that sense, the state of nature is profoundly historical, since it offers a theoretical construct for the philosopher to assess man's present condition and build a future history.[41]

Diderot links the postulate of a state of nature and an investigation into the origin and development of knowledge, which echoes the title of Condillac's celebrated essay. In the *Essay on the Origin of Human Knowledge* (1746), Condillac argues that ideas are neither innate nor prior to signs, and furthermore that although forms of communication and expression were enabled by and from the origin of language, self-reflection and reason stem from, and are only made possible by the final stage of articulate language.[42] The research conducted on the means of communication of the deaf-mutes and on the assessment of their ideas could first be interpreted as an attempt to confirm such a genealogy. In that view, like the argument used in the study of savages, deaf-mutes would be used as a marker of the evolution of language. In the same way that savages were at times equated with the beginning of a progress toward civilization, so deaf-mutes would point to the first stage of language.

Most philosophers would have agreed with Diderot's argument in *Lettre sur les sourds et muets* that the communication of thought is the main object of language (AT I, 371). At the outset though, Condillac addresses the issue otherwise, by posing that thought is made possible by (articulate) language.[43] Condillac explains in the *Essay* that the first language must have been in "the mode of speaking by action" (Condillac 1974, 171). Speaking by action means "communicating one's thoughts" (175) by gestures and inarticulate cries. This first stage of language precedes that of a mixture of words and gestures (176), itself the preliminary stage to the general use of articulate language (204). Condillac indicates that one of the main advantages of articulate language is to facilitate abstraction, and to speak of an object in its absence. In effect, the limitations of speaking by action consist in the necessary proximity to an object designating one's thought: "Now it was impossible for the language of action to disclose the situation of one's mind, but by shewing the object to which it related" (240). On the contrary, "The more the use of abstract terms was established, the more it shewed the conveniency of articulate sounds for expressing even those thoughts which seem to have the least relation to sensible things" (250).

In the perspective of a teleology toward articulate language, where the mode of speaking by action is said to correspond best with the need to express and communicate thoughts related to proximate, sensible things, and articulate language to express and communicate abstractions, what are the implications regarding the ideas believed to be held by the deaf-mute? Because he does not communicate through articulate language, the deaf-mute is found to be closer to the origin of language, to "animal language" in Diderot's words (AT I, 372). James Creech says that in Diderot's essay, the deaf-mute's silence "represents the cusp of articulation between language and ideas" (Creech 122). This is why Diderot, in a paradox that is only apparent, uses the deaf-mute in his argument to investigate the "true notions of the formation of language" (AT I, 354), and in particular "the successive substitution of oratorical signs to gestures" (AT I, 415).[44] The deaf-mute, therefore, seems to recapitulate the very history of language, or to testify exemplarily to one of its stages.

Like Diderot, Condillac uses the example of a deaf-mute to assess "the successive substitution" from the mode of speaking by action to articulate language. This occurs in the part of the *Essay* that recalls the "real story" of a young man from Chartres, who at the age of twenty-three recovered his sense of hearing and "began all of a sudden to speak" (Condillac 1974, 124). Condillac recalls that the Memoirs of the Academy of Sciences recorded in 1703 the questions that were asked of the young man, and the conclusions reached regarding his thought processes when he was deaf and after he recovered his hearing. However, Condillac remarks that the opportunity was lost to establish the chronology he is after in his *Essay*, that is to say the connection between "the progression of mental operations" and "that of language" (8):

> It were to be wished they had examined this young man concerning what few ideas he had, while he was without the use of speech; what were the first ideas he acquired after he recovered his hearing; what assistance he received either from external objects, or from what he heard said, or from his own reflexion, to form new ideas. (Condillac 1974, 125)

Since this chronology was not recorded in the Memoirs, Condillac says, "All that we can do is to supply their account by conjectures"

(125), an approach that parallels his conjecture on the origin of language or "supposition . . . in what manner this nation first invented language" (170). The parallel indicates for us a first reading of Condillac's use of the deaf-mute as a pointer to the origin of language. For Condillac, there is a connection between the progress toward articulate language and "the progress of the operations of the mind" (131). Condillac always follows the premise that "there are no ideas but such as are acquired" (15), with the following two consequences: "The first [ideas] proceed immediately from the senses; the others are owing to experience" (15). This means that for Condillac, a sensation is an idea (19). Experience and reflection function as correctives to the error of judgment that may arise from sensation (22).[45] This is why Condillac remarks that the deaf young man of Chartres had some ideas (125), and that "he could by gestures signify his necessities, and the things which might relieve them" (125–26). But he denies that he could form judgments, or reason, that is to say, combine his ideas, for lack of abstract instituted signs, without which he says it is impossible to reflect:

> As he had no signs sufficiently commodious for comparing his ideas of the most familiar kind, he very rarely formed any judgment. It is even probable that for the first three and twenty years of his life, he did not form any single reasoning. To reason is to frame judgments, and to connect them by observing their dependency on one another. (127)

Condillac consistently links the availability of a name or a sign for a thing with the possibility of thinking about it: "connect his ideas with arbitrary signs" (129). Without a sign, a thing is only accessible to attention through the perception of it, which means that attention lasts as long as the perception of the thing. This implies that the deaf-mute, who can designate only immediate, sensible things having a connection with his needs, has "no habit of contemplation and much less of memory" (126). Having no memory means, in contradistinction, having "no sign to supply the absence of things" (128–29), such a sign being available in articulate language. Condillac views the deaf-mute as living as it were always in the present, not aware of his own existence and of its continuity, in a state of lethargy.[46] The awareness of one's existence depends on what Condillac often calls "revival," the repetition of an experienced connection between sensation and idea, or more simply put, on the recollection of an idea (130). This revival is ascertained through the use of arbitrary signs, supplying the absence of the experienced connection, but designating it, or putting themselves in its place, through an operation of conscious "connection": "We cannot revive our ideas, but as they are connected with some signs" (130–31).

Condillac pursues his analysis of the "feeble traces of the operations of the mind" of the deaf-mute (128) by comparing them to the hypothesis of "a person whom we may suppose to have been deprived of all communication with society, and who with sound and perfect organs had been trained up, for instance, among the bears of the forest" (128). As was the case for the analysis of the deaf man, this hypothesis does not rest on mere conjectures, for Condillac also mentions the case of a ten-year-old boy who had been "brought up among bears" and found in 1695. The point of the comparison is to ascertain whether "sound and perfect organs" put the "wild" boy or hypothetical person in a better position to reflect than the deaf young man. The answer is negative, "because so long as he lived without conversing with the rest of mankind, he would have no occasion to connect his ideas with arbitrary signs" (129). Later on, Condillac establishes an even more forceful articulation between social intercourse and the use of signs on the one hand, and communication and the possibility of ideas on the other hand: "Since men are incapable of making any signs, but by living in society, it follows of course, that the stock of their ideas, when their minds begin to be formed, entirely consists in their mutual communication" (134).

It seems that the juxtaposition within Condillac's argument of the discussion of the deaf-mute and that of an asocialized human being suggests itself because the deaf-mute is himself represented as savage, antisocial, with no communication with others beyond his elementary needs. But Condillac complicates this position, just like Diderot when he presents the savage both as the beginning of a development toward civilization and as the intermediary between nature and artifice. For one thing, Condillac may symbolically locate the deaf-mute at the origin of language and the development of human knowledge, but the wild boy is altogether denied the use of signs (133). Unlike the deaf-mute, the wild boy does not in effect belong to the history of language, which is that of man's socialization, even at the origin, in the mode of speaking by action. Certainly, the location of the deaf-mute is determined by the privilege granted to articulate language, itself posited at the end of that development. But, as Jacques Derrida has shown in *The Archaeology of the Frivolous*, Condillac does not simply oppose speaking by action to articulate language. Derrida recalls that Condillac constantly posits that "the language of action precedes and grounds all language" (Derrida 1980, 96). He quotes Condillac's *Essay* in that respect: "here the reader will see how [the language of action] has produced every art proper to express our thoughts" (Derrida 1980, 109). And at the other end of the teleological process, it cannot be said either that articulate language, or the institution of arbitrary signs, is just a separate stage of the development, or a third kind of language:

> Thus the possibility of the arbitrary sign governs, but from its end, the totality of the progress. Consequently, articulated language, a system of arbitrary signs, is no longer one region among others within a general semiotics: it is *exemplary*. Articulated language resembles one example among others, it seems to *constitute* one, only one, of the three kinds of signs. Actually, it organizes by orienting, as the best example, the finalized totality of the semiotic process. (Derrida 1980, 112–13)

In fact, Derrida studies the motifs of analogy and "variation of insistence" (Derrida 1980, 93) in Condillac, which put into question both the "concepts of rupture and repetition" (131). For example he quotes a letter written by Condillac to G. Cramer, in which Condillac clarifies the distinction he held in the *Essay* between natural cries and signs. In Derrida's words, the difference proposed by Condillac between the two is a "difference of degree" (97).[47] For Condillac, natural cries become arbitrary signs through socialization:

> I respond that, until commerce, natural signs are not properly signs. . . . [Men] must live together to have the opportunity to attach ideas to these cries and to employ them as signs. Thus these cries merge with arbitrary signs. I presuppose that in many places. . . . But I seem to suppose the contrary and thereby place too much difference between natural and arbitrary signs. (Derrida 1980, 112)[48]

The remark that cries "merge" with arbitrary signs indicates that in commerce, but also structurally, "there are only arbitrary signs" (Derrida 1980, 110).

Furthermore, the parallel between the example of the deaf-mute and the origin of language holds mostly because of a thematic resemblance: in both instances, the language used is composed of inarticulate cries and gestures. But several moments of Condillac's examination of the deaf-mute rather point to elements constitutive of an intermediate stage of language, that is, in Condillac's terms, "a language intermixed with words and gestures" (Condillac 1974, 176). His analysis is in many respects in greater conformity with that stage than with the original "language by action." Condillac explains that the intermediate stage is characterized by the naming of sensible things (250). He describes this stage as one in which "[Men] articulated new sounds, and by repeating them several times, and accompanying them with some gesture which pointed out such objects as they wanted to be taken notice of, they accustomed themselves to give names to things" (174). This assessment is similar to that of the young man of Chartres who could "connect some of his ideas with signs" (125), but "wanted names to point out those things which had not so great a relation to himself" (126). In a brief *Mémoire* addressed to the Academy of Sciences on the subject of the deaf-mute, Pereire also holds the view that "with the exception of terms which signify visible things, almost all the words of a Dictionary are very difficult to explain to mutes, and ordinarily, on purely intellectual things, one only gives them confused and imperfect ideas" (Pereire 4).[49] Pereire's statement is close to Condillac's assessment of the intermediate stage of language, when it was possible to name sensible or "visible" things (Pereire), but not to use abstraction, which Condillac defines as "expressing even those thoughts which seem to have the least relation to sensible things" (Condillac 1974, 250).[50] Yet, Pereire's method purports to have the deaf-mutes not only "understand the value of those [words] which designate visible things, but also acquire abstract and general notions which they lack" (Pereire 8). Just as in Diderot's *Lettre sur les sourds et muets*, the deaf-mute is in fact exemplary, even in his misapprehensions of "the order of ideas" (AT I, 351) or of "the formation of language" (354). Diderot says in that respect that "It will no doubt seem odd to you to be referred to one whom nature has deprived of the faculty of hearing and speech, in order to obtain from him true notions on the formation of language. But please consider that ignorance is less distant from truth than prejudice" (AT I, 354). Creech comments that "Faced with the sensorial veil of deafness . . . the deaf-mute 'philosophizes.' He produces meanings and connections that are made both possible and necessary by his infirmity" (Creech 123). He also quotes Diderot as saying in the *Lettre* that "If he did not hit exactly upon what it was, he almost hit upon what it ought to be" (123). The instances of the *Essay* which link the deaf-mute to the intermediate stage of the development of language have further implications.

It is noteworthy that in spite of the privilege given by Condillac to articulate language, it is also designated in the *Essay* as the stage when men risk not understanding one another any longer, when communication may always misfire, just as Diderot's *Supplément* explores. In fact, Condillac finds the ideal stage for successful communication to have been at the intermediate step when only sensible objects were named: "Mankind never understood one another better, than when they gave names to sensible objects. But so soon as they wanted to pass to the archetypes . . . they began to have a great deal of difficulty to understand one another" (Condillac 1974, 254–55). This statement undermines the privilege of articulate language, because what enables abstraction and reason opens at the same time the possibility for commerce or communication to fail. On the contrary, positing the deaf-mute halfway toward abstraction allows both for a teleology toward abstraction and the description of a happy medium, in this case naming sensible objects, or successful communication.[51] The suggestion that the highest possibility of understanding among men has been left behind in the development of language also recalls Diderot's analysis of savage and civilized men. For Diderot, the savage is both the origin of the development toward civilization and a model for the possibility of happiness or intersection between natural and artificial advantages, which is itself represented as the greatest "civilized" awareness or gain. Therefore, Condillac and Diderot refer to savages or deaf-mutes in order to represent the modalities, and perhaps the inevitability of progress. Yet, in effect, both authors contest the teleology that such a description seems to entail, and more specifically the desirability or even the stability of the last stage, be it civilization, abstraction, or reason.[52] These questions are also addressed in Bougainville's narrative. His reflections on Aotourou's limited use of the French language show information about philosophical assessments of the history of language. He professes to have been "struck dumb" (Bougainville 263) by the ignorance and bad faith of the

Parisian fashionable world, who could not grasp Aotourou's difficulties when compared to the ease with which Italians, Englishmen, or Germans pick up French after a year. This led them to question Aotourou's intelligence. For Bougainville on the contrary, there should be no cause for surprise, because he traces a correlation between language and ideas. The fact that Europeans all share a similar grammar enables them to have the same ideas: "These strangers had a grammar like ours, as their moral, physical, political, and social ideas were the same with ours, and all expressed by certain words in their language as they are in French" (Bougainville 264). In contrast, Bougainville thinks that the needs in Tahiti are more simple, and do not require many signs to express them. Therefore, according to him, the relation between language and ideas in Tahiti involves the recourse to few abstract concepts, making it difficult for Aotourou to operate what Bougainville calls a translation (264):

> The Taiti-man, on the contrary, only having a small number of ideas, relative on the one hand to a most simple and most limited society, and on the other, to wants which are reduced to the smallest number possible; he would have been obliged, first of all, as I may say, to create a world of previous ideas [idées premières], in a mind which is as indolent as his body, before he could come so far as to adapt to them the words in our language, by which they are expressed. (264–65)

One recognizes in this statement the question raised by Diderot regarding the possibility of a true cultural communication between France and Tahiti. It is true that while Aotourou is assimilated to a deaf-mute, Bougainville's equally narrowed notions of the Tahitian language are not shown to impair in any serious way a productive exchange, the results of which are contained and inscribed in French. Yet, Aotourou reportedly played an important part in Bougainville's account of Tahiti. Bougainville relied on him when he depicted a less idyllic and probably more accurate Tahiti than the one he had initially presented: "I have mentioned above, that the inhabitants of Taiti seemed to live in an enviable happiness. . . . I was mistaken" (269). Moreover, Bougainville remains as alert as Diderot to the possibility of the miscarriage of communication. Aotourou's rectifications suspend self-assurance: "I shall now give an account of what I think I have understood in my conversations with him" (267). And the civilized Frenchman recalls what he heard, and first of all that he heard the "deaf-mute" speak.

In the *Supplément*, Diderot shows that incommunicability is the risk of exchange in general, not only of those between "savages" and "civilized." One is always engaged in a potential "dialogue de sourds" with others, a dialogue which falls on deaf ears. In *Lectures de Raynal*, Goggi mentions an odd anecdote involving Raynal, always in quest of information for his *Histoire des deux Indes*, and an embarrassed Horace Walpole, who was pressed for American news:

> The first testimony of Raynal asking questions about colonies to those he meets in company dates back to the year 1765. The testimony is indirect and not very favorable to Raynal: in a letter dated November 12, 1774, H. Walpole describes thus his first meeting with the abbot in Paris: "The first time I met him [Raynal] was at the dull baron d'Olbach's: we were twelve at table: I dreaded opening my mouth in French, before so many people and so many servants: he began questioning me, cross the table, about our colonies, which I understand as I do Coptic. I made him sign I was deaf. After dinner he found I was not, and never forgave me." (Goggi 19)

Walpole's recourse to deafness and inarticulateness dissimulates his lack of fluency in the other's articulate language, French, and his inability to communicate anything meaningful regarding the colonies. Raynal interprets the gesture differently, however, as a witty deliberate silence, a ploy not to inform him, or to make his own ignorance (of Walpole's ability to speak) ridiculous. It is noteworthy that the miscommunication is triggered by a discussion involving the rivalry between British and French colonizing projects. The appropriation of the other's space induced a reflection on the legitimacy of such ventures, which presented Europeans as regressive, "primitive," or "barbarous" in their greed for conquest. The depiction of civilized man as in fact primitive, and in the anecdote just mentioned, the position of deafness as a helpless refuge and an ironic weapon at the same time, show an uneasiness within Europeans about their own assumptions of superiority over and usefulness to others, non-Europeans. We have seen that concurrently with a debate regarding the legitimacy of imperialism abroad, another political discourse took place along with the aesthetic assessment of domestic space. In France, as we have seen, authors on landscape gardening fought the accusation of imitation, while acknowledging that French gardens were to a great extent appropriated and "invaded" by the English. Whether they considered their position overseas or at home, French writers were faced with anxiety and doubt as far as their territorial possessions were concerned. In the next pages, we will show how the discourse on French and English gardens developed guidelines and strategies for a successful, satisfactory, and guiltless appropriation of domestic space.

Chapter 4

Philosophical Gardens

> Is classicism merely a branch of the baroque without knowing it?
>
> —Jacques Derrida, *Dissemination*

COLONIZING SPACE

Landscape, mediating nature and culture, is made to function both as "a site of visual appropriation" (Mitchell 2) by the beholder, and as a space where the beholder himself gets encompassed, in fact becomes, in Hunt's phrase, a "figure in the landscape" (Hunt 1989). Following Mitchell and others, we have mentioned in the first chapters occasions of a political and aesthetic congruence: at a time when a discourse confirming colonization abroad also wonders about the legitimacy of such ventures, another discourse on the so-called new access to the visual beauty of domestic space occurs simultaneously. A policy of national, internal colonization can be represented with modes which obviously alter, or seem to dominate, the environment. Some would argue that this is what the French formal garden, especially in the case of Versailles, attempted to do. But construing landscape, in continuity with the garden, as a beautiful picture to be beheld, as we saw for example in Morel's treatise, is still another means serving its reification and appropriation. In other words, "innocence" is never involved in the admiration of natural beauty. In fact, the appropriation of space is made all the more possible since the construct of landscape as a beautiful picture is "engaging" for the spectator, a term often used by Watelet—we shall see to what ends—in his *Essai sur les jardins*. Bernard Kalaora says that "Patriotic sentiment through the cult of the beautiful was the equation of a conquering and expansionist civilization" (Kalaora 465). And Mitchell also points out that at the same time as imperialist ventures endeavor to annex new territories, there is "a renewed interest in the re-presentation of the home landscape, the 'nature' of the imperial center" (Mitchell 17).

We have seen so far how French and English authors developed arguments of historical, cultural, and aesthetic difference or preeminence in order to defuse the perceived threat of the other to their respective national soil. In other words, the discourse on landscape was an aesthetic pretext for a political interpretation of space, the space of a national territory, which was often seen as in danger of being invaded. But the two comments quoted above by Kalaora and Mitchell indicate a reverse link between aesthetics and politics. They suggest the extent to which, even before such an alarmist discourse is developed, the landscape has already been apprehended pictorially, and even panoptically, through the postulate of a penetrating eye, that is, through a metaphor derived from a military rhetoric of combat and invasion. In his treatise, Girardin concretely describes the relation of the spectator to the landscape as a conjunction of eyes and legs (Girardin 67). Watelet also says that "the eye moves across space" (Watelet 108). This "walking eye" is already a metaphor for the conqueror or colonist, and an immediate inference seems to be that the beholder dominates the landscape by the simple fact that he (partially or totally) sees it. The relation of the beholder to the landscape appears to be posited as one of mastery. The following pages will examine the claim made by some authors that this position of mastery varies in the French and the English styles. This will be addressed first by recalling what links the consideration of landscape to the genre of landscape painting, and their common reliance on perspective, and secondly by following some arguments linking the French formal garden to Descartes's system, and the English garden to Locke's.

SCOPOPHILIA

The definitions of landscape generally conflate space and the point of view of a beholder. Jean-Robert Pitte gives parts of the definitions of *paysage* found in several French dictionaries (Pitte I, 22), of which I will quote a few. The Furetière dictionary (1690): "An aspect of a country, the territory which extends as far as the sight can go." The Robert dictionary (1977): "The part of a country that nature presents to an observer." The *Dictionnaire de la géographie* (1974): "A part of space that is visually analyzed." The first definition of *landscape* in the Webster's dictionary (1991) is: "A section or expanse of natural scenery, usually extensive, that can be seen from a single viewpoint." Pitte comments that "the relation between landscape and sight does not seem to pose a problem to anyone" (Pitte I, 22). Later, he expands this definition, which includes then all senses as well as human practices in the very space that is beheld:

> To sum up, landscape is the observable expression by the senses at the surface of the earth of the combination between nature, techniques and human culture. It is essentially changing, and can only be apprehended in its dynamics, that is to say, in the frame of history which restitutes its fourth dimension. (Pitte I, 24)

One aspect of culture that mediates, and even to some extent creates man's relation to landscape, is painting. Pitte mentions that dictionaries always give as one definition of *paysage* the representation of a natural site (Pitte I, 22). So does Webster's dictionary in its second definition of landscape as "a picture representing natural inland or coastal scenery." Anne Cauquelin argues that "For centuries, the whole effort of Western thought has consisted in reducing what is vague in . . . 'nature'. . . . The landscape [paysage] . . . extracts from this abundant and disordered thing that natural environment is—nature—a normed, framed image, which attempts to fix limits" (Cauquelin 452), in order to induce reassurance and familiarity in the beholder. She also says that "The usual sentiment of a beautiful nature remains tied to its pictorial origin" (Cauquelin 452–53).

In "Les mots, les images," Michel Baridon has remarkably studied the etymology and function of keywords in treatises of landscape gardening published in the Renaissance and the seventeenth century, regarding in particular the visual and pictorial encompassing of a garden by the beholder. He recalls in that respect the importance of perspective in Western aesthetics, which is made manifest in paintings as well as gardens. According to Baridon's study, the Renaissance garden is to be "seen from above" (Baridon 1995, 199) and has "a short perspective" (202), whereas the Baroque garden should be "seen from afar" (199) and has "a long perspective" (202). This indicates that the position of the spectator is anticipated in the viewing of a garden as it would be in the viewing of a painting. The definitions of *perspective* that Baridon finds in dictionaries rehearse a history of approaches to vision. He mentions that for Rey [*Dictionnaire historique de la langue française* (1992)], "the word was synonymous with optics in the Middle Ages and that its specialization in painting dates back to the sixteenth century" (Baridon 1995, 200). In Furetière's dictionary (1690), the definition of perspective is "A picture which is usually put in gardens at the end of galleries in order to deceive the eye . . . by some view of a building or a distant landscape" (200). Perspective, this fundamental mode of apprehending space in the Western tradition, naturalizes an image and effaces its own artifice. It is related in Furetière's definition to the manipulation of the spectator ("in order to deceive the eye") and to the consequent theatricalization of space, where it functions as a backdrop for the eye to wander. In *Mirrors of Infinity*, Allen Weiss points out an ideological implication of perspective:

> Vision itself is a mode of placing the body in the world, among its objects, within its scenes, and the manner in which all representational systems imply the position of the ideal, putative spectator—as well as demand an optimal placement of the real, physical spectator in order to obtain the full aesthetic effect of the representation. . . . Every painting created according to the axiomatic system of one-point linear perspective has a unique viewpoint from which it must be seen. (Weiss 37)

Weiss draws out several consequences of apprehending space through the theory of one-point linear, planar perspective, in other words, the consequences of conceiving the space of a garden, or landscape, as a painting. Under this condition, the beholder loses information or is deprived of part of it: "The reduction of a visible scene to its painterly representation on a flat surface always sacrifices—within a realistic depiction of the world—a certain amount of visual information and verisimilitude due to the loss of two dimensions (depth and time)" (Weiss 35). Weiss recalls that the Renaissance system of perspective, in order to determine "the relative size of objects," relied on "the distance of the objects from the eye" and not on "the angle of vision," thereby "suppressing Euclid's eighth theorem of his *Optics*" (Weiss 35). Eighteenth-century authors are aware that space becomes flattened in the perception of a French garden. Girardin, for example, mentions that "The focal point, which is the fundamental point of symmetry, necessarily makes the objects appear flat, because the surfaces only are seen" (Girardin 124–25). Therefore, in a formal garden, all terrains "are reduced to . . . the flatness of a sheet of paper" for the beholder (Girardin 11). Following Merleau-Ponty, Weiss argues on the contrary that "Depth is the dimension of one's possibilities, one's future, where the body is the zero-degree spatiality whereby a world can take form" (Weiss 34). He shows that space is not "in front of the body" (Weiss 34), as Renaissance perspective represents it: "Rather, space surrounds the body, is before and behind, past and future, where one is both seer and object seen" (34). This definition indicates that space is not merely "viewed" from the outside by the spectator, but that the beholder is "in" the landscape. Furthermore, it prevents a reification of the landscape and announces "the very *reversibility of dimensions* that unfolds with the movements of the body" (Weiss 34). There is therefore not just one perspective on various elements in the landscape, but the spectator is also one such element; he himself can be viewed from various perspectives. Restricting this plural perspective to a single linear perspective consequently "limit[s] one's grasp of the world" (Weiss 34).

The possibility of the safe enjoyment of the space by the beholder seems to be predicated on the artificial stability of spatial positions, and on the exterior positioning of the spectator to the "picture" he contemplates. As soon as the possibility of entering the picture is evoked, the security of spatial bearings, including the spectator's own, collapses. Yet, the lack of security and stability brings about other pleasures. Some authors argue that it is precisely the passage (from outside to inside) that takes place in the change to the English style in gardening. With the change would also come the dispossession of man's mastery of the landscape.

DESCARTES AND LOCKE

Weiss generally equates the most masterful layouts in the French style, such as Vaux-le-Vicomte and Versailles, with the use of linear perspective. However, as we have mentioned, he also shows that mastery is not necessarily shared by all those who contemplate a French garden. For one thing, perspective is restrictive and limits the points of view of the beholder, and secondly, the symbolic gains (power, mastery) supposedly provided by perspective are mainly shown to return to the owner of the chateau, and in the case of Versailles, as always doubly paradigmatic, to the Sun-King.[1] This may be why eighteenth-century authors on landscape gardening often stress that "immobility" is an essential element of contemplation in a French garden: the beholder looks from one predetermined point at the garden below or in front of him. Morel writes for example that "it is a pity for the spectator if the sacred line [the main axis in the French style] does not offer in his direction anything of interest to him; he has to look there and not elsewhere" (Morel 13). Immobility, in this case, is as literal as it is a figure for social and political stasis. With immobility, a certain fatigue and disgust are felt. Watelet writes about the formal style in gardening that "the spectator perceives, guesses, and feels only a weak desire of moving" (Watelet 108).

On the contrary, the new style of gardening would represent its aims as an entry into the picture, as a motion within the space of the garden. In that respect, it is important to clarify the relation of the garden to two of its supposedly opposed references—architecture and painting. On the one hand, it is true that the new "English" style conceives itself as picturesque, that is, it openly endorses painting as the primary reference for the design of a garden, instead of architecture. Watelet says, for example, that "[the Art] which has the greatest connection with landscape gardening is that of Painting. However, Architecture has so far almost always taken care of it" (Watelet 105). But this reference to architecture functions only as far as the forms of the garden are concerned. The French garden is therefore described as the design of a horizontal plane, just as architecture decorates a vertical plane (Watelet 106). In contrast, the new style must strive to compose the forms of the landscape as a painter would the canvas of a picture: "The painter arranges and orders under the aspect favorable to his intention the objects he chooses in Nature. The decorator of a park must indeed have the same purpose" (Watelet 55). But this comment does not put into question the fact that the French style also constitutes a garden as a picture to be beheld. Watelet makes this clear when he points out the limitation that perspective brings in a painting's "arrangement" of nature: "The composition of a picture seems always the same, even if it is looked at from different points. The spectator has neither the means nor the power to alter the position" (Watelet 56). Although Watelet's remark concerns a painting, it fits the eighteenth-century notion of the viewer's static enjoyment of a French garden. This shows that both gardening styles can be compared to paintings, and that their opposition is not simply a difference of reference, to architecture or to painting. Rather, the difference consists in the position of the spectator, who is in or out of the picture, or of the landscape. The new style represents itself as an entry into the picture on the part of the beholder, emphasizing therefore not only his own motion, but the objects' changeability afforded by various perspectives: "On the contrary, the spectator of picturesque scenes in a park changes its arrangement, by changing his position" (Watelet 56).[2]

The new style also promotes a different relation to time on the part of the visitor. Watelet concludes about the spectator's enjoyment in the French, formal style that "this pleasure only lasts a few moments" (Watelet 108). On the contrary, in the gardening style Watelet is promoting, "to those who dedicate whole hours to this pleasure, [the garden designer] must uncover the beauties of his work only one after the other" (Watelet 106–107). To the attention of "a few moments" must succeed, then, the pleasant dedication of "whole hours." The new relation to time is inseparable from a deambulation within, and not a gazing into the garden. This deambulation takes an amount of time that is taken into consideration. Recommendations for appropriate ways to encourage the spectator to move into the garden are interpreted by some authors as a transposition of some of John Locke's principles in his *Essay on Human Understanding*, and of Newton's science. Baridon opposes Descartes's "systems" to the new scientific approach of "histories":

> It was a matter of keeping only to [the experiment], *following it step by step* and building the theory only at the end of the process of observation. . . . By "histories" one means, at the Royal Society, collections of minute observa-

> tions, often dated and followed up with the jealous care of proscribing any presupposition. (Baridon 1986, 439, my emphasis)

Baridon also explains that "histories" were "accounts established by respecting the chronological order" (Baridon 1995, 188). In an experiment, "particulars" were to be "successively collected" (188). As Baridon indicates, the consequence consists in an "integration of time into the vision of the world" (188). He also recalls that Locke "studied man's mental life with the method of *histories*," and that for Locke "life is a long sequence of registered *particulars*" (190). Girardin and other authors on landscape gardening apply this scientific attention to a "historical," sequential series of "particulars" in their own descriptions of "promenades" or tours of gardens.[3] They emphasize a new apprehension of space in order to prevent the effects usually assigned to the formal style. Girardin notes for example the following effect of a straight line: "Strait lines are extremely tiresome to the traveller, whose eyes are always arrived a long time before his legs" (Girardin 67). And Watelet concurs:

> An immense parterre, endless alleys, are surprising; but this pleasure only lasts for a few moments: one deliberates whether one will engage oneself [*s'engager*] to stride over these large spaces, which one look has already travelled through . . . one becomes weary of these vast and uniform dimensions . . . nothing engages [*engage*] to accelerate or slow down, like a man who would alternatively move his legs without advancing one step. (Watelet 108–109)

The question for these authors, then, becomes how to occupy time as much as how to occupy space. In effect, to fight the impression of monotony or endless repetition of time, and "disengagement," as Watelet would say, from the space under view, the gardener must fill in the space, partly in order to while away the time. In order to incite the spectator to "advance one step" and beyond, strategies are developed, encouraging an indirect approach to the whole terrain. We saw in an earlier chapter that the "new style" of gardening celebrated "the calling in of the country" (Pope) into the space of the garden. But this all-inclusiveness of the landscape in the garden is not incompatible with appeals to obstruct the view temporarily, or, as Watelet says, to "veil" it (Watelet 150), in order to induce the spectator to seek his own panorama(s), to walk in the direction he chooses, and therefore to become his own master, apparently not following a preestablished path. For Watelet, the point for the gardener is to be suggestive, not authoritarian in the arrangement of the landscape: "To engage [*Engager*], and not to constrain; here is the most pleasant of all Arts" (Watelet 26). Some authors argue that the French style tyrannizes not only nature, but the spectator himself, and furthermore, that the French garden illustrates and transposes Cartesian principles.

The second proposition corresponds to Allen Weiss's explicit aim in his study of "The French Formal Garden and 17th-Century Metaphysics": "In utilizing Cartesian metaphysics and Pascalian theology as symbols, indeed as 'captions' to the gardens, I intend to overlay certain rational fantasies with their morphological and topological correlates" (Weiss 10–11). However, Weiss states later on a difficulty involved in his project, when he says that "the Cartesian system lacks an aesthetic" because of "Descartes's notion of representation" (67). Weiss indicates one particular reason why the notion of representation in Descartes precludes in effect an aesthetic: "Truth is no longer deemed to be a function of conformity with the real world, but rather adherence to an intuitive or cognitive system of explanation" (65). In other words, truth involves a representation, but this representation is not mimetic and not referential. Yet, Weiss still claims that "we can thus easily imagine a Cartesian garden, following the example of Le Nôtre" (68). His assertion rests on a passage that he quotes from Dalia Judovitz's *Subjectivity and Representation in Descartes*: "The epistemological rejection of ocular vision [in Descartes] is replaced by the affirmation of a formal system that schematizes the visible according to logical and rhetorical paradigms" (67–68). Let us first note that if it is possible, according to Weiss, to derive from Judovitz's formulation of Descartes's project the image or the example of a garden, it is only to the extent that the French garden is already understood and all-encompassed by the definition of a "formal system" of concepts "schematizing" the terrain. This is, however, what should be in question, and which is, as it happens, problematized at times by Weiss himself. The question does not so much concern schematization, which obviously happens to a certain extent in all gardens, as it does the equivalence that seems to be established between Descartes's "*formal* system" (Judovitz) and the *formal* garden, which becomes then a "Cartesian garden" (Weiss). Is the proposed adequation between these two adjectives ("formal") just a formality? In "Vision,

Representation, and Technology in Descartes," Judovitz has delved further into the question she had tackled of the "rejection of ocular vision" in Descartes, linking it in particular to the Renaissance and Baroque pictorial traditions, such as anamorphosis, which were familiar to Descartes (Judovitz 64). Her study demonstrates that these traditions were both attacked and reappropriated by Descartes. Then, Judovitz points out that such a critique and reinvestment also occur with the concept of "vision." Following her argument will help understand the stakes of Weiss's apparently incompatible remarks (on the one hand, the absence of a Cartesian aesthetic project, and on the other hand, the very actualization of Descartes's system by Le Nôtre in the French formal garden). This double position sheds light on a structural characteristic of the French style usually omitted in eighteenth-century treatises, which consistently ignore or forget the Baroque in the seventeenth century.

Judovitz recalls that Descartes has always denounced the danger of illusion: "This invocation of illusion is invariably tied to deception and the problem of the unreliability of the senses" (Judovitz 65).[4] In his *Discourse on the Method*, Descartes writes that "because our senses sometimes deceive us, I wished to suppose that nothing is just as they cause us to imagine it to be" (Descartes 1996, 21). On the contrary, Descartes goes on, "I came to the conclusion that I might assume, as a general rule, that the things which we conceive very clearly and distinctly are all true" (22).[5] Because of the danger of illusion, Judovitz says, following Merleau-Ponty, that Descartes formulates "a theory of knowledge that seeks to move beyond resemblance" (Judovitz 73). Resemblance may be deceiving, or just an illusion. And the illusion in question refers to the apprehension of a false reality that presents itself, or can be taken to be true. Judovitz points out that the distrust of illusion leads Descartes to the point of "extending it to the visible world as a whole. . . . Descartes is in fact systematically undermining in both his scientific and philosophical writings the role of vision and its perceptual domain" (63). However, when Judovitz examines Descartes's position toward Baroque pictorial elements contributing to effects of illusion, such as the perspectival "trompe-l'oeil" and anamorphosis, she finds that Descartes is not merely critical. Jurgis Baltrusaitis has defined the effect of "anamorphosis" on the viewer in this way: "Instead of reducing forms to their visible limits, it projects them outside themselves and distorts them so that when viewed from a certain point they return to normal" (Judovitz 69). Descartes was wary of anamorphosis as an illusion; but as a critique of the limitations of ocular vision, and a projection out of what is "normally" visible, the technique was of interest to him: "Anamorphosis announces a new relation to the visible, one which conceives visual form not as a given but as a conceptual and technical construct" (Judovitz 69). Thus for Judovitz, "Descartes's critique of illusion . . . represents Descartes's assimilation of anamorphosis to his elaboration of a rationalism founded on mathematical schematism" (69).

In the same way that a pictorial tradition such as anamorphosis could be criticized and reappropriated by Descartes, so the critique of ocular vision recuperates visuality as an adequate figure for intuition and reason: "In spite of his rejection of the illusionism associated with ocular vision . . . Descartes resorts to visual metaphors to describe the nature of intuition as mental 'vision'" (Judovitz 67). Judovitz points out several consequences of this reappropriation. In particular, she shows that for Descartes, mental vision escapes the danger of illusion: "Intellectual vision is not ocular, and consequently it is no longer subject to illusion" (68). This escape is made possible because sensation and experience, which are not adequate informers of reality, are excluded from mental perception, and because the materiality of the objects is abstracted (Judovitz 78): "Descartes's paradoxical reappropriation of vision by reason . . . corresponds to an act of denunciation of its phenomenal and experiential character" (78).

Does this project, then, easily translate into, or become adaptable to principles of landscape gardening? The answer to this question depends on whether one accepts that the French style conveys an intelligibility, not sensibility, of the world. In fact, the opposition between intelligibility and sensibility is often posited as the difference between a French and English garden. Descartes can also be invoked in the context of the French geometrical style, in that for him, in Judovitz's terms, "Reduced to mathematical conventions, to the language of universal mathematics (*mathesis universalis*), nature signifies not as an image, but as a rational schema" (Judovitz 72). However, and this is the paradox mentioned by Weiss, the aesthetic transposition of Descartes's view of nature implies effecting a reverse displacement of Descartes's own metaphorization of nature ("as a rational schema"), in order to return back to forms of the sensible and the material, which Descartes was on the contrary abstracting, deducting, or "predicting" (Judovitz 76), that is, making not representable (Judovitz 81). Certainly, geometry was a preferred figure for Descartes, but it was especially a figure for the certainty and clearness of the conceptions of the mind. In other words, geometry ideally points to what is neither an "image" nor a sensation, and is mostly used by Descartes because it does not refer to an experience.[6] Therefore, as Weiss indicates, the transposition from the conceptual to the aesthetic can be effected, but only in the mode of an "emblem" (Weiss 68), or another metaphor. This statement problematizes the relation of the formal garden to clarity and intelligibility. The metaphorical French garden opens up a distance to what it would supposedly unilaterally signify. In fact, the conditions of its legibility are found to lie in an opposition or "tension" (Weiss) within its very form.

Some authors emphasize a continuity in the formal French garden, rather than a Cartesian rupture with former designs. For Thierry Mariage, the symbolic of seventeenth-century gardens directly prolongs that of the Renaissance: "Their essential principles were established well before Cartesianism can be invoked about them" (Mariage 71). He asserts instead that the effects of a seventeenth-century garden were "all in continuity with the conception of the world found in the physics of Aristotle" (71). Weiss does not altogether disagree with this view, for he points out several "tensions" within the formal garden. Admittedly for him, Versailles exemplifies "the modern quest for a *mathesis universalis*, which in the gardens of Versailles is seen in . . . the attempt to shape nature according to the human will, a task symbolized by the imposition of geometric formalism manifested in the French formal garden" (Weiss 75). In other words, the French formal garden is said to represent Cartesian principles. Mariage agrees that gardens illustrated the knowledge and scientific beliefs of the time, but unlike Weiss, he sees in the formalism of the gardens neither an imposition nor a mastery, but the "location of symbolic practices" shared by a given social group (Mariage 71). On the other hand, in his chapter on Versailles, Weiss also points out an inner contradiction between the geometry of the garden's central axis and other parts of the garden, in particular the labyrinth. In Weiss's analysis, the labyrinth represents the "finite closure" of the garden (Weiss 73), whereas the central axis represents "the perspectival utilization of the vanishing point as an overture onto infinity" (73). This tension is also assessed as one between the Baroque, with its use of the labyrinth, and the Neoclassic, with the straight line of the central axis (Weiss 73–74).

The recognition of tensions multiplies in Weiss's account, to the extent of revealing a profound ambivalence in the significance of the structure of the garden. For example, the labyrinth is represented at times as the central metaphor of the garden of Versailles (Weiss 73). At other times, though, this function seems rather to be assumed by the central axis opening onto infinity ("This infinity is the geometric and ethical point that supports the whole system" [Weiss 74]). Weiss also makes the expected point that "Louis XIV's need for order necessitated his creation of a guide to see Versailles, his own *Manière de montrer les jardins de Versailles*—especially stressing the static mode of experiencing the gardens, one divertissement at a time, each seen in proper succession" (73). Yet, he immediately qualifies this statement by adding that "it is as if the king recognized the relatively unformed, labyrinthine nature of the entirety of the gardens, and compensated for this lack of order by the royal decree that guided the visitor's vision" (73). This last statement shows that the ordered reading of the space is as much an afterthought as a planned arrangement, and does not entirely succeed in overcoming the formlessness of the garden. Therefore, the best-known symbol of the French style, Versailles, is certainly found to be formal, but not completely so. A tension has to be signalled with its opposite, with the disorder that always risks overpowering it. Because criteria such as absolutist, static, ordered, and formal are already presupposed to be those found in the French style, what is "Baroque," or does not conform to expected characteristics, often tends to be assessed as an unwanted, accidental effect of the garden. Nothing is less certain, however.

Weiss mentions crucial figures of the Baroque within formal gardens, especially in their use of "reflecting pools as major features of the landscape" (27). He recalls that specular effects and mirrors were "the archetypally baroque figure of sensibility" (69). Specularity is also manifest, in fact, along the central axis, starting from the chateau of Versailles, with its large "Fountain of Apollo" in the middle of the perspective, and the further view of the canal. This means that a contradiction is at work in the very opposition that is constituted within the arrangement of the central axis, itself a major structuring element of the garden. The contradiction occurs between the "baroque figure of sensibility," represented by the mirrorlike waters of the Fountain and the canal, and the geometric intelligibility of the axis. Similar apparent incompatibilities are also evinced in the Hall of Mirrors within the chateau. In his commentary on the Hall of Mirrors, Weiss doubles again his interpretation. First, he offers a baroque reading of the Hall: "This gallery provided the ultimate specular baroque spectacle: each gesture is doubled, each movement is observable from all sides, each representation represented" (72). He then describes the figure of geometrical infinity reflected or inscribed within the baroque effect: "And, seen in the infinitely reflective depths of the mirrors, across the expanses of the garden's length, is the reflected double of infinity at the vanishing point as the sun enters the gallery at sunset" (72). Weiss explains that the "infinity" of the central axis is itself but a double or a reflection of the very movement of specularity ("the infinitely reflective depths of the mirrors"), which underscores the constant intermingling of the Baroque and Classicism in the so-called classical, formal, or French garden. Yet, Weiss ultimately ascribes the effects of the Hall of Mirrors to the king and to geometry, both kinds of absolute power, that is, the power of the conceptual, preexisting the actual or the sensible: "Here, the king and his solar and geometric doubles reign—in the last moment of baroque splendor within a neoclassic realm" (72). The certainty of the assignation of this return interrupts the subtle interplay of Weiss's argument. The Hall of Mirrors could be interpreted instead as a location where even the image of the king is doubled to infinity, made reproducible, evincing in Weiss's words "the fissure of appearance and being" (69). Mariage has also shown that the taste for reflections, for example in fountains or canals, as it is expressed in the poetry of the seventeenth century, shows an awareness of the fact that they "both embellish and blur the projected image" (Mariage 73), in opposition, therefore, to a static, controlling ambition.[7] Such studies demonstrate that the signification of the structure of the classical garden is not unified or unilateral. The garden inscribes within its form a baroque division or specularity which doubles and troubles the apparent certainty of formal effects. In other words, the whole effect of the French garden has to be determined not in spite of but by this division and inner contradiction.

REPETITION AND DISPLACEMENT: CONDILLAC

When French eighteenth-century treatises on landscape gardening written in the 1770s assert that they are breaking with the formal style, then, they systematically silence the inner structural division within the French garden. They also underplay, as we have seen in a previous chapter, their repetition of English treatises or the specular effect of their own enterprise. The "labyrinthine" tension within the Versailles garden, for example, complicates the claim that we have examined earlier of a passage from "system" (the French style) to "history" (the new style) in the experience of the beholder and visitor of a garden. The concept of history in the scientific sense—that is, the avoidance of presupposition in the chronological recording of an observed experiment—is of course not simply invented by the new science (Newton and his followers). In fact, Descartes's narrative of the *cogito* or of the thinking subject is not foreign to this notion and experience of history. The very terms *experience* and *experiment* also need to be addressed, especially if they are used as a mere shortcut to one of the poles of an opposition with a priori systematic thought.[8] For one thing, as d'Alembert showed in the article "Expérimental" of the *Encyclopédie* (VI), the very concept of "experiment" may point both to a system and to a history, in that it is used at times in the sense of the confirmation of a theory (as in a demonstration, or the verification of parts of a system); whereas on other occasions, experiment is said to anticipate on and contribute to the elaboration of a new axiom (in a chronological chain akin to "history").[9] This indicates that experimental science accepts and includes some of the ways in which systematic thought functions.[10] The very history of the scientific meaning of the word *history* could be traced, not as a rupture with Descartes, but through him (in particular in his notion of a deductive *process*). At least since Bacon's argument in favor of *historia* or observation, the concept of history has become inflected when differently taken up by scientists like Descartes, Locke, and Newton.

If eighteenth-century treatises celebrate the gardening forms they recommend as a novelty or a rupture with the formal French garden, it is however noteworthy, as we have seen in preceding chapters, that they often describe the task of the gardener as a "return" to more natural delineations. It will be recalled that Morel, for example, says that in Guiscard, "the course of the terrain . . . has recovered its natural bend" (Morel 271). Understanding the new as a return to, or the repetition of former traits has important implications. Consistently in these treatises and in many other texts of the Enlightenment, what is new is considered as what was already there, under one's very eyes, but was not given proper attention. D'Alembert says for example that "a little thought on the nature of bodies, together with the observation of the phenomena which surrounded them, should have, it seems to me, caused philosophers to discover these laws [of motion, etc.] much earlier" (VI, 301). Likewise, Condillac devotes some thoughts to the concepts of origin as well as repetition, in particular in the *Essay*. This fact is significant, especially since Condillac has been called Locke's disciple and spiritual son, making his work, therefore, itself a sort of repetition. Thomas Nugent, who translated Condillac's *Essay* into English (1756), stresses several times in his introduction that "[Condillac] has followed the footsteps of the celebrated Mr. Locke" (Condillac 1974, vii). At the beginning of *The Archaeology of the Frivolous*, Jacques Derrida uses an epigraph from Karl Marx, which assesses Condillac's genealogy precisely in these terms: "Locke's *immediate* pupil, Condillac, who translated him into *French*, at once applied Locke's sensualism against seventeenth-century *metaphysics*" (Derrida 1980, 29). This commentary presents Condillac's work as a rupture (against Descartes) and a repetition (of Locke). However, Derrida remarks in his essay that Condillac's work addresses time and again the question of novelty as that which repeats a former rupture, therefore not simply ushering in something else. For example: "The philosopher who marks out a trail is the one who repeats (by generalizing) the fact of an earlier rupture, which both transposes and extends that fact" (Derrida 1980, 42). Therefore, the seeming opposition between rupture and repetition, or between "open[ing] a trail" and "recommencing an operation" (Derrida 1980, 43) is critically addressed by Condillac. Derrida adds: "Thus Locke inaugurates—but *after* Bacon and Newton. Condillac inaugurates *after* Locke" (42). It is not only the origin or the new which becomes opened by Condillac's integration of repetition in the very gesture of "inauguration." The figure of repetition itself gets affected because what is repeated is at the same time a variation, in a double movement which Derrida sums up thus when he examines Condillac's treatment of analogy: "Invention by analogy, perhaps, is the most general formula of this logic" (43). Therefore, the repetition of Locke introduces a difference in Condillac: "The science of human understanding, as properly inaugurated by Locke, is repeated, corrected, and completed by Condillac—particularly concerning the decisive question of language. But he will do nothing less than found it: finally and for the first time" (43).

In eighteenth-century treatises on landscape gardening, the same logic of inauguration and/as repetition is discernible. There, the issue will often be not so much to criticize the legitimacy of a prepared effect than its achieved success in the former garden. The point for their authors is to reconsider effects in their efficacy, not their validity. This is true, above all, of the notion of the garden (or at other times, Nature) as a spectacle. Nowhere does one find questioned the purpose of looking at a landscape as if it were a beautiful object meant for the spectator's pleasure.[11] On the contrary, all these treatises strive to make the experience of the spectator more assuredly enjoyable. Certainly, one method which will be recommended to enhance that experience is that of an increased participation in the spectacle on the part of the beholder, unlike the declared static experience afforded by a formal garden. But this does not imply that the garden becomes any less a spectacle, an object from which to derive a certain pleasure. In fact, the emphasis put in gardening treatises on the effects of landscape on the spectator can be seen as an attempt to classify and analyze what, in natural surroundings, causes specific feelings or emotions in man, in order to reproduce them with constant success. For instance, Watelet considers that in parks, "passive affections" are elicited at the sight of "the arrangement of prospects, and with the help of some artificial objects" (Watelet 49). What he calls into question, then, is not the wish to induce "affections," but the result of the attempt: "But is it enough for these affections to be prepared? Is their effect very sure? Should not those to whom they are meant also be disposed to receive and feel them? This is what rarely happens" (Watelet 49). Watelet and others do not oppose, therefore, the view that effects are desirable in a garden, including traditional effects of the French garden such as surprise and admiration. Rather, they analyze the means that may be taken to produce these impressions infallibly in the beholder; moreover they attempt to ascertain conditions which would make them persist longer. This gesture shows, in Gilles Clément's words, that the concept of "the garden as the prolongation of an ordered thought" (Clément 1990, 8) has not disappeared in the eighteenth century, even though the modalities of that "ordered thought" have been modified because of the increasing disaffection with the formal garden. To that end, authors of gardening treatises have recourse to notions that Condillac has studied in the *Essay*, such as the principles of attention, liaison or connection, association, impression, and perception.

CONDILLACIAN EFFECTS: ATTENTION

Condillac writes that "The perception or the impression caused in the mind by the action of the senses, is the first operation of the understanding" (Condillac 1974, 27). For Condillac, all perceptions are noticed by the mind, though many are forgotten. In that respect, it is not indifferent to our discussion of gardens as an object to be beheld, that he should provide three examples connected with a spectacle or with sight: the first is that of a play in a theater (29), the second concerns reading (32), and the third the viewing of a historical picture (33). These examples are given to illustrate the process by which out of "several perceptions of which we have a consciousness at the same time, it frequently happens that we are more conscious of one than the other" (28), while some are immediately forgotten. The increased consciousness of a particular perception is what Condillac calls "attention," an operation which also implies the selection of a specific object from the variety of those capable of impressing the senses at a given time: "Thus to be attentive to a thing, is to be more conscious of the perceptions which it occasions, than of those which other objects produce by solliciting our senses in the same manner" (30). Condillac derives several consequences from his analysis of attention; some bear directly on our discussion of the effect of gardens on spectators.

First, he notices the necessity of attention, in the sense of selective consciousness, for an effect to be achieved, and further for memory to function:

> If acting upon the senses with an almost equal force, [the several objects around me] produce perceptions in my mind, all of them very near in the same degree of vivacity; and if I yield to the impression they make, without striving to have a greater consciousness of one perception than another, I shall retain no idea at all of what has passed within me. (34)

This statement could be an apt caption for the effect of the French garden as it is recounted in landscape gardening treatises of the eighteenth century. Their authors are precisely denouncing the "same degree of vivacity" in the design of the French garden, which produces not only monotony and boredom, but a lethargy also mentioned by Condillac as a likely consequence: "What happens with this work executed with all the regularity and neatness possible? The spectator perceives, guesses, and feels only a weak desire of moving" (Watelet 108); "I shall retain no idea at all of what has passed within me. It will appear to me as if my understanding had been all this time in a kind of lethargy" (Condillac 1974, 34).

Authors of landscape gardening treatises emphasize the difficulty of sustaining attention for a very long time, and propose to implement a variety of "scenes" (Watelet 69) in gardens in order to counteract the failure of attention. For Watelet, "the first principle is to intermingle ceaselessly motives of curiosity which engage [*engagent*] to move, with objects which attach and invite one to stop" (105). The principle of the "engagement" of attention depends on the process of "acceleration and slowing down," or the motion and pause that Watelet mentions. Alternating contrasting scenes through different objects and impressions is a way of keeping the visitor's attention alert and consistent. Girardin also recommends a design in which "you are immediately led to wander through walks . . . where what you see ceaselessly engages, and gives you an interest in what you do not see" (Girardin 19); and he adds that "In every work where the attention is divided, there is an end of all interest" (20). For these authors, unlike what they evaluate as the general object of the French garden (an effect of surprise obtained once and for all, which means for a little time, with the consequent attending boredom for the spectator), the new garden should have a general effect which can be assessed only at the end of a sequence, as a series of contrasting impressions. This can be linked to Condillac's remark that

> Experience shews that the first effect of attention is to make those perceptions which are occasioned by their objects to continue still in the mind, when those objects are removed. By this means a chain or connexion is formed amongst them, from whence several operations, as well as reminiscence, derive their origin. (Condillac 1974, 38)

When moving from one scene to another, replacing one object of interest with the next, the visitor experiences a paradoxical continuity, that of attention, which is elicited and sustained by means of a discontinuous chain of objects or scenes. Strolling through the garden provides the experience of an unfolding (akin to a narrative) of perceptions coalescing into a general effect.[12] The effect is conveyed by objects which absent themselves in succession, but the disruption between scenes does not prevent the absent object from "continuing still in the mind" (Condillac). On the contrary, attention is maintained through the unexpected juxtaposition of contrasting objects viewed in sequence, so that the new object gains in retrospect an additional effect from the removed scene. According to Morel, the variation of scenes is a "game which excites curiosity by continual changes, and which sustains attention by repeated surprises" (Morel 82). Condillac precisely says that attention consists in the ability to "point out the difference in the series of perceptions which I have felt" (Condillac 1974, 34). Because authors on landscape gardening assess the attention of the spectator as tenuous, and the desired effect (surprise, awe, admiration) as uncertain in a French garden, they suggest methods to keep attention more surely focused. However, the effort to elicit attention should not for these authors abruptly contradict the principle of connection or liaison which is deemed essential in new gardens, especially because, as we have seen earlier, connection is thought to be the very principle of Nature. For example, Morel reproaches the classical French garden for providing surprise at the expense of coherence: "This is why gardens, in which each bosquet is made into a particular scene which is independent from what follows and what precedes it, are so cold as to say nothing to the soul" (Morel 329). Even irregularity and disruption must respect the "natural" principle of liaison: "If one abandons to whim what is a necessary sequence of constant and known causes, one will only produce bizarre effects . . . for these forms, though irregular, are not without rules" (Morel 88). Therefore, the effects of surprise must obey a "natural" rhythm.

One method suggested to elicit attention is to interpolate in the point of view of the spectator intriguing objects which arrest his gaze.[13] Characteristically, however, treatises immediately signal a risk involved in the purposeful obstruction of space. Though the monotony caused by the French garden is said to be a direct function of the all-encompassing view it affords, blocking the view may induce in the spectator not only a positive curiosity but also alarm and insecurity. This is why while the spectator is encouraged to explore the space of the garden, a particular emphasis is put at the same time on helping him derive ease and enjoyment from his panorama.

Watelet for instance notes that "Spaces produce discoveries, and lead the gaze. . . . Besides, the sight which extends itself needs to be relieved in its effort" (Watelet 70–71). Both Watelet and Morel address the issue of the weariness felt by the spectator in an apparently endless expanse, when they describe a "bocage" that each included in their layouts (in Moulin-Joli and Guiscard), in order to encourage movement and "relieve" the gaze. Watelet describes his bocage as located within

> an inconsiderable space, in which the variety of planes, the irregularity of the terrains, the curves of the banks, the unsymmetrical aspect of the trees, the slopes, the islands and dykes which ensure its communication, afford such a striking diversity that one does not desire to get out of the little enclosure where one finds oneself rather *stopped* than shut in. (Watelet 139, my emphasis)

This is one of the moments of the alternating principle, or the fostering of "difference" in Condillac's words (Condillac 1974, 34), that Watelet proposes in order to sustain the visitor's interest and attention: a moment of pause ("stopped") should succeed that of motion. According to Watelet: "A pretext to stop will be presented, such as a picturesque point of view which attaches, or an unexpected object which suspends the footsteps while fixing the gaze" (Watelet 27). He pursues his description of the bocage by narrating his own incentive to move:

> I let my gaze wander. The bocage which I have just sketched *arrested* it. It offered me at the distance of half a quarter of a league a prospect pleasant

> enough to make me desire to enjoy it more perfectly. . . . I did not resist this impression. . . . I strolled toward a place which called me by the effect of a secret sympathy. (Watelet 140–41, my emphasis)

If Watelet points out the need to tease the curiosity of the viewer, he also emphasizes that it must never be done in a disquieting fashion. The gaze must be neither wearied nor worried. Attention is sharpened by a hidden, or better still, a partially visible object, but the point is not to shock the viewer by a disturbing effect. In that respect, Watelet praises another location in the garden where "the sight, veiled as it were, penetrates however through the foliage" (Watelet 151). He then remarks that "Intervals are filled by trellis work assembled in lozenges, which, by letting water be perceived, reassure the gaze" (151–52). This precision shows that when space is not visible, directly and in its entirety, it may become potentially threatening to the viewer, an unwanted consequence of the effort to sustain the visitor's attention. Morel also seems to be aware of that risk, and to defuse its possibility, when he mentions that in the bocage he designed in Guiscard, "[the trees] which are perceived, make us, by their agreeable aspect, seek those which they hide, and invite us to visit them in hope of a new pleasure" (Morel 49). He also depicts in the same bocage "agreeable and close points of view which become invisible and reappear on purpose" (53). Likewise, Watelet notes: "I have discovered agreeable prospects; then I have lost sight of them, in order to find them with more pleasure" (Watelet 25). The pleasure in question should always be "agreeable," or effortless: "The enjoyment of the country must be a fabric of desires excited without affectation, and of satisfactions fulfilled without effort" (Watelet 22). Thus, complete visibility is paradoxically a sure way not to see anything, because it triggers no desire to see, and objects must be partially visible, but not in a disturbing fashion for the spectator's ease. Watelet also notes that the enjoyment he prepares for the visitor requires that the landscape be seen in proximity, not from afar:

> The soul which extends itself with the gaze, certainly enjoys, but vaguely, beauties which lead it too far from itself. It must be surrounded much more closely, in order to be inspired; less distracted, it must feel in sweet musing sensations that it takes pleasure in taking account of. (Watelet 155)

Girardin makes the same point, in terms which imply that the space thus discovered by a closer look is also appropriated by the visitor:

> When a traveller is going over hills and high places which command a great extent of country, his eyes wander to all the different points, as on a map; but of all that he sees, *nothing is familiar to him, nothing properly belongs to him*, nothing is within his reach, nothing detains his gaze or his steps: in descending the hill, if he sees near his path a soft valley, the entrance of which is guarded by groups of trees happily disposed; if he perceives a cool spring under a little tufted wood, and giving freshness to the grass on its borders, immediately a secret charm attracts and fixes him. Upon the heights, it was the universe to him; this is a resting place, a *habitation which nature offers to man*. (Girardin 45–46, my emphasis)

The consequences of "entering" the picture also are, therefore, that the visitor domesticates the landscape, makes himself at home within surroundings which can become tame, "familiar," and "properly" his. Space is annexed as man's possession.

Girardin's remark sheds light on two characteristics of eighteenth-century treatises which derive from considering the effects sought in a garden. First, since the new garden should be divested of an authoritarian control over the spectator's direction (of his gaze as well as of his steps), the variation of scenes is also a way to incite the beholder to choose a path of his own, which appropriately fits his current frame of mind. In that respect, Condillac also remarks that attention depends on what he calls one's "constitution": "Our attention is drawn by external objects, in proportion as they are more relative to our constitution, passions, and state of life" (Condillac 1974, 35). These "psychological" considerations are of extreme importance for authors of gardening treatises. Watelet describes for example a possible stroll in Moulin-Joli, in which he stresses the harmony of the landscape with the visitor's mood, while praising the skillful artistic dissimulation in the design of the path:

> The slope of the terrain where I am walking is softened, and the paths follow slight curves. They do not tend geometrically where I purport to arrive; they are not too winding, in order not to delay my walk. And is it not what best fits men? Nothing is more similar to the course of our ideas than these traces they form in the vast country. . . . Indecision is doubtless a more convenient state for us than accuracy, and it is more natural than precision. (Watelet 24–25)

Later on, Watelet celebrates again designs providing "effects which are more perceived than their principles" and "an indecision full of pleasantness" (107). "Indecision" is then promoted instead of the supposed mastery over the spectator in the French formal garden, and the uncertainty of the walk or of the effect is found to be pleasurable. It is clear, however, that these so-called new tactics still involve the gardener's manipulation of the visitor.

In fact, and this is the second characteristic, studies on sensations are solicited in order to understand better "the most perfect relations between the outside objects, the senses, and the frame of mind" of the spectator (Watelet 13). Girardin devotes one chapter of his essay to the discussion of "the power of landscape over the senses, and, through their interposition, over the soul" (chapter 15, 134). He notes that

> It is by the emotion of pleasure or of repugnance, that our senses indicate the fitness or unfitness of things with regard to ourselves; a cord, more or less drawn up, gives such or such vibrations, and the nerve struck more or less forcibly or frequently, raises in us an idea, a recollection, a sensation, or a pain. (Girardin 135)

Like Condillac, Girardin goes on to say that "every idea originates in the senses" (135). But what is specific to authors on landscape gardening is that they wish to use the knowledge of the link between the senses and the soul (or the mind) in order to produce deliberately a given effect on the visitor. For Condillac, "to occasion [attention] no more is wanting, than that one object act upon the senses with greater force than another" (Condillac 1974, 51). Once this premise is accepted, it is possible to consider implanting objects in the landscape deliberately, in order to act on the senses and achieve a predetermined effect on the visitor. Girardin, for example, writes that "it is so much the more essential to know how to employ them [the senses], as they may serve to prepare the mind, and put it into different dispositions" (Girardin 135–36). In that respect, though Morel values the principle of continuity as intrinsic to Nature, he does not entirely reject the effect of having this expectation defeated, in order to induce new associations and effects in the visitor:

> [L]et us remark in passing that this expectation, when it is deceived, is the source of contrasts and striking transitions . . . objects, according to their associations, trace in the mind a sequence of simultaneous and successive images which, setting one another off to advantage, strengthen the present impressions and prepare to the effects which will succeed them. (Morel 328–29)

Watelet also says that when designing a plantation, "it is necessary to foresee fully the effect that [the trees] will produce" (66). Girardin explains best how such effects operate, through what he calls an "analogy" between outward sensations and inward ideas: "The soft sensations which its aspect [nature's] excites in us (by an analogy that no man can fail to feel), insensibly bring to our souls voluptuous and touching impressions" (Girardin 18). Or later: "In such situations as these, one feels all the force of that analogy between physical charms and moral impressions" (147).

But Watelet mentions a difficulty as soon as "more meditated nuances" are planned to move the visitor (Watelet 77). It occurs when in addition to a picturesque design, the gardener seeks to provide a poetical effect. Girardin explains what motivates such an attempt in terms that precisely spell out the specific reaction that is desired in the spectator, behind the general purpose of producing effects: "The picturesque scene gives pleasure to the eyes . . . the poetical scene interests the mind and memory by bringing before us Arcadian scenes" (Girardin 141–42). The object of a garden or landscape, therefore, is not only to be pleasing or beautiful to the eye, but also to represent to the spectator cultural landmarks which will reinforce and justify his own participation in the spectacle. The inscription of the poetical in a garden also shows that landscape as such, provided it were possible to have a landscape "as such," would risk escaping familiarity and consequently readability, unless interpreted through cultural bearings. In *Essais sur la peinture* (1765), Diderot clearly shows the link between the eye and the mind's eye. For him, senses are solicited in a landscape in order to conjure up a cultural vision:

> It is sure that high mountains, ancient forests, and immense ruins are imposing. The accessory ideas they awaken are great. Whenever I please, I will have Moses or Numa descend from them. The sight of a torrent which falls with a loud noise through abrupt rocks whitened with its spray will make me shudder. If I do not see it, but hear its din from afar: Thus, I will say to myself, have famous scourges passed through history. The world remains, and all their exploits are no more than an empty, lost noise which amuses me. (Diderot 1996, 479)

The poetical effect is activated through literary, artistic, or sometimes philosophical reminiscences, so that the effect is inseparable from a cultural affect.

CONDILLACIAN EFFECTS: IMAGINATION, MEMORY, REMINISCENCE

Watelet points out that the benefit of such reminiscences lies in the pleasure of cultural participation or recognition. But in his analysis, it depends on the possibility for imagination to function, by establishing comparisons between what the object suggests and the visitor's own musings, that is, by establishing a chain or series of links between the perceived object and other ideas. Condillac makes this point when he describes what is involved in recollection: "The attention given to a perception that actually affects us, revives its sign: this reminds us of others to which it bears some relation: these renew the ideas with which those signs are connected: these ideas recall other signs or other ideas to our minds, and so on successively" (Condillac 1974, 47–48). Yet, Watelet remarks:

> In the arrangement of these scenes, in which the poetical and the picturesque are joined, the aim is to renew, with the help of the Spectators' memory, some threads of these [mythological] ideas. . . . [W]hat obstacles, most of them impossible to overcome, are opposed to their effect! Think of the little mobility of most imaginations. . . . The only resource left is some buildings, some monuments and approximations of sites and accidents, through which one strives to recall the ideas one had in mind. (Watelet 78–80)

Condillac sums up the difference between imagination, memory, and reminiscence in these terms: "The first renews the perceptions themselves; the second brings to our minds only their signs or circumstances; the third makes us discern them as perceptions which we had before" (Condillac 1974, 44). Like Watelet, Condillac points out the weakness of some imaginations; according to Condillac, the reason for this weakness is that imagination and memory are more developed as the connection of ideas through the use of signs increases: "All men cannot connect their ideas with equal force, nor in equal number: and this is the reason why all are not equally happy in their imagination and memory" (49). For Condillac, therefore, imagination and memory, in order to function at will, or as he says, to be "in our power" (49), depend on the ability to pay attention to the connection between a perception and another idea:

> I therefore believe I have a right to conclude that the power of reviving our perceptions, their names, or their circumstances, proceeds entirely from the connexion which the attention has established between these things, and the wants to which they are related. Take away this connexion, and you destroy the imagination and memory. (49)

Recollecting is evoking a connection, or a liaison of different, though related ideas. As Condillac also argued in his *Traité des systèmes*: "The imagination owes its liveliness to the force of the connection of ideas, and its extent to the multiplicity of ideas that are recalled on the occasion of a single one" (Condillac 1982, 134). He adds that "this is the principle to which the mind owes all its discrimination, fecundity, and extent" (135).

The part given to imagination and reminiscence in treatises on landscape gardening is important for the effect to be fully felt and appreciated by the visitor. Girardin describes for example what happens when the spectator encounters a "happy spot" (140) in his walk: "Our mind is delighted to find an image of these descriptions which have given us so much pleasure; reminiscence immediately places there all the attributes rendered sacred by poets" (Girardin 140–41). Therefore, when (or since) imagination is largely deficient, as Watelet notes, it follows that the gardener must have recourse to what he calls an "approximation" of an idea, in particular through the use of a telling representation or image of that idea (for example a tombstone may evoke melancholy, or a revery on mutability, transitoriness, mortality, etc.). Watelet mentions the desirability of "renew[ing], with the help of the Spectators' memory, some threads of these [mythological] ideas" (Watelet 78–79). Girardin also admits that the poetical "attributes" that imagination spontaneously places in a happy spot are sometimes already literally found there, perhaps because, like Watelet, he would concede that not every visitor has the requisite imagination: "Such is poetical landscape, whether exhibited to our view by nature in some favoured spot, which has escaped the general destruction, or created anew by the hand of taste" (Girardin 141). This "recreation" is probably why Morel consistently denounces the poetical garden as artificial. Like Watelet, he remarks that "these representations are far from producing the effects that the Composer has in mind" (Morel 383), and that a poetical garden "says nothing to the imagination, and even less to the soul" (384). But for him, this consequence is unavoidable, either because of the lack of available cultural reminiscence, or that of precision in the images used. He observes that "they are so little known, so equivocal, that they rarely recall the ideas that were attached to them" (383). On the contrary, the pleasure afforded by what he calls "natural gardens" requires in his opinion "neither erudition nor preliminary reflection" (385–86). However, if Morel disputes the cultural participation to be derived from poetical gardens, he still agrees that a universal reaction, that of sensibility, can be induced in seeing a garden: "It is enough, in order to find it attractive, that one should have the degree of sensibility that Nature has granted to almost all men, because her expression is not equivocal . . . she is clear and precise, and nobody hesitates on the character she presents" (386). Therefore, for Morel as for Watelet and Girardin, a manipulation of the visitor is possible, in that seeing a scene in appropriate conditions will elicit the desired feeling in the spectator.

The combination of the picturesque and the poetical testifies to the reversibility of seeing and feeling: in Girardin's words, "sentiment consists in the manner of seeing things" (Girardin 133). The fact that it is recommended that "cultural" references should be interspersed with the garden's other features indicates the extent to which such signs are necessary for space to become readable at all. Watelet and Girardin are not averse to using inscriptions which dispel what might be obscure in a particular scene. Watelet describes the characteristics of such a spot:

> Inscriptions and selected short passages, engraved on trees or on columns and obelisks would cultivate the impression that the whole would have inspired, that is to say, a sweet melancholy, a pleasant distraction in which noble and elevated sentiments would merge, where remembrance and reality would mingle, where the moral would uphold the poetical. (Watelet 114)

Watelet gives as an example of possible inscription a sign that he placed near a stream in Moulin-Joli: "Here the water, with liberty, / Meanders and reflects the object which surrounds it. / From its frankness it receives its beauty; / Its crystal pleases, and flatters no one" (Watelet 157). The anonymous "Tour of Ermenonville," which describes a stroll through Girardin's park, gives several instances, among which is an inscription found on a rock with these words from Thomson: "Here studious let me sit, / And hold high converse with the mighty / dead" (Girardin 64); and another posted in "the grotto of verdure": "Delightful verdure! You rest the eyes and tranquilize the heart, your effect is that of tender harmony, which pleases nature, and makes it sweet" (Girardin 74–75). The last inscription and Watelet's sign show that the purpose of such inscriptions is to convey straightforwardly to the visitor the appropriate reaction expected of him. The effect is carefully fielded, channeled, and this precision marks the limit of the "indecision" recommended at other times in the treatises. The content of the inscriptions also reveals what sort of "pleasure" is generally meant by their authors (with the exception of Morel). Not only should the visitor experience a pleasurable cultural participation; the spectacle should also foster reflection. This may be why, in the dedication to one of the editions of his essay, Girardin gives as the etymology of *paysage* the tendentious meaning of "pays des sages" ["country of the wise"] (Girardin 9).

PHILOSOPHICAL GARDENS

The inclusion of ruins and statues in gardens contributes to the discourse on imagination and reminiscence found in treatises of landscape gardening. According to Girardin: "Besides the picturesque effect, some emblematical character may be given to the ruin, which will exert with pleasure imagination or reminiscence" (Girardin 127–28). Diderot wrote extensively on what he named "the poetics of ruins," especially in his *Salons*, and the main effect he ascribes to ruins is that they induce revery and melancholy in the spectator (Mortier 91). The ruin is a temporal reminder of greatness destroyed, the spectacle of which emphasizes the contrast between the past and the present, or simply of the passage of time, of man's mortality.[14] As such, Diderot finds ruins more striking than an intact building (Mortier 92). In his study on the motif of ruins, Roland Mortier credits Diderot for having been the first to consider them not only as a memorial of past times, but as an aesthetic object sufficient in itself (92). Anne Betty Weinshenker has also shown that together with "expressions of pleasurable gloom at the sublime and awesome thoughts" generated by painted ruins (Weinshenker 321), Diderot formulates a new response to their aesthetic appeal: "Decay of earthly glory, although sorrowfully inevitable, may also prove beneficial, and Diderot reacts joyfully to this possibility. In this context, ruins remain the symbol of impermanence, but they are viewed with affirmation, not despair" (Weinshenker 321–22), as a promise of future social justice. Mortier adds that Diderot's meditation on ruins is often "more prospective than retrospective. The ruin makes one reflect less on what was than on what will be, or more precisely *on what will be no longer*" (Mortier 93).

Other authors of the eighteenth century, such as Delille, suggest that the ruin should be integrated to the landscape. In Morel's treatise, this is the only acceptable form of ruins. They should not be artificial, because "they will interest only as far as, venerable by their antiquity, the still existing parts will make known, without a painful effort, the general form and destination of the monument, of which they are the remains" (Morel 231–32). He makes the interesting point that the "proof" of the veracity of the ruin lies in the vegetation that covers it: "the trees that grow on its foundations, the ivy on its walls and the moss and grass that cover them will prove its decrepitude" (232). The ruin's effect is at its most poignant when nature overgrows a former monument of human greatness. However, because of its structure and of its aspect, the ruin is in itself well adapted to the vegetal, which suggests that more than a reintegration to the landscape, the point is to recognize that it already belongs there. The ruin looks natural: "They are very properly employed in landscape, because the variety of their shapes, their colour, and the green with which they may, in part, be covered, make them unite much better with the surrounding objects than new constructions" (Girardin 127). Thus, Girardin and others do not find that the artifice constituted by the ruin, that is, the fact that it represents the remains of a human construction warrants its exclusion from the garden. In fact, Weinshenker quotes a passage from Diderot's *Salon de 1767*, which indicates that Diderot considers the ruin as a temporal phenomenon which affects natural surroundings as well as man-made productions, undermining further the distinction between the two. The passage elaborates "the ideas that ruins awaken in me": "What is my ephemeral existence, in comparison with that of that rock which collapses, that valley which grows hollow, of that forest which staggers? I see the marble of tombs fall to dust; and I do not want to die!"

(Weinshenker 312). Therefore, the ruin both looks natural and ruins nature, at least as much as it does culture.

Mortier points out a particular suitability of the motif of the ruin to a garden, in that like gardens, "ruin is always the point of encounter between nature and art" (Mortier 10). Similarly, ruin is both a reminder of classic antiquity, and an anticlassical feature. Mortier explains that "Initially, the word 'ruin' was always the equivalent of 'Roman ruin'" (21). The privilege of Classicism is one of the constant references of landscape gardening, as we have shown earlier, but the inclusion of ruins in gardens is in keeping with a contradictory impulse, which manifests itself for instance in the attempt to break away from symmetrical patterns, or in the recourse to "Chinese" motifs. In that respect, Weinshenker indicates that ruin was of interest in the eighteenth century precisely because it could be "associated with anticlassical tendencies: irregular and incomplete objects offered a fascination beyond that of integral ones" (Weinshenker 328).[15] Diderot says of the ruin that it "awakens in me an accessory idea which touches me, by reminding me of the instability of human things" (Weinshenker 310). His terms suggest a parallel with Watelet's recommendation, the aim being in both cases to "touch" the spectator. For Watelet, "indecision" is an apt strategy to move the visitor, both sentimentally and literally. Likewise, Diderot finds in the ruin an image of "instability" which is both fascinating and pleasurable. In this case, reminiscence supports a philosophical reflection on man's existential condition.

The deliberate inclusion of various objects to uphold reflection may explain why statues are as much in favor in the new style as they were in the formal garden. The poet Delille complains of those who wish to remove pseudo-classical statues from gardens, because, according to him, "In Athens and in Rome nourished, / Our childhood has known their smiling enchantment; / Were not these gods farmers and shepherds? / Why then close your woods and your orchards to them?" (Mortier 123). This desire corresponds to the belief in the possibility of sharing common cultural reminiscences, as well as it provides a "Georgic" legibility to the landscape in which the statue is included. Watelet also proposes to integrate statues for the edification of the visitor: "In apparent spots, the statues of famous men, executed with art and care, would be offered, so that after having inspired the desire of looking at them, one should feel elevated by their perfection from the idea of the image to that of the wise and of the hero" (Watelet 113). The elevated feeling to be elicited by the contemplation of the statue is however more likely to occur, Watelet adds, if its pose is lifelike. This concern is expressed in a remarkable passage:

> The statues would be isolated and straight, others would be seated or grouped. One would have chanced not to raise them on pedestals whose narrowed plane makes their immobility more apparent. Some would be placed on a low base; others would be seated on antique beds or would seem to converse under open porticoes. (Watelet 113)

Diderot testifies to the same sensibility in a letter he wrote to Sophie Volland (May 10, 1759), on the occasion of a visit of the gardens of Marly. He describes a few statues, one of which "struck me by its simplicity, the strength and the sublime of the idea" (Diderot 1970, 41). Generally, though, he thought that there were too many statues in the park. He justifies the small number he prefers by saying that

> Statues must be viewed as beings who love solitude and who look for it, such as poets, philosophers, and lovers, and these beings are not common. A few beautiful statues hidden in the most distant spots, far from one another, who call me, that I seek or that I encounter, who arrest me and with whom I converse for a long time. . . . " (40)[16]

If the statue "speaks" through the intermediary of cultural recollection, the visitor responds in turn by his reactions, feelings, or thoughts. The garden is the pretext and the occasion of an encounter with the "rustle of language."

Girardin is the only author to suggest that personal reflection or feeling should only be a first step toward a vaster perception, that of man's social surroundings. The picturesque garden (whose object was to move the mind or soul through the sight) opened up the spectator's prospect not only to the national territory, but also to the poverty of the French peasants. This awareness is called "philosophical" by Girardin:

> A virtuous man, called back to the country, by the real enjoyment of nature, will soon feel that the sufferings of humanity make the most painful of all spectacles; if he begins by *picturesque* landscapes which please the eyes, he will soon seek to produce *philosophical* landscapes which delight the mind. For the sweetest and the most touching spectacle is that of an ease and a universal content. (Girardin 150)

Girardin proceeds to make suggestions for the development of rural economy, in terms, however, that are often comparable to the characteristics of the picturesque garden. He recommends for example to have "the land continually under [the master's] eye" in order to improve the productivity of the farm (Girardin 151). As for the cottager's wife, "this view of her possessions would attach her to her country, and make even the air she breathed more delightful to her" (157). Whether it concerns the idle visitor or the working peasant, Girardin tends to consider landscape through the same sentimental lens.

If eighteenth-century treatises explicitly address the issue of a perceived excessive power over the spectator of a landscape, they still silently legitimize the appropriation of the space. This happens because the domestication of space is depicted as involving first an awareness of the land's natural beauty, and then a patriotic link to the land (or "attachment to [one's] country" in Girardin's words), which can succeed in hiding the violence of the gesture of purported domination, or nationalism. This violence is all the more insidious since it presents itself as the (at first glance, harmless) sentiment shared by a community in the face of natural surroundings. The next pages will examine attempts made today to break away from the notion and description of a sentimentalized nature.

Conclusion

The Future of the Garden/ The Garden of the Future

> We're tired of trees. We should stop believing in trees, roots, and radicles. They've made us suffer too much.
>
> —Deleuze and Guattari, *A Thousand Plateaus*

THE GARDEN IN MOVEMENT IN THE HISTORY OF LANDSCAPE GARDENING

Gilles Clément's recent theoretical work and layouts (in particular in La Vallée, and the André Citroën Park in Paris) address the question of man's sentimentalization of the landscape through his concept of "the garden in movement" (*jardin en mouvement*). Clément does not assume that it is entirely possible or even desirable to break away from a gardening tradition. He endorses the setting up of "discrepancies" (Clément 1990, 73), rather than new paradigms, in relation to the visitor's expectations. Likewise, the garden in movement is established on possibilities found in a plot of land that has gone fallow. According to Clément, one of the interests of the fallow land is its "aesthetic incoherence" (Clément 1990, 99). The terms *discrepancy* and *incoherence* suggest the disavowal not only of the possibility of rupture but also of that of novelty, by means of a simultaneous exposition and displacement of the desires that man projects on to a garden. What is most important in Clément's work is the fact that he openly relinquishes man's desire of comprehending the garden, both in the sense of appropriation and understanding. Indeed, one of his proposed explanations of the effects of "discrepancy" is that "the discrepancy comes from the feeling of perfectly understanding and, however, not to have understood everything" (Clément 1990, 70). The principles behind the garden in movement illustrate the adhesion to *and* rejection of the history of landscape gardening at work in the notion of discrepancy.

Clément makes several arguments that show continuities with past principles, including those of the eighteenth-century treatises I have studied so far. The very notion of making "movement" apparent in the garden was, it will be recalled, what authors of the eighteenth century claimed as their new contribution to landscape gardening. Thus, Clément proposes to "manage mobility" (Clément 1990, 99) or make "mobility visible" (Clément 1990, 46). The emphasis on vision is another continuity, as is the realization that some kind of management is unavoidable: "The 'Garden in Movement' proposes an alternative, but the term garden implies management, the control of man over space" (Clément 1995, 528). Finally, his claim that his gardening method promotes "a space of liberty" (Clément 1994, 66) takes up an important motif of eighteenth-century treatises. In an important sense, Clément is a historian of gardens, and makes this history visible in his layouts. Fallow land is interesting for him not only in aesthetic terms, but also because, in his analysis, it is the trace or "memory of a former era" in a landscape (Clément 1990, 54). However, he denounces a history that would be a nostalgic attachment to the past.

Clément inscribes the concept of the garden in movement within a larger reflection on biological movement in which man should integrate himself (Clément 1990, 99). Yet, this view implies that man needs to entrust himself to life, or to the future, and should not cling nostalgically to the past. Instead of endorsing nostalgia, Clément approves of changes, even of disconcerting transformations: "The ties that one has to structures make us desire them to be immutable. But the garden is the privileged terrain for permanent changes. The history of gardens shows that man has constantly fought against these changes" (Clément 1990, 24). Nostalgia can happen after a destructive cataclysm, or, conversely, when a parasitical plant takes over domestic plants, in other words, whenever the familiar landscape is transformed. Clément points out that the lament over supposed ecological disasters, for example regarding "kudzu" (a Japanese creeping plant), reveals the wish to preserve an untouched landscape: "The discourse which aims at integral ecological protection is evidently nostalgic" (Clément 1990, 34). He emphasizes instead the "power of invention of nature" (34), and explains that if a land were left uncultivated, or alone, it would tend toward the state in which it used to be before man's intervention, for example, a forest in Europe. This ultimate stage is called a "climax: an optimal level of vegetation" (Clément 1990, 42). Fallow land provides access to the climax of the landscape (Clément 1990, 36). Even a climax is not the dead end of an evolutionary process, but can "recycle itself" (Clément 1990, 45). Such positions forbid a sentimental reading of landscape. Even demographic increase, urbanization, and pollution are defined by Clément as the modifiers of climax, but not its opposite: "One may wonder what the climax of a garbage dump is. What plants grow easily and reproduce themselves there?" (Clément 1990, 45). Clément insists that man's distress at the sight of natural transformations is not warranted. In that respect, fallow land reveals man's unease (the terrain has become wild) and his failure to be aware that it is the sign of a landscape in evolution, in "an essentially dynamic state" (Clément 1990, 39). What particularly interests Clément in his projects of gardens in movement is to derive a lesson from "the vagabond behavior" of plants in fallow land (Clément 1990, 64). In fallow land, vagabond plants do not keep to the space initially assigned to them; they migrate, or, as gardeners also say, colonize the terrain of their own accord. In the André Citroën Park, in which Clément implemented fallow land, the point has been first of all to apply principles elaborated elsewhere (especially in La Vallée, where Clément found a terrain which had been left uncultivated for at least twelve years).

THE ANDRÉ CITROËN PARK: "SHARING THE SIGNATURE"

With his reflection on the signature of a landscape, Clément is within the critical tradition which describes a dual responsibility for its form (man's and nature's). It is generally argued that a landscape is a mediation between man and nature, which often implies, in stronger words, that it is in effect largely man-made. This statement is often formulated as a criticism of man's inappropriate handling of nature. In keeping with his confidence in nature's self-regenerative power, Clément wonders if man's intervention in the landscape is not overemphasized, that is, if it does not betray an anthropocentric or sentimental reflex (such as man's guilt over his "destruction" of nature): "The planetary landscape is recognized as anthropic. What is the true part due to man?" (Clément 1995, 523).

Clément has few qualms about the intervention of the gardener, granting him even more responsibility than usual in the formation of the garden in movement (Clément 1994, 66). When he suggests that the garden in movement should share the signature between man and nature (Clément 1995, 530), he also reiterates the traditional definition of a gardener's input. He only specifies that some parts of the garden are more exclusively under the direction of the gardener than others. In the André Citroën Park, the garden in movement is said to share the signature with the gardener, whereas the gardener's signature is exclusive in another part, the serial gardens. If we were to summarize hastily at this point, it could be said that for Clément, the serial gardens are more artistic or formal than the garden in movement. We are again within the parameters of the eigtheenth-century rejection of art or formality. However, Clément displaces the grounds of that rebellion.

Clément narrows man's concerns regarding nature down to two opposite poles: man wants a clearing when there is a forest, and he wants clean water when there is a swamp. He is afraid of forests and swamps (Clément 1990, 7). Hence, he structures or formalizes what frightens him. But having done so, he is afraid anew, this time of the forms with which he thinks he presumed to denature his environment. This new fear happens because form is often conceived (this was the case during the eighteenth century) as a restrictive power which forcefully immobilizes what should be left unbounded. The constraint of mobility is then dramatized, as we have seen in an earlier chapter, as an absolute or arbitrary power. Clément rejects the pathos of that metaphor: "In reality, one must admit that any garden, any landscape, carries within itself, at the very moment when it is watched, the disappearance of the forms which reveal it" (Clément

1995, 531). Clément suggests that man's control of nature through form is a figure of speech, rather than a metaphor for unjust power. After having mentioned the gardener's supposed exclusive signature in the serial gardens, Clément cautions that "this point of view is reductive, it caricatures the implementation in order to make it understood" (Clément 1995, 531). It is perhaps the case, as Joël Gilles claims, that any understanding of what constitutes landscape is made possible by a *discourse* about man's control of nature: "In order to have a landscape, the brutal fact of nature must be constrained to the verb" (Gilles 19). This is why Clément indicates that the serial gardens are not in fact conceptually opposed to the garden in movement. Instead, both gardens modalize movement differently: the garden in movement evinces "a great liberty of form and event," and the serial gardens "appear as 'freeze images' of a discourse valorizing mobility and invention" (Clément 1995, 531). The discourse on movement becomes interchangeable with movement itself.

With the serial gardens, and other parts of the André Citroën Park, like the canal and the hothouses, Clément shares his signature with the tenets of the gardening tradition. Clément has explained the function of the serial gardens as a symbolic reference to movement: "Their particularity has to do with the *analogical mode of reading based on simple correspondences*. This system enables each of them to be given a *colored dominant note*, the *choice of a material*, and a *relation to the five senses*" (Clément 1994, 71). Clément also assigned a planet, and a day of the week to each serial garden. For example, the red garden is associated with taste, and iron is the metal chosen, the planet is Mars, and the day of the week is Tuesday. Not surprisingly, this is one of the parts of the garden that has been most appreciated by the public, and Clément notes the public's aptitude at reading space analogically (Clément 1994, 67). This is part of the tradition that we examined in the last chapter, which consists in interpreting the garden through cultural bearings. In the case of the red garden, the enlightened public can relish the associations made in the martial garden (iron), with the color of the planet Mars (red), the choice of the day of the week (Mars/Mardi-Tuesday), and so on. Undertones of alchemy (the serial gardens' chosen metals go from lead to gold) further metaphorize movement, as in transmutations. Moreover, Clément notes a fundamental relation to water in the garden in movement, as well as in the serial gardens.

It will be recalled that in the eighteenth century, authors were insisting that water in a garden is always an eloquent figure of variety and liberty. For Clément, too, water figures movement: all the serial gardens present water in some form, except the last which represents the sun (Clément 1994, 72), the ultimate metaphor of unrestrained flow. Moreover, the figure gets inverted in the case of the garden in movement, which, even though it does not include water, appropriately "represents" it: "The garden in movement (number 1), taken as the initial figure, represents the source of all sources—the sea (its aspect of hollows and swellings evokes the swell of the sea)" (Clément 1994, 72). The importance of water in Clément's design increases the possibility of the legibility of the park, an issue that he explicitly addresses in connection with the serial gardens. Not only is the visitor on familiar ground when he is required to provide an analogical reading. An interpretive ease comes to him at the sight of recognizable features from the gardening tradition. For example, in the east of the garden, two hothouses are separated by a "peristyle of water" (Clément 1994, 72), which recalls the water-jets in the French style. Likewise, the park includes a canal, but unlike in formal French gardens, it does not occupy a middle perspectival position, but is decentered (in the south). In fact, "*water is distributed within the frame* and not in the middle. It forms the container of the park on four of its sides, the Seine being taken as one of them" (Clément 1994, 72). In that sense, the Seine forms the figure of a flowing frame. Clément takes up a tradition such as the canal in a park, and quotes it, contributing to the tradition as much as displacing it. The André Citroën Park testifies to the need to recall, not to eliminate, most available gardening traditions of the Western garden: "Nature-Movement-Architecture-Artifice" (Clément 1994, 73) coexist in the park. Yet, there is one tradition that Clément's designs put into question deeply. It is the necessity of man's presence in the garden, his viewing the park in order to "constitute" it.

GARDEN WITHOUT MAN

Clément's landscape project "places man, not at the heart of the process as it is usually understood (heading it), but swept away by it"

(Clément 1995, 528). "[Man] is not consulted. Could the new gardens be made without him?" (Clément 1990, 5). The André Citroën Park is a garden without human representations, such as statues. In the east, high hothouses take parodically the position of the palace or the mansion commanding a view of the garden and further surroundings. The position has been sligthtly decentered, but with a mock-parterre in front, and the peristyle of water, as well as the peristyle of trees and the canal, the hothouses are arguably occupying the place usually reserved for man's habitation, or in the eighteenth century, for the palace. Yet, the house holds plants, not humans: nature is displayed without the need of man. At one of the possible entrances to the park, the black garden, ensconced in a cryptic construction topped by circuitous black waters, seems to mourn man's disappearance. This funereal memorial is built at the threshold, closest to the city, not to the Seine: man's activity near-by, beyond the limits of the park, is a contrastive suggestion of man's spectrality within the garden.

Deleuze and Guattari have remarked the centrality of the tree in Western thought (Deleuze and Guattari 18), and proposed a "rhizomatic" model (18) against its logic (which is not in their analysis merely a logic of roots, but also of tracings and genealogy). This countermove opposes "plant[s] with deep roots that cling to slopes" (19), though it can sometimes traverse them. "Unlike trees or their roots, the rhizome connects any point to any other point, and its traits are not necessarily linked to traits of the same nature" (21). There are few trees in the André Citroën Park. Instead, there is grass, and moss in the water, grass and moss being two rhizomatic plants, which are not deeply or vertically rooted in a soil. For Clément, moss relates to movement, as a sign of transition to what will exclude it: "a landscape in miniature, an initial order of a future series where moss itself will have disappeared" (Clément 1990, 23). Moss is not a sign of permanence. Allen Weiss has also emphasized the use of moss in Zen gardens, in an environment deprived of trees: "There are no trees, shrubs, or flowers—there is only the moss that grows on the rocks. Such moss, like the patina of ancient bronzes, is the valued trace of the passage of time in an otherwise timeless . . . setting" (Weiss 11). The garden in movement, in which "good" plants (flowers) and "bad" grass (weeds) "are next to each other and cross each other's paths" (Clément 1990, 49), gets permanently modified. This happens because plants "appear and disappear in unexpected places of the garden" (Clément 1990, 50), so that the paths themselves are never the same: "The perpetual modification of spaces of circulation and vegetation justify the term movement" (Clément 1990, 51–52). The garden in movement functions like a rhizomatic space: "[The rhizome] has neither beginning nor end, but always a middle (*milieu*) from which it grows and which it overspills" (Deleuze and Guattari 21).

The reactions of the public to the André Citroën Park show that such a space meets with resistances. Some are perhaps unavoidable. For example, to the physical movement of the plants corresponds "a network of privileged circulations" (Clément 1994, 66) on the part of the public, and this circulation unwittingly constrains the movement, by tracing a definite path in the garden. As if instinctively, the public attempts to channel what "overspills." Another reaction betrays the wish to bring a sentimental attitude back to the garden, to experience it as comforting: "When they speak of this space, several evoke their childhood. The reference is not . . . to fallow land as an abandoned social space" (Clément 1994, 67). Clément interprets childhood as a new and vagabond spirit (67), but the reference to childhood by some visitors can equally be associated with attempts to reinvest the garden with already learned codes of legibility.

These codes are above all based on the primacy of vision in man's experience of the garden. Because Clément deemphasizes the centrality of man in connection with the landscape, vision is not granted any privilege in the project of the garden in movement. This implies that landscape should not be a panorama, which man's eye can encompass. Nor should a narrowly focused garden scene be the pretext for man's meditation. Vision follows axes, and eighteenth-century designs avoid that monotonous rule by tracing curves instead. Still, in spite of the change, the eye is again solicited along a given direction. Instead, Clément's garden in movement seeks to avoid a predetermined line of vision, or at least to foster conditions in which it will be unexpectedly modified. He favors tall grasses in the garden in movement, where man's gaze becomes inessential: "It is a forest of grasses in which the man-insect enters" (Clément 1990, 90). This image (of plants taller than man, in which man can be incorporated, but without being granted a central position) illustrates several effects of Clément's project. Unlike in the eighteenth century, man's entry into natural surroundings is not construed as a possibility of either knowledge or self-reflection, two modes which purport to use nature for man's ends. Likewise, when man becomes an "insect" in the garden in movement, the realization entails no awed narrative about nature's sublime. In fact, the image serves to present a space which is indifferent to man's gaze, and which can live on autonomously, not only without man, but also after him. The garden would be different without man's tending, but it would *be*, which means that it is in effect always tending toward man's disappearance. This awareness permeates Clément's project. The wistful reaction of some visitors to the André Citroën Park shows how a nostalgic reading of the garden in movement attempts to sidestep this perhaps uncomfortable insight of their vanishing, of the end of man, his becoming-animal, or his spectrality.

Therefore, Clément's garden in movement also prevents a nationalist reading of the space of the garden. Clément says of the André Citroën Park that it is "an unusual place. . . . Understood at first as a space of liberty, it is occupied as such, that is to say, freely, with all the questions that the use of a place whose rules are still unknown poses" (Clément 1994, 66). The public park is not construed as an exclusive place, or a place of exclusion. The garden refutes modes of appropriation, and functions instead in the way Jacques Derrida has described in his analysis of "khôra": "Hermeneutic *types* can inform, they can give a form to *khôra*, only to the extent that, inaccessible, impassible, 'amorphous' . . . it *seems to receive* these types and *give a place* (*donner lieu*) to them" (Derrida 1993, 28). The garden remains indifferent to, and unaffected by, man's interpretive moves. As a rhizomatic space, the garden in movement is not based on the integrity of the soil, but "deterritorializes" the terrain (Deleuze and Guattari 15). Clément's project points toward a conception of space that is not nationally anchored, in contrast to eighteenth-century treatises. Refusing a sentimentalized interpretation of nature is also a way of overcoming the traditional response of attachment to one's land, or one's national soil. By insisting on the undeterminable movement of the garden, Clément points to another ethics of inhabiting space. It should remain unprogrammed, left open to possibilities, not planned strategies. The André Citroën Park proposes an experience of communality, not nationality, and of hospitality, not appropriation. This layout challenges the inscriptions of nationalism, property, and self-reflection that eighteenth-century treatises harbored. In keeping with the history of landscape gardening, however, Clément's designs and theoretical work contribute to a larger reflection, shared in its main arguments by several of his contemporaries, on man's ethical relation to "others," including his natural surroundings. This reflection suggests a fundamental displacement of man's position in relation to others. In that view, man's function would not be secondary to nature (the eighteenth-century argument about landscape gardening), but, as Clément would have it, accidental to it. The André Citroën Park opens both man and garden to a promise of a different and noncalculated future.

Notes

INTRODUCTION. THE SEEDS OF DISCORD

1. Throughout this book, I have silently modified existing translations from French whenever appropriate. All other translations are mine.

2. In her analysis of the Elysée and especially of the waters within it, Peggy Kamuf points out a double inscription in the structure of the garden: "The garden is not a simple space. Its doubleness—or duplicity—is indeed the *source* of its fertility" (Kamuf 1982, 113). She later identifies two sources which were used to form the waters of the Elysée. One comes from the stream which supplies the garden water-jet, in other words it corresponds to Julie's father's favored French style; the other comes from a public spring which used to damage the main road on its way to the lake, corresponding to disordered nature: "Thus, the excess of the father's pure artifice has been joined to the excess of a natural source—the public spring—run awry in its rush toward the common level of the lake. The Elysée is the joint product—the child, so to speak—of a subterfuge which preserves a father's vanity and harnesses and encloses a gravitational flow. Once again, it is important to remark the doubling which takes place, the fact that the Elysée is supplied by two different sources" (Kamuf 1982, 115). Neither exclusively one nor the other, the Elysée uses both sources for its own purposes.

3. Robert pointed it out himself when he reportedly showed the king "these monuments of arts, which, isolated, do not have a pleasant aspect any longer and seem to participate in the ruin of the first [dead nature]" (de Cayeux 72).

4. In his treatise promoting the new style, which was published in 1776, Jean-Marie Morel refers in passing to the felling of the trees of Versailles, and argues that it would be a mistake to "change the genre" of the gardens of the king's palace (18), in spite of his endorsement of new principles.

5. See for example Ann Bermingham's *Landscape and Ideology: The English Rustic Tradition, 1740–1860*, John Barrell's *The Dark Side of the Landscape*, Simon Pugh's edition of *Reading Landscape: Country—City—Capital*, and W. J. T. Mitchell's collection of essays, *Landscape and Power*. The following passage exemplifies the thrust of these studies: "The landscape garden's aesthetic effect depended on a completely nonfunctional, nonproductive use of land. Most historians of the landscape garden fail to consider that its size and appearance related directly to the rescaling and redesigning of the real landscape through enclosure. Whereas the garden put a premium on informal and irregular plantings and earthworks, enclosure divided the landscape and regularized its appearance. . . . As the real landscape began to look increasingly artificial, like a garden, the garden began to look increasingly natural, like the preenclosed landscape" (Bermingham 1986, 13–14).

6. In the introduction to their edition of *Le Jardin, art et lieu de mémoire*, Monique Mosser and Philippe Nys write that, during the eighteenth century, the landscape designer becomes recognized as an artist whose status is comparable to that of a painter or an architect. They add that this recognition "happens at a time when several questions are raised at once—landscape, the sublime, and political liberty and ethics tied to the status of imagination" (Mosser 1995, 16).

CHAPTER 1. NATURAL NATURE

1. In one of his *Newtonian Studies* which reverses Voltaire's title of the fourteenth letter, entitled therefore this time "Newton and Descartes," Alexandre Koyré sums up the two philosophies in these terms: "The protracted struggle for and against Descartes and Newton transformed both of them into symbolic figures; the one, Newton, embodying the ideal of modern, progressive, and successful science, conscious of its limitations and firmly based upon experimental and experiential-observational data which it subjected to precise mathematical treatment; the other, Descartes, symbol of a belated, reactionary—and fallacious—attempt to subject science to metaphysics, disregarding experience, precision, and measurement, and replacing them by fantastic, unproved, and unprovable hypotheses about the structure and behavior of matter" (55–56). Koyré adds a few lines later, however, that "This is, of course, the Newtonians' image" (56).

2. See Koyré, 56ff. Newtonian attraction was taken by the Cartesians to reintroduce the notion of "immediate action at a distance, that is, an occult quality" (56), which Descartes's philosophy had rejected.

3. This is a point repeatedly underscored in Koyré's essay on "Newton and Descartes": "It is difficult to acknowledge one's debts to one's enemies. Now Newton's thought, nearly *ab ovo*, had been formed and developed in opposition to that of Descartes. Accordingly, we cannot expect to find praise, or even historical

justice, for Descartes. . . . We, however, have to try to be more impartial" (65). Koyré gives several examples of Descartes's unsuccessful formulations, which, however, influenced Newton. For instance, "Descartes's formulation of the principle of inertia, which placed motion and rest on the same ontological level . . . inspired his own [Newton's]" (65); "Here we are dealing only with Newton's first law of motion, that of inertia, and it is enough for us to have shown that, in its conception as well as in its formulation in the *Philosophiae naturalis principia mathematica*, Newton was directly influenced by Descartes" (79); regarding space, "Newtonian demonstrations, in their spirit, are deeply Cartesian" (86–87); about Newton's concept of infinity: "Which is undoubtedly true. But it is also purely Cartesian" (88).

4. Koyré concurs: "Thus, modifying somewhat the celebrated statement of Newton, made in his famous letter to Robert Hooke, we could, with truth, say that if Newton saw as far as he did, and so much farther than anybody had seen before him, it was because he was a giant standing on the shoulders of other giants" (11), including Descartes.

5. Likewise, Yvon Belaval underscores the intricacy of the links between science, or philosophy, and national considerations, when he points out that "when Voltaire wanted to publish his *Elements de la Philosophie de Newton*, 'the bias for Cartesianism was to the point that the chancelier d'Aguesseau refused a privilege [authorization to publish] to M. de Voltaire' . . . for one claimed then that 'not being a Cartesian is being a bad Frenchman'" (352).

6. "The concept of Enlightenment" examines some consequences of the endorsement of and emphasis on progress: "Adaptation to the power of progress involves the progress of power, and each time anew brings about those degenerations which show not unsuccessful but successful progress to be its contrary. The curse of irresistible progress is irresistible regression" (Horkheimer and Adorno 35–36). This essay also specifies what power is at work within the project of the Enlightenment: "Enlightenment is totalitarian" (6). See also Daniel Brewer's *Discourse of Enlightenment* (1993, 4–5). He indicates that "this other story reveals what a mythologized Enlightenment covers up, namely, its own double bind, the inability to prevent the critical practice of Enlightenment from turning or being turned back upon itself" (5).

7. In fact, the vogue of the English style of landscape gardening in France apparently occurred in the years following Jaucourt's article. See for example an entry of 1774 in the duc de Croÿ's *Journal*: "And it is only after the last Peace of 1763 that the French good society, having started traveling to England, brought from there the new taste" (de Cayeux, 64). De Croÿ, who went to England himself in 1766, found it difficult to appreciate the English style, as the *Journal* of his voyage testifies: "It is there that we started seeing in its perfection the new rustic taste, which requires some reflection in order to feel its beauty" (18). See also a similar account of d'Holbach's visit to England in Diderot's letter to Sophie Volland dated September 20, 1765. According to Diderot, d'Holbach was "dis-

contented with the gardens, where the affectation of imitating nature is worse than the monotonous symmetry of art" (Diderot 1970, 940).

8. Let us recall here some moments of that history as it is summed up by Hunt in his introduction to *The Genius of the Place*. Le Nôtre died in 1700. In England, "The dominant, mediating taste . . . by the end of the seventeenth century was French" (Hunt and Willis 8). But this prevalent taste had been contested and was about to give way to the movement known as the English landscape garden movement, with William Kent in particular in the forefront. Kent died in 1748, and the gardens he designed in England, the most famous of which is Stowe, were considerably written about and discussed in England and abroad. His layouts of gardens had been heralded earlier in English literature (one example is Milton, who is quoted in English at the end of Jaucourt's article on gardens), and were supported by numerous contemporaries of Kent's, including Pope, but also powerful Whigs, such as Lord Burlington. The English landscape garden movement conceived itself as a response to and a rejection of the French style. By the 1750s, it was commonplace to think that a clear opposition existed between the French and the English styles. Kent's designs were in turn criticized, and a history of reactions against him would include the movement around Lancelot "Capability" Brown, himself contested at the end of the century by exponents of the picturesque (Chambers, Knight, Price).

9. The primacy of nature in gardening is still endorsed today, as can be seen for example in Gilles Clément's current theory of "the garden in movement," elaborated in particular in the André Citroën Park in Paris. While recognizing a dimension of artifice in gardening, Clément proposes man's "collaboration" with nature, "to the extent of conceding a superior part than that of the gardener to the possible inventions of nature" (Clément 1995, 530). However, as we shall see later, Clément criticizes man's attempt to legitimize his acts or conceptualizations when referring to "nature."

10. For example, she says that "there is evidence to demonstrate that the French were familiar already in the seventeenth century with the elements characteristic of the eighteenth-century picturesque garden" (Wiebenson 7). She also shows that some reputed English features, such as the "ha-ha," had been advocated at an earlier stage in France (8). See also Michel Baridon (1986, 430).

11. That the garden has an essential relation to power is the argument of the collection of articles, *Landscape and Power*. In his essay "Imperial Landscape," W. J. T. Mitchell says that "As a fetishized commodity, landscape is what Marx called a 'social hieroglyph,' an emblem of the social relations that it conceals" (15). He also reminds us that "The Enclosure movement and the accompanying dispossession of the English peasantry are an internal colonization of the home country, its transformation from what Blake called 'a green & pleasant land' into a landscape, an emblem of national and imperial identity" (17).

12. See Jean Lauxerois: "The Renaissance imaginary has configured the modern site of memory, by superimposing to it the site of Rome, both mythical and referential. This location constitutes the Western memory of modern Times" (95). On the interpretation of the Renaissance see Hunt (1986, 11–15).

13. See also Jaucourt's description of the classical garden: "Not only did they offer the spectacle of cultivated lands . . . in the midst of Rome, but also superb palaces and large places for pleasure, or country houses meant to rest pleasantly away from the rush of business" (*Encyclopédie VIII*, 459).

14. I extend here Miller's insight into the double character (rustic and/or architectonic) of the garden grotto to describe the mode of gardens in general (see *Heavenly Caves*). See Hunt's *Garden and Grove* for a study of the influence of the Italian garden on the English. Paul Vernière points out that the same antecedents are also found in the French style, though they are often silenced by French authors: "It is too often forgotten that the garden of Lenôtre is heir to the Italian gardens of the 15th and 16th centuries" (271). In that respect, Jaucourt not only does not mention any French gardening practice before the time of Louis XIV, but he immediately juxtaposes his account of the French style to his discussion of Roman classical gardens. Therefore, he altogether omits the discussion of Italian Renaissance gardens. On French gardening before Le Nôtre, see for example Franklin Hazlehurst's study on Boyceau de la Baraudière, Thierry Mariage's *L'univers de Le Nostre*, Michel Baridon's "Les mots, les images."

15. In her edition of Louis XIV's *Manière de montrer les jardins de Versailles*, Simone Hoog mentions for example that "The alleys which lead to these two gates [of the Ball Room] are, in keeping with a habit dear to Le Nôtre, either oblique or curved, and they do not bring the visitor in the axis of the bosquet, but sideways, in order to preserve surprise and to distill effects" (80). She also quotes Charles Perrault's description of the Labyrinth: "It is called Labyrinth, because there one finds an infinity of small alleys so mixed up together that is is almost impossible not to lose one's way; but also, in order for those who do get lost, to be allowed to do so pleasantly, there is no detour that does not present several fountains at once to the sight, so that with each step one is surprised with some new object" (79).

16. "We have remarked before how the exploitation of the constraints of the site and its insertion in the environment were the fundamental criteria of the conception of gardens in the first half of the seventeenth century. This observation puts into question again the division between the English garden and the French garden on the basis of the naturalism of the former and the tyrannical rationality of the latter. But things are even less simple, for Le Nostre, though he finds himself, on the issue of the change of style, irremediably categorized by art history, evinced conceptions that one would rather tend to attribute to Alexander Pope, Robert Morris, or Hubert Robert" (Mariage 105).

17. Also, though for Boyceau and Girardin, nature is so contradictorily defined in respect to geometry, it is worth noting that for both their position is compatible with a shared understanding of nature as variety. This assessment of nature is a standard definition in eighteenth-century treatises. But Franklin Hazlehurst explains that it is also the case for Boyceau. According to this landscape gardener, geometry is the figure of nature's essential "congruity," which is then reconciled with variety: "One of Boyceau's basic theorems is the idea of congruity amidst diversity found in Nature" (29). He quotes Boyceau: "Following the teachings Nature gives in so much variety, we feel the most varied gardens are the most beautiful" (32).

18. In his *De la composition des paysages* (1777), René de Girardin notes that "The Doric order in general succeeds better than any other in landscape, from the columns having no base, and therefore being planted and united better with the ground to the eye, and from the proportions (unconfined by the laws and rules of Paris) being closer to primitive construction, and consequently to nature" (118).

19. Jacques Derrida's remarks on invention in "Psyche" illuminate the position I have described in the example of Robert's "Bath of Apollo"—not an innovation, but not a repetition of the same either: "How can an invention *come back* to being the same, how can the *invenire*, the advent of time-to-come, come to come back, to fold back toward the past a movement always said to be innovative? For that to happen it suffices that invention be possible and that it invent what is possible. Then, right from its origin . . . it envelops in itself a repetition; it unfolds only the dynamics of what was already *found there*, a set of comprehensible possibilities that come into view as ontological or theological truth, a program of cultural or technoscientific politics (civil or military), and so forth. By inventing the possible on the basis of the possible, we relate the new—that is, something quite other that can also be quite ancient—to a set of present possibilities, to the present time and state of the order of possibility that provides for the new the conditions of its status. . . . And yet . . . [t]he very moment of this fabulous repetition can, through a merging of chance and necessity, produce the new of an event" (Derrida 1989, 59).

20. I will discuss mainly Jean-Marie Morel and Girardin, but also Watelet and Carmontelle. As of the 1770s, a number of treatises on "the new style" were published in France. See Daniel Mornet's remark in *Le Sentiment de la Nature*: "In 1731, the Académie française had proposed as a topic: '*The progress of landscape gardening under the reign of Louis the Great.*' The topic was not treated. Fifty years later, there would have been twenty candidates to celebrate the beauties of English gardens" (236).

21. Jean de Cayeux explains that Morel has some legitimate grounds behind his claim of being the designer of Ermenonville: "We owe him in any case the Pavilion of the boccage, the Temple of Muses, the Tower of Gabrielle and the two bridges" (93). De Cayeux adds that Girardin became irritated with him and put

an end to their collaboration. See also Wiebenson for details on Watelet (64ff.), Girardin (70ff.), Morel (75), Carmontelle (76ff.).

22. This is the case of Whately's treatise, which was soon translated into French by Latapie (Paris, 1771). See also Voltaire's *Lettres philosophiques*, a first English edition of which appeared in 1733, one year before the French publication.

23. Let us note that some seventeenth-century authors, like Charles Perrault, had defined the task of the artist as the research of ideal beauty, which may not be found in nature. Perrault said that "it is not enough for a painter to imitate *the most beautiful nature,* such as his eyes see it, but that he must go beyond, and strive to grasp the idea of the beautiful, that not only pure nature, but even beautiful nature never reached" (Ehrard 259). Eighteenth-century writers, like Jaucourt for example, were also aware, as we have mentioned, that art "embellishes" nature. In *Les Beaux-Arts réduits à un même principe* (1746), abbé Batteux had again referred to the notion of "Beautiful Nature." But in his *Lettre sur les sourds et muets*, and the *Traité du Beau*, Diderot was to take this concept to task. In the second essay, Diderot gives his well-known definition of the beautiful as "a set of relations" [rapports] (AT X, 35), and observes, in Ehrard's words, that "in order to judge the relative beauty of a production of nature, we should have an exhaustive knowledge of nature in its entirety" (323). Authors like Morel and Girardin seem to follow Diderot's recommendation of studying (or "knowing") nature before invoking its beauty.

24. See also Mariage's comment quoted earlier (note 16), and Michel Baridon in "Les mots, les images" (1995, 194–95).

CHAPTER 2. NATIONAL NATURE

1. A similar point is made by Paul Vernière. He points out "the persistence into the eighteenth century of the Lenôtre garden" (271).

2. By giving his own treatise on landscape gardening the title *Observations on Modern Gardening*, Whately also implied such an equivalence. Whately's French translator, Latapie, made the connection even more explicit by rendering the title as *L'art de former les jardins modernes ou l'art des jardins anglais* [*The Art of Forming Modern Gardens or The Art of English Gardens*] (Paris, 1771).

3. Let us add in a note a remarkable anecdote, which Morel also adds in a note. Here is the story: "I once accompanied a woman in one of these modern Gardens, where one sees a numerous collection of buildings of all kinds shut in a small space. . . . When she had walked through it, and saw that we were about to leave it, she ingenuously said, '*Let's go and see the garden*'" (355). Morel lets the woman speak the truth, with the very ("ingenuous") voice of nature: the result is that an "English," modern garden does not look natural.

4. Hunt quotes a contemporary French comment by Le Rouge (*Détails des Nouveaux Jardins à la Mode* [Paris, 1776–87]) that concurs with Walpole's observation: "Everyone knows that English gardens are only an imitation of those of China" (Hunt and Willis 33). Wiebenson complicates the issue and points out a further division when she says: "The interest of the French in Kent, as a Chinese-inspired garden designer, may be explained by the fact that by the end of the 1770s, when the popularity of the *jardin anglo-chinois* had reached its peak, the characteristics of the 'Chinese' garden had come to be accepted by some French garden theorists and designers as French, while those of the moral gardens were considered to be English" (Wiebenson 35). Carmontelle's *Jardin de Monceau* represents for Wiebenson "the philosophy behind the *jardin anglo-chinois*" (76).

5. In a section entitled "The French garden. Letter to a friend" (138ff.), Watelet also seems to describe features characteristic of the English style, but in the reversal we have just mentioned, he chooses to call them "French." This garden is Watelet's Moulin-Joli. Watelet also says that "the parks that we dispose on the new principles, are designated by the name of a Nation which we imitate in some customs of little interest, with an often ridiculous affectation" (50).

6. See also a comparable analogy established by Monique Mosser in the case of eighteenth-century France: "Thus, well before the irruption of medieval and Celtic fashions, of the invasion of Bards and troubadours, it seems that a small number of scholars and amateurs found on the national territory, aside from any authority of the Greeks and Romans, enigmatic traces and forms, which were likely, however, to put into question the classical theory of architecture and above all to pose the problem of origins in a new light" (Mosser 1983, 55).

7. This is what Pope and other authors call "the calling in of the country." For example, Pope's *Epistle to Burlington*: "Consult the Genius of the Place in all; / That tells the Waters or to rise, or fall, / Or helps th' ambitious Hill the heav'ns to scale, / Or scoops in circling theatres the Vale, / *Calls in the Country*, catches opening glades, / Joins willing woods, and varies shades from shades" (Pope 138, my emphasis).

8. Such a view is of course tendentious. We have mentioned earlier the connection established by Ann Bermingham, among others, between the process of enclosure on the part of big landowners and the cultural discovery of the countryside in Britain. One aesthetic effect of enclosure was that "each new property was bordered, usually by hedges. . . . Inevitably, the newly enclosed landscape of neatly hedged fields looked small in scale compared with the unbroken commons and wastes that it replaced. 'Extent and freedom' took refuge in the landscape garden that aimed precisely at 'disguising or hiding the boundary' and 'making the whole appear the production of nature only'" (Bermingham 1986, 13).

9. See Mariage about the seventeenth-century French garden: "Of course this opening of the garden to space is the affirmation of a domination, but beyond this appearance remains the essential fact, which is the exportation of its criteria of

order to the whole territory" (105). As for the eighteenth century, Bermingham explains that as landscape gardens became larger, "Not only did they absorb village commons within their boundaries, but occasionally whole villages that stood in the way of a prospect or an improvement were destroyed and rebuilt elsewhere" (Bermingham 1986, 11). She also says that unpleasant objects were excluded from a prospect. The preferred pleasing views were "glimpses of meadows, lakes, or church spires framed by trees" (14).

CHAPTER 3. TRADE WINDS

1. Jean Tarrade and Henri Verdier mention that Choiseul started a policy of reforms of the French army, and in particular the development of the French navy, as early as 1761, that is before the end of the war, to prepare for revenge against the British. Verdier quotes in that respect a letter from Choiseul written in 1762, before the Peace of Paris: "The best is to make peace, I agree, at whatever cost, and to work in concertation with the King of Spain on our navy and our colonies, to mend our disgraces in a few years. We have to expect beginning the war again at the same level in five years; we will cut Germany off, but we will ward off our enemies and will attack them before they are prepared" (Verdier 109).

2. D'Holbach's rather negative impressions of England after a trip undertaken in 1765, for example, are reported by Diderot in some letters to Sophie Volland. In his letter dated "Sunday [October 6, 1765]," Diderot writes: "Do not believe that the distribution of wealth is unequal only in France." And: "The monarch seems to have free hands for the good, and bound hands for the evil; but he is as much and more the master of everything than any other sovereign. Elsewhere the court orders and makes itself obeyed. There it corrupts and does what it likes, and the corruption of the subjects is perhaps worse in the long run than tyranny" (Diderot 1970, 943). The question of corruption had also been raised by Diderot in the article "Représentants" of the *Encyclopédie*: "English members of Parliament, who have long been worthy of praise, have succumbed to corruption and have all too often handed over their constituents to the avidity of those who want to plunder them" (*Encyclopédie* XIV, 145).

3. See Montesquieu's *Spirit of the Laws* (1748): "The purpose of these colonies [in America] is to engage in commerce under better conditions than one has with neighboring peoples with whom all advantages are reciprocal. It has been established that only the mother country can trade with the colony, and this was done with very good reason, for the goal of the establishment was to extend commerce, not to found a town or a new empire" (391).

4. There were three revised editions of Raynal's work (1770, 1774, 1780). The edition I am referring to is the last (Geneva: Pellet, 1781), generally in translation (1798).

5. In "Aux mânes de Diderot," Meister asked: "Who does not know today that nearly one third of this great work belongs to him?" (AT I, XVII).

6. For the identification of Diderot's participation in Raynal's work, see in particular Anatole Feugère's "Raynal, Diderot et quelques autres historiens des deux Indes," Herbert Dieckmann's *Inventaire du fonds Vandeul*, Michèle Duchet's *Diderot et l'Histoire des deux Indes ou l'écriture fragmentaire*, and Gianluigi Goggi's *Diderot, Mélanges et morceaux divers. Contributions à l'Histoire des deux Indes*. Elsewhere, Goggi notes that "if one considers the manuscripts of the 'fonds Vandeul' which gather passages of the *Histoire* . . . one finds that the passages of Raynal's work are copied according to the text of the third edition" (Goggi 35).

7. See for example in the introduction: "If, in after ages, this work should still be read, it is my wish, that, while my readers perceive how much I am divested from passions and prejudice, they should be ignorant of the kingdom which gave me birth, of the government under which I lived, of the profession I followed in my country, and of the religious faith I professed: it is my wish, that they should only consider me as their fellow-citizen and their friend. . . . Raised above all human considerations, it is then we soar above the atmosphere, and behold the globe beneath us. . . . From thence it is, that I have been enabled to cry out, I am free, and feel myself upon a level with the subject I treat" (Raynal 1798, I, 3).

8. See among others, Michèle Duchet (1971, 129sq.; 170sq.), Gianluigi Goggi (19–20), Jean Tarrade (I, 73), Benot (156). In his introduction to selections from the *Histoire*, Yves Benot notes: "After the disasters of the Seven Years War, the loss of Canada, India and of Saint-Louis of Senegal . . . [the *Histoire des Deux Indes*] aimed to pave another way for colonization (French, of course), gather in the Encyclopedic manner the useful knowledge in this area, incite the French, as Choiseul wished, to turn their attention overseas" (Raynal 1981, 6).

9. However, Hans Wolpe also provides a detailed appendix on "Diderot et l'*Histoire des deux Indes*" (Wolpe 186–252), and notes that it is only for lack of timely awareness of Diderot's *Fragments imprimés* and *Pensées détachées* that he did not point out that some of the most remarkable elements of the *Histoire* are also found in the Fonds Vandeul, that is, written by Diderot (251).

10. Michèle Duchet gives similar answers to her own question in her article "Où chercher alors l'auteur?" (Duchet 1991, 11).

11. The concern regarding a potentially declining nation is expressed by Raynal near the end of the *Histoire* when he mentions that "The sedentary life is the only favourable one to population. The man who travels leaves no posterity behind him" (Raynal 1798, XIX, 489). This statement can be seen as a corrective to (though it does not completely invalidate) his general praise of "commerçants," who are described as nomadic and uprooted. On the issue of demographics, see Matthew Anderson's assessment that the eighteenth century witnessed "the unprecedented multiplication of the number of inhabitants in Europe," but in spite of this demographic surge, "the whole century is haunted by the specter of

depopulation. Under the influence of mercantilist and physiocratic theories, it is a commonplace to affirm . . . that a nation must 'multiply' . . . in order to ensure its power and its glory" (Papin 145).

12. Véron de Forbonnais's article, "Colonie," of the *Encyclopédie*, describes colonization (in ancient history) as a way to remedy an excessive population in a given land: "Thus the diverse regions of the earth became populated little by little, in proportion as one could not feed its inhabitants. Such is the first kind of *colonies*: need occasioned it" (*Encyclopédie* III, 648).

13. Véron de Forbonnais's article, "Colonie," also posits an interesting view of what might be termed "pure commerce," that is, commerce dissociated from conquest and settlement, nomadic, and not sedentary: "In India, they only consider the English as merchants, among the great nations of Europe who trade there; *doubtless because they are the least powerful there as far as possessions are concerned*" (*Encyclopédie* III, 649, my emphasis).

14. See however a contribution of Diderot against this position: "It was in this point of view, which can only be applied to the state of nature, that the European nations considered America when it was first discovered. They counted the natives for nothing, and imagined they were sufficiently authorised to seize upon any country, if no other nation of our hemisphere were in possession of it. Such was constantly and uniformly the only public right observed in the New World, and which men have not even been ashamed to justify, in this century during the late hostilities" (XIII, 310–11).

15. *Lectures de Raynal* addresses in several articles the question of Raynal's position on colonialism and slavery. Jacques Chouillet sums up the issue when he mentions the coexistence of "a 'tough' message and a 'soft' message" in Raynal's *Histoire* (Chouillet 1991, 375), that is, both conformism and revolutionary propositions.

16. Throughout his celebrated *Voyage* (first published in 1771), for instance, Bougainville records, along with his circumnavigation, acts of taking possession of "all the lands discovered" (Bougainville 238). Bougainville feared English expansionism, and significantly saw England as "this rival nation" (Bougainville 328). He is always prompt to underscore potential interest in some lands on the part of the British (e.g., "The English now frequent the Moluccas very much; and this is doubtless not done without some design" [444]). Like Raynal regarding Guiana, Bougainville, who had participated in the battle and surrender of Quebec, was conversely favorable to the establishment of a colonial empire overseas that would parallel the British empire. His newly discovered possessions are not only supposed to be profitable to France. They are also intended to foil the potential gain of another European nation, such as Britain. On that question, Jean Meyer remarks: "That there was an aspect of Franco-British competition in the attempts of circumnavigation of the second half of the eighteenth century is apparent in all the texts" (Meyer 36). He also links Choiseul's policy of revenge

with the attempted expansion of Guiana and colonialism in the South Seas: "The other political aspect—of immediate politics—is found in the conjunction of the myth of the Southern [austral] continent and the need for a colonial compensation, after the losses sustained after the Peace of Paris. The Bougainville expedition goes together with the great attempt—even more of a perfect failure—of the development of Guiana. . . . Consequently, the discovery of Southern lands was supposed to offer a counterpart to these political failures of the war and its aftermath" (Meyer 27). Likewise, Maurice de Brossard gives the gist of one of Bougainville's instructions signed by the king on October 26, 1766: "Let us not let ourselves be distanced by the English in the economic conquest of these unknown lands reputed rich in precious ore, and in that of the Asian markets of China. Also let us seize spice islands. Let us take possession by planting poles with French arms" (de Brossard 56). In the context of her discussion of French Anglophobia at the time of the American War of Independence, Frances Acomb has also shown that "among all save the most Anglophile Frenchmen . . . France appeared . . . to be a nonimperialistic power with a mission to defend the rights of men and peoples against aggression. This concept of a mission was suffused with the idea of liberty. In this case, however, liberty meant chiefly, not civil or political liberty, but what was called 'the freedom of the seas.' . . . In eighteenth-century France it meant . . . the destruction of the whole maritime commercial superiority of the English nation" (Acomb 73).

17. In *The Spirit of the Laws,* Montesquieu writes that "Commerce cures destructive prejudices, and it is an almost general rule that everywhere there are gentle mores, there is commerce and that everywhere there is commerce, there are gentle mores" (Montesquieu 338). In the next chapter, he adds that "The natural effect of commerce is to lead to peace. Two nations that trade with each other become reciprocally dependent" (338).

18. "When these colonies shall have acquired that degree of culture, knowledge [lumière, Raynal 1781, XIX (421)], and population, which is suitable for them, will they not detach themselves from a country [patrie (421)] which had founded its splendour upon their prosperity? We know not at what period this revolution will happen, but it must certainly take place" (Raynal 1798, XIX, 487). See the famous passage (one of Diderot's contributions) in Raynal: "This is the decree pronounced by fate upon your colonies: You must either renounce them, or they will renounce you" (Raynal 1798, XIII, 273). See also Chouillet's assessment of contemporary projects to Raynal's, such as Brissot's "project of *white* independence" (Chouillet 1991, 378).

19. This network of associations between commerce and "development," civilization, etc., may conversely contribute to an understanding of what Marshall Sahlins has called the concepts of an "earlier anthropology": "The so-called primitive societies were never so isolated as an earlier anthropology, obsessed by an evolutionary concern for the pristine, was pleased to believe" (Sahlins viii). In this case, the supposed isolation of non-European nations is seen as a corollary of their primitiveness.

20. See the same focus in Montesquieu's *Spirit of the Laws*: "The consequence of the discovery of America was to link Asia and Africa to Europe. . . . Europe has reached such a high degree of power that nothing in history is comparable to it" (Montesquieu 392).

21. This part of my analysis is profoundly indebted to Georges Van den Abbeele's reflections on travel in *Travel as Metaphor*, and his article, "Utopian Sexuality and Its Discontents," on Diderot's *Supplément au voyage de Bougainville*.

22. In Michèle Duchet's words, a crisis in Enlightenment "around 1770, leaves in disarray the generation who made the *Encyclopédie*" (1963, 137). Stephen Werner also mentions that the late Enlightenment is "a period generally characterized as one of pessimism and self-doubt" (Werner 271).

23. "Since the bold attempts of Columbus and of Gama, a spirit of fanaticism, till then unknown, hath been established in our countries, which is that of making discoveries. We have traversed, and still continue to traverse, all the climates from one pole to another, in order to discover some continents to invade, some islands to ravage, and some people to spoil, to subdue, and to massacre" (Raynal 1798, XIX, 489).

24. See Michèle Duchet's comment about "a conception of history, which is that of Enlightenment, and which *The Spirit of the Laws*, followed by the *Essai sur les moeurs* illustrate brilliantly between 1748 and 1755; neither providence, nor chance, but a system of forces, a chain of causes and effects, and the inexorable part of time which gives power to the most audacious" (Duchet 1971, 92–93).

25. In his essay *What Is Enlightenment?* Kant's well-known answer was: "*Enlightenment is man's emergence from his self-imposed immaturity. Immaturity* is the inability to use one's understanding without guidance from another. This immaturity is *self-imposed* when its cause lies not in lack of understanding, but in lack of resolve and courage to use it without guidance from another. *Sapere aude!* Have the courage to use your own understanding!—that is the motto of enlightenment" (Kant 41).

26. In his "Discours sur la nature de l'églogue" (1688), Fontenelle had summed up thus the pleasure of pastoral poetry: "The idea does not fall precisely on the management of the countryside, but on the little care one is laden with, on the idleness one enjoys; and, what is the most important, on how little it takes to be happy" (Fontenelle 1991, 390).

27. "The Tahitian is close to the origins of the world and the European near its old age. The gulf between us is greater than that separating the new-born child from the decrepit dotard" (Diderot 1992, 40).

28. Unlike Rousseau also, he does not believe in the necessity of positing (the hypothesis of) a dispersed state of nature: "I do not believe that this solitary life, attributed to our ancestors, is in human nature," Voltaire says (Voltaire 1963, I, 23). Diderot holds similar views in Raynal's *Histoire*: "Thus it is that the first

founders of nations are satirized, under the supposition of an ideal and chimerical savage state. Men were never insulated in the manner here described. They bore within themselves a germen of sociability, which was incessantly tending to unfold itself" (Raynal 1798, XIX, 224).

29. Van den Abbele points out that this is the position of "exoticism," another aspect of colonialism: "Contradiction is resolved, domesticated, by a certain law of the home or economics (*oiko-nomia*) which brings difference back into the comfortable, familiar orbit of the same. Exoticism is apprehended as appropriation, as colonialism" (Van den Abbeele 1984, 44–45).

30. Edouard Glissant shows that tolerance is not a corrective to, but the very moral justification of what he calls "system thinking": "the appeal to tolerance (or to pity), which is the luxury of system thinking [pensées de système]" (Glissant 1996, 90).

31. Diderot repeats a similar statement in one of his contributions to Raynal: "If I laugh inwardly at the imbecility of the man who gives me his gold for iron, the so-called imbecile also laughs at me who yields him my iron, of which he knows the usefulness, for his gold, which is useless to him" (Raynal 1798, VIII).

32. I am not discussing here whether Diderot's example of interest as a universal motive is accurate or not. My question, whether the risk of alterity is encompassed by the practices of the "self," is general, and not limited to that example. Marshall Sahlins has tackled the issue in his *Islands of History*, when he discusses the different interests vested in trading with the British in Hawaii (and Polynesia) in the eighteenth century (e.g., Sahlins 8). One of Sahlins's points serves to show that while it is the case that "interest" was at stake in such a trade, no unity of response was elicited from the Hawaiians. He points out in particular that issues of class and gender struggles have to be taken into account when assessing the participants in, and the nature of the trade undertaken. The complexity of such responses is not sufficiently recognized by the "self": in European narratives, "others" tend to be seen as a homogeneous group, with no class interests or other internal divisions.

33. The Tahitian's speech in Diderot's *Supplément* rewrites a passage in Bougainville's *Voyage* that perhaps betrays bad conscience (if smugly): "This venerable man . . . even retired without answering our civilities, without giving any signs of fear, astonishment, or curiosity; very far from taking part in the raptures all this people was in at our sight, his thoughtful and suspicious air seemed to shew that he feared the arrival of a new race of men would trouble those happy days which he had spent in peace" (Bougainville 1967, 220–21).

34. Cook's *Journal of a Voyage around the World*, undertaken between 1768 and 1771, ends with a "Concise Vocabulary of the Language of Otahitee" [Tahiti]. The glossary includes the word *Tio* and its translation, "a friend" (Cook 133). The phonetic rendering of the Tahitian word for "friend" rather evokes violence for French speakers: *taïaut* ("tally-ho") is a term used in hunting to designate the

hunter's cry when he sees his prey. In English *tio* may suggest *tie*, as in tying or binding. Behind the professions of friendship to Tahitians lie competing imperialist projects between France and England. This is testified in Bougainville's *Voyage*. He reports that before he left Tahiti he "took possession" of the island: "I buried near the shed, an act of taking possession, inscribed on an oak plank, and a bottle well corked and glued, containing the names of the officers of both ships" (Bougainville 1967, 238). He immediately adds that he did the same in all the lands where he set foot: "I have followed the same method in regard to all the lands discovered during the course of this voyage" (238). Bougainville finds out later that the British had disembarked on Tahiti shortly before him: "I learnt from Aotourou, that about eight months before our arrival at his island, an English ship had touched there. It is the same which was commanded by Mr. Wallace [Wallis]" (273). Rickman's *Journal of Cook's Last Voyage* specifies in its introduction that "Captain Wallis discovered . . . Otaheite . . . and returned to England, May 1768" (Rickman xxxiii–iv). The competing claims of "discovery" are further illustrated in an anecdote related by Bougainville. He says that on an island he found in the sand an English inscription, which was an act of possession similar to his: "A sailor belonging to my barge, being in search of shells, found buried in the sand a piece of a plate of lead, on which we read these remains of English words, HOR'D HERE, ICK MAJESTY'S. There yet remained the mark of the nails, with which they had fastened this inscription, that did not seem to be of any ancient date" (Bougainville 327). The surprise at finding "a monument of an enterprize similar to our's" (328) does not prevent Bougainville from pursuing his own practice. However, Bougainville's *Voyage* also represents the natives' accurate reading of the European appropriation of their land. On coming upon the tree on which the English sign was nailed, he concludes that "The savages had doubtless torn the sign off and broken it in pieces" (Bougainville 327). The Tahitian women also reportedly pointed out the inconsistency between friendship and violence on the part of the French: "The women, who were all in tears, fell at his feet, kissed his hands, weeping and repeating several times, *Tayo, maté*, you are our friends, and you kill us" (Bougainville 236).

35. This wish was not granted, for Aotourou died on the voyage home, in Ile de France (see Jacques Proust's introduction to Bougainville 1982, 11).

36. A passage of Rousseau's *Second Discourse* also testifies to a disjunction within civilized man, a disjunction from oneself which is not apparent in "savages": "The savage lives within himself, whereas social man, constantly outside himself, knows only how to live in the opinion of others; and it is, if I may say so, merely from their judgment of him that he derives the consciousness of his own existence" (Rousseau 1967, 245). This disjunction forbids happiness for "social man." Diderot would agree that no happiness is possible for civilized man: "How far we are from both nature and happiness!" (Diderot 1992, 71). However, Diderot, who often promotes the right to happiness, is also wary of the political risk of "brutishness" (Diderot 1992, 73) of happy citizens. This is why he always condemns enlightened despotism, as the way of permanently enslaving grateful

subjects. The discussion of "brutishness" occurs at the end of the *Supplément* in a passage that unexpectedly links the condition of Tahitians with that of Venetians: "Let me just remark that nowhere but in Tahiti will you find the condition of man a happy one, nor is it elsewhere even tolerable, apart from in a little backwater of Europe" (Diderot 1992, 73). This comparison might indicate that Diderot was not unaware of some "despotic," totalitarian effects of his Tahitian utopia.

37. Moreover, woman in civilization evinces for Diderot the same tension between nature and artifice characteristic of civilized man, yet with an additional emphasis: "More civilized than we are on the outside, they have remained real savages inside" (*Sur les femmes* AT II, 260). Van den Abbeele provocatively links Diderot's assessment of women at the end of the *Supplément* with the work's textuality: "Inevitably, we are forced to face the crucial hermeneutical problem posed by the irreducible polyphony of this text, namely that of determining to what extent any of these conflicting voices can be said to be that of its author. Indeed, A's comment that women say perhaps the opposite of what they think seems nowhere more applicable than to the case of Diderot's own textual practice" (Van den Abbeele 1984, 50).

38. See Glissant's advocacy in *Caribbean Discourse* of the passage from the Same to the Diverse: "The Same, which is neither the uniform nor the sterile, punctuates the effort of the human spirit to transcend that universal humanism that sublimates the particulars (nationals). . . . But, in order to feed its claim to the universal, the Same required (had need of) the flesh of the world. The other is its temptation. Not yet the Other as project of agreement, but the other as matter to sublimate. . . . The Diverse, which is neither the chaotic nor the sterile, signifies the effort of the human spirit towards a transversal relation, without universalist transcendence" (Glissant 1989, 97–98).

39. Diderot believes that it is possible to find this "medium." Yet, he is immediately attentive to the difficulty involved not only in finding it, but more importantly, in bringing mankind to embrace it: "And even if it were found, what authority would be capable of directing the steps of man to it, and to fix him there?" (Raynal 1798, IX, 275). Diderot is always wary of the various possible forms of "enlightened despotism," writing often that people should not be coerced, not even into happiness. And precisely as far as happiness is concerned, Diderot does not recommend unlimited, "civilizing" progress, though he believes it is possible to defer its present limit. He admires the Tahitians for having "stopped" when they found the point of happiness (Papin 129). See also his comment after his argument quoted earlier that "It is not, however, that I prefer a savage to a civilized state": "But the more I reflect upon this point, the more it seems to me, that from the most rude nature to the most civilized state, every thing is nearly compensated, virtues and vices, physical good and evil. . . . I imagine that nature hath set certain bounds to the felicity of every considerable portion of the human species, beyond which there is nearly as much to lose as to gain" (Raynal 1798, VI, 467).

40. For example, although the following passage refers to "savage man," the attributes given him, such as solitude, no speech, etc., apply to man in the state of nature: "savage man, wandering about in the forests, without industry, without speech, without any fixed residence, an equal stranger to war and every social tie, without any need of his fellows . . . " (Rousseau 1967, 207–208). The term *savage* is therefore used loosely in that quotation, unlike in the following passage, where the distinction between "savage" and the state of nature is maintained: "And it is so much the more ridiculous to represent savages constantly murdering each other to glut their brutality, as this opinion is diametrically opposite to experience, and the Caribbeans, the people in the world who have as yet deviated least from the state of nature, are to all intents and purposes the most peaceable in their amours" (Rousseau 1967, 206). Yet, it is noticeable that even while making the distinction, Rousseau uses the "savage" as a verification of his hypothesis on the state of nature.

41. See also Papin (118).

42. Chouillet analyzes the ways in which this thesis reverses Locke's genealogy of ideas (Chouillet 1973, 159–60). Therefore Condillac's essay is both aimed against Descartes (ideas are not innate, or a priori) and against Locke.

43. However, it should be pointed out that if Diderot's essay posits at times the preexistence of thought to language, as is the case in his well-known passage concerning the state of the mind as "a moving picture [tableau] from which we ceaselessly paint" (AT I, 369), his subsequent analysis of hieroglyphic language, for instance, shows the irrelevance of such a priority, to the extent that it would be as right to say the reverse, or that "our understanding is modified by signs" (AT I, 369). On the issue of the reversibility of the priority of thought to language in *Lettre sur les sourds et muets*, see James Creech's analysis (particularly Creech 128–33).

44. See Creech 122ff.

45. This is therefore Condillac's answer to Cartesians, who are wary of the delusion provided by the senses. Here is Condillac's extended argument: "If, for example, I see at a distance a square building, it will appear to me to be round. Is there then any obscurity or confusion in the idea of rotundity, or in my applying it? No: but I judge this building to be round, and there lies the mistake. When I say that all our knowledge proceeds from the senses, we must not forget that this is to be understood so far as this knowledge is derived from the clear and distinct ideas which those senses contain. As to the judgments which accompany them, they can be of no service to us, till their defects have been corrected by experience and reflection" (Condillac 1974, 22). In the example just given by Condillac, the clear and distinct idea would be that of rotundity, and the defective judgment would be the assumption that the building is round. Incidentally, the reference to a "clear and distinct idea," though it is used here against, and differently than in Descartes, is itself a Cartesian notion.

46. This is doubtless why Charles-Michel de l'Epée, Pereire's contemporary and self-styled competitor, claims that until he invented a method to teach them, deaf-mutes were considered to be "half-automata" (de l'Epée 9, 141).

47. Here is the context of Derrida's phrase: "As with all of Condillac's concepts . . . the gap or deviation is not that of a structural opposition but of a difference of degree: a subtle, gradual, infinitely differential transition from one quality to another, as from one quality then back to itself again" (Derrida 1980, 97).

48. About the intermediate stage of language, Condillac also writes in the *Essay*: "And yet when once they had acquired the habit of connecting some ideas with arbitrary signs, the natural cries served them for a pattern, to frame a new language" (Condillac 1974, 174). And near the end of the *Essay*, he explains that "every language has been formed after the pattern that immediately preceded it. In the mode of speaking by action we have beheld the blossom, as it were, of articulate sounds" (299).

49. De l'Epée's main purpose in his *Véritable Manière d'instruire les sourds-muets* is to show his opposition to this view, and to demonstrate that on the contrary, it is possible for a deaf-mute to have "metaphysical ideas" (12): "Since there is no word which does not signify something, there is also nothing, even if it is independent from our senses, which cannot be clearly explained in an analysis consisting of simple words" (12). De l'Epée thinks that "there is not a more natural link between metaphysical ideas and articulated sounds that we hear, than between those same ideas and written characters that we see" (109). He also notes that "the deaf-mutes do not mistake the different figures of each letter which strongly strikes their eyes any more than we mistake the different sounds which we hear" (21).

50. Even though, in a gesture we have already mentioned, Condillac will claim a minimal difference between the naming of sensible and abstract things: "The most abstract terms come from the first names which were given to sensible objects" (Condillac 1974, 249–50).

51. This position is also found in Rousseau's *Essay on the Origin of Languages* and Diderot's *Lettre sur les sourds et muets*. In both essays, Rousseau and Diderot point out that with the gradual disappearance of gestural language, language has lost its "energy," and that the "perfection" of articulate language (Diderot) is also what marks its decadence. In her article on Rousseau's *Essay*, "Origins," Peggy Kamuf points out in Rousseau's analysis "a pattern whereby differences or distinctions will be marked in two ways: as differences from each other (no two national languages are alike) but also as differences from the origin, as departures from the original manifestation of speech as such. . . . And that is why stories about origins so frequently end up being fables about lost wholeness" (Kamuf 1989, 455).

52. In his manual, de l'Epée quotes a positive assessment of his method by Condillac, which illustrates well Condillac's complex view toward his own

account of a progress toward articulate language: "[M. de l'Epée] has only one way of giving [his students] ideas that are not provided by the senses, which is to analyze them and have them analyzed with him. Therefore, he leads them from sensible to abstract ideas by simple and methodical analyses, and it is easy to judge how advantageous his language by action is, compared to the articulated sounds of our governesses and instructors" (de l'Epee 95–96).

CHAPTER 4. PHILOSOPHICAL GARDENS

1. "The system of linear perspective is thus a social and historical system of exchange by means of articulating diverse subjects as potential viewers, interchangeable and identical before a given scene. . . . At Versailles—structured according to the optical and symbolic signification of the central alley leading from the chateau to infinity—it is rather a sign of the Sun-King's hyperbolic hubris" (Weiss 62–63).

2. Morel concurs and he follows the same line of argument. He first shows that a painting always brings the same site to view, in the same perspective, which evokes the position of the spectator in a French formal garden: "Look at the work of a painter, it only presents the same site: whatever point it is seen from, the diverse objects which compose it are always shown in the same order; all the effects of perspective are the same" (Morel 376). Then, Morel presents the aims of the new garden as an entry into the picture: "On the terrain, the diverse positions of the Spectator nuance the effects and vary the perspectives. Doubtless he only sees the same things and in the same order from the same place; but if he transports himself a few steps away, if he goes up or down, then immediately, as if the objects were mobile, the scene changes, it offers him new tableaux and presents him other combinations" (376–77).

3. See for example Girardin's descriptions of Ermenonville, the anonymous account of "A Tour of Ermenonville," Watelet's section entitled "The French garden. Letter to a friend," which describes his garden, Moulin-Joli, and Morel's descriptions of Guiscard and Ermenonville.

4. Stressing the unreliability of the senses was a position taken against scholastics, as this passage from the *Discourse on the Method* shows: "Even the philosophers in the Schools hold it as a maxim that there is nothing in the understanding which has not first of all been in the senses . . . neither our imagination nor our senses can ever assure us of anything, if our understanding does not intervene" (Descartes 1996, 24). On the contrary, Locke will argue that the conditions of possibility of knowledge are derived from the senses.

5. However, Jacques Derrida has shown that even though Descartes elaborates a notion of doubt "beyond whose reach will be only the truths of nonsensory origin, mathematical truths notably" (Derrida 1978, 46), he still considers the possi-

bility of the reliability of the senses, for example in the First *Meditation*. Derrida quotes Descartes: "But it may be that although the senses sometimes deceive us concerning things which are *hardly perceptible, or very far away*, there are yet many others to be met with as to which we cannot reasonably have any doubt" (Derrida 1978, 45). Derrida adds: "There would be, *there would perhaps be* data of sensory origin which cannot reasonably be doubted" (45).

6. See for example a passage in Descartes's *Discourse on the Method* which makes a parallel between the certainty of the demonstrations of geometricians and that of the existence of God. Characteristically, the reference to the certainty of "the object of the geometricians" does not necessarily entail the certainty of the existence of the object: "I went through some of their simplest demonstrations, and having noticed that this great certainty which everyone attributes to these demonstrations is founded solely on the fact that they are conceived with clearness, in accordance with the rule which I have just laid down, I also noticed that there was nothing at all in them to assure me of the existence of their object. For, to take an example, I saw very well that if we suppose a triangle to be given, the three angles must certainly be equal to two right angles; but for all that I saw no reason to be assured that there was any such triangle in existence" (Descartes 1996, 23). See also Judovitz's commentary on the use by Descartes of the figure of the chiliagon in the Third *Meditation* as "a mathematical figure whose thousand sides resist visualization" but does not prevent, in Descartes's words, the "conception" of the figure (Judovitz 80).

7. Mariage says that "the subterranean world was . . . one of the main centers of interest of the culture of the seventeenth century" (Mariage 75). In that respect, he mentions that "in the seventeenth century, lakes were considered to be the *eyes of the ocean* and were thought to communicate with it through subterranean conduits. This idea which comes from Aristotle is also found in Descartes, in his work entitled *Les Météores*. Sources are therefore resurgences of the sea, and all waters communicate. The adductions of water in gardens, pools and fountains are therefore understood as the complements of the hydrological system of the planet, and are therefore part of the subterranean world" (75).

8. In the *Encyclopédie,* for example, d'Alembert says that "Descartes . . . made some forays into experimental physics, but he recommended it more than he practiced it" (*Encyclopédie* VI, 301). In his postface to Descartes's *Discours de la méthode*, Jean-Marie Beyssade also notes that "In this epistemological model, experiment is not absent but it is subordinated. At first, the most common experiments are sufficient to confirm the principles of physics, which draw their certainty from elsewhere, from metaphysical deduction. . . . As one gradually progresses towards the particular, experiment becomes more necessary, and more difficult" (Descartes 1973, 134).

9. The second instance is what d'Alembert recommends for the future of experimental physics. D'Alembert first complicates the notion of experiment by dividing it in two. For him, "experimental physics revolves around two points that must

not be confused, *experiment* properly speaking, and *observation*" (VI, 299). The difference between the two is that observation must "see well . . . the spectacle of nature," whereas experiment "create[s], so to speak, through the different combination of bodies, new phenomena to be studied" (299). The two are complementary: "Experiment, among several advantages, has that of extending the domain of observation. . . . Observation, by the curiosity it raises and by the gaps it leaves, leads to experiment; experiment brings back to observation" (300). Then, d'Alembert disagrees with the hierarchy and confirming structure usually posited between theory and practice in physics, which is also a way of undermining the strict opposition we have mentioned between system and history. He is far, however, from simply dismissing theory, conceding that theory can sometimes spare itself the recourse to experiment. The interest of his position concerns experiment, which is not merely in his view the confirmation of theoretical findings. For example, regarding the laws of motion, d'Alembert writes that experiment brings out a difference to theory, which serves truth, while not invalidating theoretical results: "The only true usefulness that experimental research can provide the physicist on the laws of balance, motion, and in general on the primitive affections of bodies, is to attentively examine the difference between the result given by theory and that provided by the experiment, and to use that difference skilfully. . . . Such is the method that the greatest physicists have followed, and that is the most appropriate to cause science to make great progress, for then experiment will not simply be used to confirm theory, but, differing from theory without shaking its foundation, it will lead to new truths that theory only could not have reached" (301). The privilege of theory is not denied, but experiment is claimed to be more than a demonstration, an important tool for the discovery of truth.

10. In that respect, Condillac's *Traité des systèmes* (1746) is exemplary in its reconciliation of "facts" and "systems." He postulates on the one hand that "the only proper scientific principles are established facts," and on the other hand that "true systems, the only ones that merit the name, are based on principles of this last kind" (Condillac 1982, 3). Later on in the treatise, he also says: "So let us conclude that we can construct true systems only in cases where we have enough observations to grasp the interconnection of phenomena" (139).

11. See for example Morel's chapter 2, entitled "Of the Spectacle of Nature and of the advantages of the countryside": "Among all the objects that strike our gaze, there is none of which the impressions are as vivid, there is none which has such a universal empire over man's heart, than the spectacle of Nature" (Morel 23). Or Girardin: "And indeed, what human magnificence can be compared to the vast spectacle of nature?" (Girardin 18–19). In *Essais sur la peinture*, Diderot confirms the notion that nature is a spectacle, but he goes further when he argues that the experience of the spectator of a landscape and that of the viewer of a landscape painting are reversible: "If we happen to walk in Tuileries, Boulogne, or some remote spot of the Champs-Elysées . . . the aspect of a branch, of a leaf, arrests the gaze, and suspends conversation. . . . Our steps involuntarily stop; our

gazes move across the magic canvas, and we exclaim: What a picture! It seems as though we considered nature as the result of art. And reciprocally, if it happens that the painter repeats the same enchantment on the canvas, it seems as though we looked at the effect of art as that of nature" (Diderot 1996, 478).

12. In that respect, if the sense of sight is privileged, as in the French formal garden, it should be noted that other senses are also solicited. For example, Girardin writes: "In a situation of picturesque beauty, where nature unconfined displays all her graces, the emotions of pleasure we receive from sight by the effect of such a landscape, are encreased by agreeable impressions upon the other senses; such as the fresh smell of the young grass; the opening leaves of the spring, expanded by the vivifying electricity of a warm shower; the soft murmuring of streams, which give new life to the verdure; or the tender concert of the birds singing among the branches. Then the hearing and smell, less quick than the sight to seize the objects, but also less roving, and more intimately affected, powerfully assist in conveying to the soul every delightful impression" (Girardin 139–40).

13. In *Salons*, Diderot demonstrates the same attention to details in paintings, but he insists that no impression of confusion should be fostered in the spectator. He often mentions that the spectator's gaze should be guided, and in the *Salon* of 1763, he reproaches Boucher for failing to do so in his pictures: "Between all these details, which are all equally well finished, the gaze does not know where to stop. . . . When one paints, must one paint everything? Please leave something to my imagination" (Diderot 1996, 247).

14. Girardin describes the following sight in one of his walks in Ermenonville: "A plantation of laurel and myrtle, in which there still remains an ancient altar, the perfume of flowering shrubs with which the island is covered, and the ruins of a little antique temple, sufficiently indicate that it was heretofore consecrated to love; but now it is only a passage, and the house of the ferryman is supported against the almost unrecognizable ruin of the temple" (Girardin 60–61).

15. See also Mortier: "The preference given to the fragmentary over the integral, to mutilated marble over the intact statue, this choice is part of an aesthetic which is both *classical* in its object and *anticlassical* in its spirit" (Mortier 102).

16. There is a similar passage in Diderot's *Salon* of 1761: "Generally there must be few figures in temples, in ruins and in landscapes, which are places where silence must almost not be broken; but these figures must be exquisite. They are usually people who pass by, meditate, wander, live or rest" (Diderot 1996, 223).

Bibliography

Acomb, Frances. *Anglophobia in France 1763–1789. An Essay in the History of Constitutionalism and Nationalism*. Durham: Duke University Press, 1950.

Althusser, Louis. *Politics and History: Montesquieu, Rousseau, Hegel and Marx*. Trans. Ben Brewster. London: NLB, 1972.

Baridon, Michel. "Jardins et Paysage: Existe-t-il un style anglais?" *Dix-huitième siècle* 18 (1986): 427–47.

———. "Les mots, les images et la mémoire des jardins," *Le Jardin, art et lieu de mémoire*. Ed. Monique Mosser, Philippe Nys. Besançon: Les Editions de l'Imprimeur, 1995.

Belaval, Yvon. "La crise de la géométrisation de l'univers dans la philosophie des Lumières." *Revue internationale de Philosophie* VI, 21 (1952): 337–56.

Benot, Yves. *Diderot, de l'athéisme à l'anticolonialisme*. Paris: François Maspero, 1970.

Bermingham, Ann. *Landscape and Ideology: The English Rustic Tradition, 1740–1860*. Berkeley: University of California Press, 1986.

———. "System, Order, and Abstraction: The Politics of English Landscape Drawing around 1795," *Landscape and Power*. W. J. T. Mitchell, ed. Chicago: University of Chicago Press, 1994.

Bhabha, Homi. "DissemiNation: Time, Narrative, and the Margins of the Modern Nation," *Nation and Narration*. London and New York: Routledge, 1990.

———. *The Location of Culture*. London and New York: Routledge, 1994.

Bougainville, Louis-Antoine de. *Voyage autour du monde par la frégate du roi La Boudeuse et la flûte L'Etoile*. Introduction: Jacques Proust. Paris: Gallimard, Folio, 1982.

———. *A Voyage Round the World*. Trans. John Reinhold Forster, F.A.S. London: J. Nourse, 1772 (Reprint: New York: Da Capo Press, 1967).

Brewer, Daniel. "Diderot and the Image of the Other (Woman)," *L'esprit créateur* 24, 1 (Spring 1984): 53–65.

———. *The Discourse of Enlightenment in Eighteenth-Century France: Diderot and the Art of Philosophizing*. Cambridge: Cambridge University Press, 1993.

de Brossard, Maurice. "Le voyage de Bougainville dans le contexte de la découverte, de Byron à Cook," ed. Michel Mollat du Jourdin. *L'importance de l'Exploration Maritime au Siècle des Lumières (A propos du voyage de Bougainville)*. Paris: Editions du Centre National de la Recherche Scientifique, 1982.

Carmontelle (Carrogis, Louis). *Jardin de Monceau*. Paris: Delafosse, 1779.

Cauquelin, Anne. "Paysage et environs: une logique du vague." *Critique* 577/578 (Juin–Juillet 1995): 449–58.

de Cayeux, Jean. *Hubert Robert et les Jardins*. Preface Michel Serres. Paris: Editions Herscher, 1987.

Chabanon, Michel Paul Gui de. *Epitre sur la manie des jardins anglois*. Paris: s.n., 1775.

Chouillet, Jacques. *La formation des idées esthétiques de Diderot, 1745–1763*. Paris: Librairie Armand Colin, 1973.

———. "Postface: Raynal face à l'horizon d'attente des Lumières," *Lectures de Raynal. L'Histoire des deux Indes en Europe et en*

Amérique au XVIIIe siècle. Studies on Voltaire and the Eighteenth Century 286. Lüsebrink, Hans-Jürgen and Manfred Tietz, eds. Oxford: University of Oxford Press, 1991.

Clément, Gilles. "Identité et signature," *Le Jardin, art et lieu de mémoire*. ed. Monique Mosser, Philippe Nys. Besançon: Les Editions de l'Imprimeur, 1995.

———. *Le Jardin en mouvement*. Paris: Pandora Editions, 1990.

———. *Le Jardin en mouvement. De La Vallée au Parc André Citroën*. Paris: Sens et Tonka, Editeurs, 1994.

Condillac, Etienne Bonnot de. *An Essay on the Origin of Human Knowledge*. trans. Thomas Nugent. New York: AMS Press, 1974. (Reprint of the 1756 ed., London: J. Nourse).

———. *Philosophical Writings (A Treatise on Systems; A Treatise on the Sensations)*. Trans. Franklin Philip, Harlan Lane. Hillsdale, N.J.: Lawrence Erlbaum, 1982.

Cook , James. *Journal of a Voyage Round the World, In His Majesty's Ship Endeavour*. London: T. Becket and P. A. de Hondt, 1771 (Reprint: New York: Da Capo Press, 1967).

Creech, James. *Diderot. Thresholds of Representation*. Columbus: Ohio University Press, 1986.

de Croÿ, Emmanuel. *Journal d'un voyage en Angleterre en 1766. Revue Britannique* 3 (mars 1895): 7–53.

Deleuze, Gilles, and Félix Guattari. *A Thousand Plateaus*. Trans. Brian Massumi. Minneapolis: University of Minnesota Press, 1987.

Derrida, Jacques. *The Archaeology of the Frivolous: Reading Condillac*. Trans. John P. Leavey, Jr. Pittsburgh: Duquesne University Press, 1980.

———. *Khôra*. Paris: Galilée, 1993.

———. *The Other Heading: Reflections on Today's Europe*. Trans. Pascale-Anne Brault and Michael B. Naas. Bloomington: Indiana University Press, 1992.

———. "Psyche. Inventions of the Other," *Reading de Man Reading*. Ed. Lindsay Waters and Wlad Godzich. Trans. Catherine Porter. Minneapolis: University of Minnesota Press, 1989.

———. *Writing and Difference*. Trans. Alan Bass. Chicago: University of Chicago Press, 1978.

Descartes, René. *Discours de la méthode*. Commentaries Jean-Marie Beyssade. Paris: Librairie Générale Française, 1973.

———. *Discourse on the Method and Meditations on First Philosophy*. Trans. Elizabeth S. Haldane and G.R.T. Ross. New Haven: Yale University Press, 1996.

Dézallier d'Argenville, Antoine-Nicolas. *Voyage pittoresque des environs de Paris*. Paris: 1755 (other editions: 1762, 1768, 1779).

Diderot, Denis. *Encyclopédie ou Dictionnaire raisonné des sciences, des arts et des métiers par une société de gens de lettres*. Paris: Briasson and Le Breton, 1751–65.

Article "Colonie" (Véron de Forbonnais), III: 648–51.

Article "Encyclopédie" (Diderot), V: 635–48.

Article "Expérimental" (d'Alembert) VI: 298–301.

Article "Jardin" (de Jaucourt), VIII: 459–60.

Article "Représentants" (Diderot), XIV: 143-46.

———. *Lettres à Sophie Volland. Oeuvres complètes* 5. Paris: Le Club français du livre, 1970.

———. *Oeuvres* III. Paris: Editions Robert Laffont, 1995.

———. *Oeuvres* IV. Paris: Editions Robert Laffont, 1996.

———. *Oeuvres complètes*. [AT]. Ed. J. Assézat and M. Tourneux. Paris: Garnier Frères, 1875.

———. *Supplément au voyage de Bougainville*. *Political Writings*. Trans. and ed. John Hope Mason and Robert Wokler. Cambridge: Cambridge University Press, 1992.

Duchet, Michèle. *Anthropologie et Histoire au siècle des Lumières*. Paris: François Maspero, 1971.

———. "L'*Histoire des deux Indes*: sources et structure d'un texte polyphonique," *Lectures de Raynal. L'Histoire des deux Indes en Europe et en Amérique au XVIIIe siècle. Studies on Voltaire and the Eighteenth Century* 286. Lüsebrink, Hans-Jürgen and Manfred Tietz, eds. Oxford: University of Oxford Press, 1991.

———. "Le Primitivisme de Diderot." *Europe* 405–406 (janvier–février 1963): 126–37.

Ehrard, Jean. *L'idée de nature en France dans la première moitié du XVIIIe siècle*. Paris: Albin Michel, 1994. (Reprint: 1963)

Fontenelle. *Oeuvres complètes* II. Paris: Librairie Arthème-Fayard, 1991.

———. *Elogium of Newton*. In Cohen, I. Bernard, ed. *Isaac Newton's Papers and Letters on Natural Philosophy*. Cambridge: Harvard University Press, 1978. [Reprint of London: J. Tonson, 1728]

Francastel, Pierre. "La replantation du parc de Versailles au XVIIIe siècle," *Bulletin de la Société de l'histoire de l'art français* (1950): 53–57.

Gilles, Joël. "Quand la peinture fait paysage." *Recherches POIETIQUES* 2, (Printemps/Eté 1995): 18-30.

Gillispie, Charles Coulston. "Fontenelle and Newton." In Cohen, I. Bernard, ed. *Isaac Newton's Papers and Letters on Natural Philosophy*. Cambridge: Harvard University Press, 1978.

Gilpin, William. *A Dialogue upon the Gardens of the Right Honourable The Lord Viscount Cobham at Stow in Buckinghamshire* (1748). Introduction John Dixon Hunt. Los Angeles: Augustan Reprint Society 176, University of California, 1976.

Girardin, René-Louis de. *De la composition des paysages*. Paris: 1777.

———. *An Essay on Landscape, or, On the Means of Improving and Embellishing the Country Round our Habitations*. Trans. Daniel Malthus. New York: Garland, 1982. Reprint of London: J. Dodsley, 1783.

Glissant, Edouard. *Le Discours antillais*. Paris: Editions du Seuil, 1981.

———. *Caribbean Discourse: Selected Essays*. Trans. J. Michael Dash. Charlottesville: University Press of Virginia, 1989.

———. *Introduction à une poétique du divers*. Paris: Gallimard, 1996.

Goggi, Gianluigi. "Quelques remarques sur la collaboration de Diderot à la première édition de l'*Histoire des deux Indes*," *Lectures de Raynal. L'Histoire des deux Indes en Europe et en Amérique au XVIIIe siècle. Studies on Voltaire and the Eighteenth Century* 286. Lüsebrink, Hans-Jürgen and Manfred Tietz, eds. Oxford: University of Oxford Press, 1991.

Guy, Basil. *The French Image of China before and after Voltaire. Studies on Voltaire and the Eighteenth Century* 21. Geneva: Institut et Musée Voltaire, 1963.

———. Trans. and ed. of Prince de Ligne. *Coup d'Oeil at Beloeil*. Berkeley: University of California Press, 1991.

Hazlehurst, Franklin Hamilton. *Jacques Boyceau and the French Formal Garden*. Athens: University of Georgia Press, 1966.

d'Holbach, Paul-Henri Thiry. *Le Système de la nature, ou des lois du monde physique et du monde moral* (1770). Paris: Librairie Arthème-Fayard, 1990. 2 vols.

Horkeimer, Max, and Theodor W. Adorno, *Dialectic of Enlightenment*. Trans. John Cumming. New York: Continuum, 1997.

Hoog, Simone, ed. *Manière de montrer les jardins de Versailles, par Louis XIV.* Paris: Editions de la Réunion des Musées nationaux, 1992.

Hunt, John Dixon. *The Figure in the Landscape*. Baltimore: Johns Hopkins University Press, 1989.

———. *Garden and Grove: The Italian Renaissance Garden in the English Imagination: 1600–1750*. Princeton: Princeton University Press, 1986.

———. *William Kent, Landscape Garden Designer*. London: A. Zwemmer, 1987.

Hunt, John Dixon, and Peter Willis, eds. *The Genius of the Place: The English Landscape Garden 1620–1820*. Cambridge: MIT Press, 1988.

Judovitz, Dalia. "Vision, Representation, and Technology in Descartes," *Modernity and the Hegemony of Vision*. Ed. David Michael Levin. Berkeley: University of California Press, 1993.

Kalaora, Bernard. "L'artiste: Un *homo faber* des lieux." *Critique* 577/578 (Juin–Juillet 1995): 458–68.

Kamuf, Peggy. *Fictions of Feminine Desire. Disclosures of Heloise*. Lincoln: University of Nebraska Press, 1982.

———. "1754? Rousseau Writes His *Essai sur l'origine des langues.* Origins," *A New History of French Literature*. Ed. Denis Hollier. Cambridge: Harvard University Press, 1989 (455–60).

Kant, Immanuel. "An Answer to the Question: What Is Enlightenment?" *Perpetual Peace and Other Essays*. Trans. Ted Humphrey. Indianapolis: Hackett, 1983.

Koehn, Nancy F. *The Power of Commerce. Economy and Governance in the First British Empire*. Ithaca and London: Cornell University Press, 1994.

Koyré, Alexandre. *Newtonian Studies*. Cambridge: Harvard University Press, 1965.

Lauxerois, Jean. "Le jardin de la mélancolie," *Le Jardin, art et lieu de mémoire*. Ed. Monique Mosser, Philippe Nys. Besançon: Les Editions de l'Imprimeur, 1995.

Lefebvre, Georges. Review of Frances Acomb's *Anglophobia in France 1763–1789*. *Revue historique* CCVIII (Juillet–Septembre 1952): 97–100.

de l'Epée, Charles-Michel, Abbé. *La véritable manière d'instruire les sourds et muets confirmée par une longue expérience* (1784). Paris: Librairie Arthème Fayard, 1984.

Mariage, Thierry. *L'univers de Le Nostre*. Liège: Pierre Mardaga, 1990.

Meyer, Jean. "Le contexte des grands voyages d'exploration du XVIIIe siècle," ed. Michel Mollat du Jourdin. *L'importance de l'Exploration Maritime au Siècle des Lumières (A propos du voyage de Bougainville)*. Paris: Editions du Centre National de la Recherche Scientifique, 1982.

Miller, Naomi. *Heavenly Caves: Reflections on the Garden Grotto*. London: George Allen and Unwin, 1982.

Mitchell, W. J. T., ed. *Landscape and Power*. Chicago: University of Chicago Press, 1994.

Montesquieu. *The Spirit of the Laws*. Trans. and ed. Anne M. Cohler, Basia Carolyn Miller, Harold Samuel Stone. Cambridge: Cambridge University Press, 1989.

Morel, Jean-Marie. *Théorie des Jardins*. Paris: Pissot, 1776.

Mornet, Daniel. *Le Sentiment de la Nature en France de J. J. Rousseau à Bernardin de Saint-Pierre*. Paris: Hachette, 1907.

Mortier, Roland. *La poétique des ruines en France*. Geneva: Librairie Droz, 1974.

Mosser, Monique, and Philippe Nys. "Introduction." *Le Jardin, art et lieu de mémoire*. Ed. Monique Mosser, Philippe Nys. Besançon: Les Editions de l'Imprimeur, 1995.

———. "Le rocher et la colonne: Un thème d'iconographie architecturale au XVIIIe siècle." *Revue de l'Art* 58–59 (1983): 53–74.

Papin, Bernard. *Sens et fonction de l'utopie tahitienne dans l'oeuvre politique de Diderot. Studies on Voltaire and the Eighteenth Century* 251. Oxford: University of Oxford Press, 1988.

Pereire, Jacob Rodrigue. *Mémoire que M. J. R. Pereire a lu dans la séance de l'Académie Royale des Sciences du 11 juin 1749, et dans lequel en présentant à cette compagnie un jeune sourd et muet de naissance, il expose avec quel succès il lui a appris à parler* (slnd).

Pitte, Jean-Robert. *Histoire du paysage français*. 2 vols. Paris: Editions Tallandier, 1983.

Pope, Alexander. *Epistles to Several Persons (Moral Essays). Poems* III–2. Ed. F. W. Bateson. London: Methuen, 1951.

Raynal. *Histoire philosophique et politique des Etablissements et du Commerce des Européens dans les deux Indes*. Geneva: Pellet, 1781.

———. *Histoire philosophique et politique des Etablissements et du Commerce des Européens dans les deux Indes* (selections). Edited with an introduction Yves Benot. Paris: Maspéro, "La Découverte," 1981.

———. *Philosophical and Political History of the Settlements and Trade of the Europeans in the East and West Indies*. Newly translated from the French by J. O. Justamond, F.R.S., London: J. Mundell, 1798 (Reprint: New York: Negro Universities Press, 1969).

Rickman, John. *Journal of Captain Cook's Last Voyage to the Pacific Ocean*. London: Newberry, 1781 (Reprint: New York: Da Capo Press, 1967).

Rousseau, Jean-Jacques. *Essay on the Origin of Languages in Which Something Is Said about Melody and Musical Imitation*. Trans. Victor Gourevitch. New York: Harper and Row, 1986.

———. *Julie ou la Nouvelle Héloïse. Oeuvres complètes* II. Paris: Gallimard, Pléiade, 1964.

———. *The Social Contract and Discourse on the Origin of Inequality*. Edited, revised anonymous translation Lester G. Crocker. New York: Washington Square Press, 1967.

Sahlins, Marshall. *Islands of History*. Chicago: University of Chicago Press, 1985.

Stone, Lawrence, ed. *An Imperial State at War: Britain from 1689 to 1815*. London and New York: Routledge, 1994.

Tarrade, Jean. *Le Commerce colonial de la France à la fin de l'Ancien Régime: L'évolution du régime de "l'Exclusif" de 1763 à 1789*. 2 vols. Paris: PUF, 1972.

Thomson, James. *The Complete Poetical Works*. Ed. J. Logie Robertson. London: Oxford University Press, 1908.

Todorov, Tzvetan. *The Conquest of America. The Question of the Other*. Trans. Richard Howard. New York: Harper and Row, 1984.

Van den Abbeele, Georges. *Travel as Metaphor. From Montaigne to Rousseau*. Minneapolis: University of Minnesota Press, 1992.

———. "Utopian Sexuality and Its Discontents: Exoticism and Colonialism in the *Supplément au Voyage de Bougainville*." *L'esprit créateur* XXIV, 1 (Spring 1984): 43–52.

Verdier, Henri. *Le Duc de Choiseul*. Paris: Nouvelles Editions Debresse, 1969.

Vernière, Paul. *Lumières ou Clair-obscur?* Paris: PUF, 1987.

Voltaire. *Essai sur les moeurs et l'esprit des nations et sur les principaux faits de l'histoire depuis Charlemagne jusqu'à Louis XIII*. 2 vols. Paris: Editions Garnier Frères, 1963.

———. *Lettres philosophiques ou Lettres anglaises*. Introduction and edition Raymond Naves. Paris: Garnier Frères, 1962.

———. *Philosophical Letters*. Trans. Ernest Dilworth. New York: Bobbs-Merrill, Inc., 1961.

Walpole, Horace. *The History of the Modern Taste in Gardening*. In Chase, Isabel Wakelin Urban. *Horace Walpole: Gardenist*. Princeton: Princeton University Press, 1943.

Watelet, Claude-Henri. *Essai sur les jardins*. Paris: Prault, 1774.

Weinshenker, Anne Betty. "Diderot's Use of the Ruin-Image," *Diderot Studies* XVI (1973): 309–29.

Weiss, Allen S. *Mirrors of Infinity: The French Formal Garden and Seventeenth-Century Metaphysics*. New York: Princeton Architectural Press, 1995.

Werner, Stephen. "Diderot's *Supplément* and Late Enlightenment Thought." *Studies on Voltaire and the Eighteenth Century* LXXXVI (1971): 229–92.

Whately, Thomas. *Observations on Modern Gardening*. New York: Garland, 1982.

Wiebenson, Dora. *The Picturesque Garden in France*. Princeton: Princeton University Press, 1978.

Wilson, Kathleen. "Empire of Virtue: The Imperial Project and Hanoverian Culture c. 1720–1785," *An Imperial State at War: Britain from 1689 to 1815*. Ed. Lawrence Stone. London and New York: Routledge, 1994.

Wolpe, Hans. *Raynal et sa Machine de guerre*. Stanford: Stanford University Press, 1957.

Index